The Unquiet Woods

The Unquiet Woods

Ecological Change and Peasant Resistance in the Himalaya

TWENTIETH ANNIVERSARY EDITION

RAMACHANDRA GUHA

with a new preface by the author and three new critical essays by

AMITA BAVISKAR
JOAN MARTINEZ-ALIER
PAUL SUTTER

permanent black

Published by
PERMANENT BLACK
'Himalayana', Mall Road, Ranikhet Cantt,
Ranikhet 263645
perblack@gmail.com

Distributed by
ORIENT BLACKSWAN PRIVATE LTD
Bangalore Bhopal Bhubaneshwar Chandigarh
Chennai Ernakulam Guwahati Hyderabad Jaipur
Kolkata Lucknow Mumbai New Delhi Patna
www.orientblackswan.com

The first edition of this book was published in India by Oxford University Press in hardback in 1989 and the University of California Press, Berkeley, in 1990. It was typeset in Baskerville by P.K. Ghosh at Eastend Printers, 3 Dr Suresh Sarkar Road, Calcutta 700014. A second, expanded edition was published by Oxford University Press in 1999. The present Twentieth Anniversary Edition of 2010, the book's third edition, photographically reproduces pp. 1–196 of the Eastend typesetting of the 1989 edition. All other pages have been freshly typeset in Baskerville.

ISBN 978-81-7824-378-8

Printed and bound by Manipal Technologies Limited, Manipal

MIX
Paper | Supporting responsible forestry
FSC™ C043100
FSC www.fsc.org

for

Amma, Appa, and Suja

Contents

Preface to the Twentieth Anniversary Edition

Chance and contingency play their part in history, and in the life of the historian. This book would never have been written—or published—had I not bumped into Rukun Advani at the wedding reception of a mutual friend on 6th September 1982. We knew each other slightly, for we had been in the same college hostel in the mid 1970s. Back then he was bookish and I a cricketer, and so we had not had much to say to each other. At this reception, however, it was as though he was the Ancient Mariner and I the Wedding Guest: there was so much to speak about. He had just joined Oxford University Press (OUP) as an editor and wanted to know what I had been up to since college. I told him I was halfway through a doctoral dissertation and described what my research was about, and he immediately said: 'There may be a book in there. Send me the thesis when it is finished.'

At that stage I had not even published a newspaper article. I was enjoying my research, however, and vaguely felt that there might be an article or two that I could publish once it was completed. I hoped to place these in scholarly journals such as the *Indian Economic and Social History Review* (*IESHR*) and *Contributions to Indian Sociology*. Research articles were all that I thought I could, or would, produce. This may have been because I was the son and grandson of scientists who had themselves published dozens of papers but never a book. More likely it was because my mental and intellectual horizons did not permit me to think I could undertake an exercise so comprehensive and definitive as to merit publication between hard covers.

In October 1983 I published my first paper—not in *IESHR* or *Contributions* but in the *Economic and Political Weekly* (*EPW*). The next year I had an essay accepted in *Subaltern Studies*. These papers got me my first job, at the Centre for Studies in Social Sciences in Calcutta, one of the few genuinely interdisciplinary research centres in India. I had no more ambitions–from my thesis at any rate.

But Advani had other ideas. I do not think he regularly read the *EPW*, but within the OUP he was the point man for *Subaltern Studies*. He had read and edited for publication my essay in that series; at his request, I sent him a copy of the thesis. Over the next few years, we worked on converting it into a book. I may not have been the first to discover that he had a sharp mind, a keen sense of literary style, and a reassuring knowledge of the process of book making.[1] So I owe him a special debt–it is not just that he made *The Unquiet Woods* a better book by his editing, or at any rate less flawed; without him there would have been no book at all.

To be sure, even before I met Advani at that wedding, I had incurred substantial debts to others. I was thinking of studying factory workers for my dissertation when the sociologist of science Jayanta Bandyopadhyay suggested I investigate the Chipko movement instead. Subsequently, had a peasant in Mandal (a village in the upper Alakananda Valley) not alerted me to protests of the past in his region, I would not never have thought to scour around in the archives for historical antecedents to Chipko. Had the government not introduced a new (and draconian) forest bill in 1982, I would not have had the incentive to trace the continuities between colonial and post-colonial forest policies. In retrospect it seems the work of chance and contingency, each time–for it was an accident that I met Professor Bandyopadhyay, a coincidence that I met that particular peasant, and my good fortune that the government chose to introduce their bill bang in the middle of my own research.

The core text of this anniversary edition of *The Unquiet Woods* is exactly as first printed in 1989 by Oxford University Press, Delhi,

[1] My opinion of Rukun Advani's editorial skills is shared by, among very many others, the mutual friend at whose wedding we were thrown together. This is K. Sivaramakrishnan, who was then an outstanding and upright officer of the Indian Administrative Service, and who is now Professor of Anthropology and Enviromental Studies at Yale University. In the process of making this transition he has written his own books, and had them edited by Advani, both at the OUP and at Permanent Black.

and in the year following by the University of California Press, Berkeley. A decade later a new, expanded second edition of the book was published, again by Advani at Oxford University Press. That second edition added an epilogue to the original text, along with an appendix outlining Indian environmental history between 1989 and 1999. For this third Twentieth Anniversary Edition I have brought that epilogue up to date, while three fellow environmental scholars have done me the great and undeserved honour of contributing essays on the relevance of the book to India and the world.[2] I will not here anticipate the book's contents, allowing new readers to encounter it with, I hope, fresh eyes and an open mind. But I think I should at least answer this question: Twenty years later, how does this book, written by a young man, read to its now middle-aged author?

When *The Unquiet Woods* was first published, reviewers and readers, even when they disagreed with some of its emphases or conclusions, were all agreed that it was very well written. Rereading the book, this is an opinion that I cannot entirely share. To be sure, the narrative is powered along by the passion of the author, the excitement with which he presents his discoveries from the archives. The fact that there is an abundance of quotes from primary sources perhaps contributed to making the narrative less bland than it would have otherwise been. But the author's own prose is, at least in retrospect, too stiffly sociological for my taste. Over the years, as I have become less a sociologist and more a historian and biographer, I have tried to write a less cluttered, more conversational, and I think more accessible prose. For all its freshness, *The Unquiet Woods* remains the work of a first-time academic writer.

Apart from cutting out some of the jargon, what changes would I make in the book two decades down the road? At twenty-five I was, politically speaking, a romantic left-wing populist; at fifty I am a pragmatic, middle-of-the-road, liberal. Were I to rewrite *The Unquiet Woods* now I would not, all the same, impose my new political persona on it. I may not always agree with the positions taken by the young man I once was, but I must allow him his youth, his energy, and his idealism.

[2] These three essays have made redundant the second edition's appendix on Indian environmental history 1989–1999, so that appendix has not been reproduced in the present edition.

I would, however, make some changes in substance. One reviewer, the historian Rashmi Pant, pointed out that for a work of environmental history *The Unquiet Woods* had paid surprisingly little attention to demography. This was a fair criticism–I should really have discussed, at greater length, the growth in the populations of humans and domestic animals in the Uttarakhand Himalaya, and the impact that more villagers and more cattle have had on patterns of cultivation and migration.

I also particularly regret not having access to one key archival source. This pertained to the protest movement in Rawain, described on pp. 72ff. of *The Unquiet Woods*. I knew that the files of the newspaper *Garhwali*, published in Hindi out of Dehradun, had covered the movement *in extenso*, for its editor, Bishambar Datt Chandola, had been in sympathy with the protesting peasants. The files were now in the possession of Chandola's daughter, Lalita Devi Vaishnav, who was a retired college principal. She allowed me access to the material she had, except for the crucial months of June–December 1930. This was because the reports of the Rawain incident over those six months had prompted a libel case, brought against the editor by the government. The government won the case, and Mr Chandola was briefly imprisoned. I can only speculate why, despite her generosity otherwise, Mrs Vaishnav kept those particular issues from me. It may have been that the memory of her father's perhaps unjust imprisonment was still painful; or that (as one of her own students speculated) she planned to write a biography of him, in which case she had rather not let anyone else see evidence on the most important and controversial period of his life.

Some pages on demography, and access to the *Garhwali* for the second half of 1930, would have made this a better and more rounded book. For the rest, I have no complaints, and many happy memories. I was born and raised in Dehradun, which is now the capital of the state of Uttarakhand. However I am by ethnic origin and background not a hillman but a Tamilian. Working on the social history of Uttarakhand allowed me to develop a closer and more meaningful relationship to the territory of my birth and upbringing.

The two authentic *paharis* who did most to make me a honorary Uttarakhandi were also, and perhaps not coincidentally, the two scholars who taught me the most about the region. The first was Thakur Shoorbeer Singh Panwar, an uncle of the Maharaja of Tehri Garhwal, and a sort of amateur historian himself. While working in the service of the Maharaja he had accumulated a range of documents and letters pertaining to the modern history of Garhwal. These were kept in a room of his large house in Dehradun's Dalanwala area; in which room I cannot say, since I was never allowed ingress. Thakur Saab would meet me in the verandah; then, depending on what turn our conversation was taking, would disappear inside and bring out a single document relevant to the discussion. This he held out for me to see and take notes from—never, I believe, did he permit me to hold any of his papers in my own hands.

To these dribs and drabs from his personal archive, Thakur Saab added some insights of his own. One was fundamental—the origin of the word *dhandak*, and the significance of what this form of customary rebellion meant to the social and political history of Tehri Garhwal (cf. pp. 67ff. below). On a more personal level, he assured me that despite my southern origins I could still be counted as an authentic son of the soil. He pointed out that the town and valley of Dehradun were both in and out of the hills, as made clear in a folk ditty which went: '*Dehradun mein ronda chan/ Garhwali aur Khatmali/Khatmali bhi Garhwali/Pur bhola na janan Garhwali.*' To translate this sympathetically: 'In the valley of Dehradun there live both us hill people and them plainsfolk. Them plainsfolk cannot speak our language, yet still we may count them as being in some ways our own.'

Appropriately, my second friend and teacher came from the other, and sometimes rival, part of Uttarakhand, namely Kumaun. In 1981 and 1982, as I worked in the archives in Delhi, Dehradun, and Lucknow, in several files I ordered I saw the name of 'Shekhar Pathak' entered before mine. Most times he was the only other person who had seen the file besides me. I knew then that I had to meet the man in the flesh. Which I soon did: in his office at Kumaun University, high above the lake in Naini Tal. He was, even at first sight, a deeply impressive man—tall, slim, surrounded by students, speaking at a fast clip about an astonishing range of subjects—ecology, history, geology, culture, language—all, however, only as they pertained to his beloved Himalaya.

I was delighted to make the acquaintance of this remarkable, and remarkably knowledgeable, man. But for Shekhar Pathak I was not an entirely unwelcome visitor either. There were other people with whom he climbed through 18,000 foot high passes; other people with whom he consulted while bringing out his outstanding journal, *Pahar*; other people with whom he marched to protest against this or that action of an unfeeling government. But till I arrived at his doorstep there was really no one else he could speak to about forgotten files in the archives. Among his multiple passions, this one at any rate was shared by no one but myself. His historical work had focused on the opposition to *begar* (forced labour) in Uttarakhand; mine was on the opposition to commercial forestry. The two movements had both peaked in the early 1920s; and, as we found through the course of speaking to one another, the conjunction in time of these two popular grievances had played a crucial role in catalysing opposition to colonial rule, and in the growth of a radical nationalist consciousness in the hills. In our conversations we spoke about the sociology and politics of protest, but we also exchanged details on minutiae—relating to particular letters, particular files, particular newsreports from the 1920s and 1930s that one of us had seen and wanted the other to see.

My debt to Shekhar Pathak's published work will be evident later in this book—as in the footnotes to Chapter V. In the preface to the first edition I had also inserted a footnote to the effect that he was then writing what would be 'the definitive history of the Chipko Andolan'. Twenty years later, that book has not yet appeared—perhaps I had put *nazar* by announcing it in advance. At any rate, Professor Pathak has had his hands full to overflowing with other (and arguably more important) matters. In these two decades he has brought out, almost single-handed, nearly twenty fat volumes of *Pahar*; published, in book form, his thesis on begar; published an acclaimed biographical study of the pioneering trans-Himalayan traveller Nain Singh Rawat; been to Tibet twice; walked the entire breadth of Uttarakhand four times; made countless high-altitude treks in Himachal, Arunachal, Sikkim, and Nepal; attended to a serious accident suffered by his son; and gone through a near-death experience himself. For all this, Shekhar Pathak has not entirely forgotten the promise he made to me—and to himself. When I spoke to him last, he was in Gopeshwar, working through the extensive files of the Dashauli Gram Swarajya Mandal, the 'mother' organization of the Chipko movement. So perhaps that definitive history will appear yet. It will, if I know my man and his subject, be certainly worth the wait.

If Shoorbeer Singh Panwar made me feel at home with that reassuring ditty, Shekhar Pathak did the same by presenting me a copy of his book on the begar abolition movement with these words inscribed on the fly-leaf: '*apne* pyare Ram ko'. That possessive pronoun 'apne' was used in the individual and collective sense–I was, it seems, dear to the author, and dear also to Uttarakhand, the region (now state) of which he was not just the leading intellectual but more or less the living embodiment. That inscription would not have been written had Professor Pathak not read and approved of the thesis on which *The Unquiet Woods* is based. His words, and in particular that single word 'apne', have meant more to me than any number of favourable reviews or reprints of *The Unquiet Woods*.

I have written earlier of the intellectual deficiencies in this book; but there is also one personal regret. The book was proofed, partly edited, and typeset by the legendary P. K. Ghosh of Eastend Printers, Calcutta. At the time, I was working in the Institute of Economic Growth; when the packet of proofs arrived there, I walked across to the Delhi School of Economics, and into the office of the distinguished sociologist André Béteille. He was, as ever, at his portable Olivetti typewriter, and as he looked up I thrust the packet in front of his nose with these words: 'Here are the proofs of my first book.' Fortunately, Professor Béteille was able to excuse my boastfulness on account of my youth, and because he had himself written a dozen books, some of them, indeed, typeset by the self-same P.K. Ghosh.

Those proofs were exquisite–to touch, to hold, to look at, and to feel. The type was set in Baskerville, a beautiful and elegant font; and the paper exuded the warm, authentic smell of the best kind of hot metal press. There are no presses or printers like that any more. Hence my abiding regret that, on one of the many changes of residence that I have made since 1989, I misplaced those proofs. I should have kept them more securely, and perhaps even framed some sample pages–not because they were of my first book, but because they were among the last works of art produced by one of the greatest of modern printers.

My first printer is now gone, but fortunately my first editor labours on. That *The Unquiet Woods* now appears in its latest (and surely last) incarnation under the imprint of Rukun Advani's Permanent Black, its print line indicating a press headquartered so appropriately for my book in Kumaon's pretty hamlet of Ranikhet, is to me a matter of almost indescribable joy–and relief.

RAMACHANDRA GUHA
Bangalore, 8th May 2009

Preface to the First Edition

Since the early seventies a wave of social movements has swept Uttarakhand, the region embracing the eight hill districts of the state of Uttar Pradesh.[1] By far the best known of these movements is the peasant initiative against commercial forestry, the Chipko movement. Chipko has been followed in rapid succession by movements directed at the siting of large dams, the environmental consequences of mining, and the sale and consumption of illicit liquor in Uttarakhand. At the time of writing the region is once again astir, in the grip of a renewed call for a separate hill state.

These movements have helped Uttarakhand emerge from a position of relative obscurity to one which more accurately reflects its ecological and cultural importance to the life of the subcontinent. Himalayan deforestation is by now widely recognized as India's most pressing environmental problem. It has attracted wide attention, as has the chain of events which has come in its wake: the eroding basis of subsistence agriculture, large-scale outward migration, and the creation of a 'moneyorder' economy in the villages of Uttarakhand. Meanwhile, Chipko has almost universally been hailed as a significant step forward in the fight to save Himalayan ecology and society from total collapse. While this attention is certainly welcome, what it tends to obscure is that Chipko, like the processes of ecological and social fragmentation which it attempts to reverse, is itself only part of a much longer history of resistance and protest. As this work shows, Chipko is the last in a long series of peasant movements against commercial forestry which date from the earliest days of state intervention, i.e. the closing decades of the nineteenth century.

This study was originally conceived as a sociology of Chipko. Despite the token genuflection to the movement in national and

[1] These eight districts are Pauri, Chamoli, Tehri, Uttarkashi, and Dehradun (which collectively constitute 'Garhwal'); and Almora, Pithoragarh and Nainital (which constitute 'Kumaun').

international debates on ecologically sound development alternatives, and its widespread coverage in the media, there was a surprising lack of sociologically informed analyses of the movement. Perhaps the media attention itself contributed to this lacuna: by assimilating the movement to the modern discourses of feminism, environmentalism, and the revival of Gandhism, it glossed over the local roots of Chipko, its embeddedness in the specific historical and cultural experiences of the Uttarakhand peasantry. Meanwhile, with the emergence of several wings within the movement, such accounts as did exist were seriously vitiated by the a priori partisan stance they took in favour of one or other wing of Chipko.[2] In the circumstances, a non-partisan analysis of the movement, which would in addition restore Chipko to its original home, seemed long overdue. A sociological perspective significantly reveals that the most celebrated 'environmental' movement in the Third World is viewed by its participants as being above all a *peasant* movement in defence of traditional rights in the forest, and only secondarily, if at all, an 'environmental' or 'feminist' movement. At the same time, a historical approach contributes to a decentring of Chipko, by showing it to be part of a much longer tradition of peasant movements in the Himalaya. Consequently, this study has turned into a more general history of ecological decline and peasant resistance in this region, whose main focus is on recovering the history of forest-based resistance within which Chipko is a small though undoubtedly distinguished part. In this sense my study is both more and less than the history and sociology of the Chipko movement.[3]

As it happens, this shift towards a more historically rooted analysis coincided with the timely arrival of the Subaltern Studies project. That series, as well as the individual monographs on peasant movements by some of its contributors, notably David Hardiman, Gyanendra Pandey, and Ranajit Guha, has greatly enriched our understanding of the origins and modalities of tribal/

[2] See, in this connection, the exchange between Jayanta Bandyopadhyay/ Vandana Shiva and myself in *Seminar*, New Delhi, issues of February, June, August, and November 1987.

[3] The definitive history of the Chipko Andolan is currently being written by Dr Shekhar Pathak of Kumaun University, a person uniquely qualified for the task; for he is perhaps the leading historian of modern Uttarakhand and an activist in Chipko from its inception in 1973.

peasant movements in the nineteenth and twentieth centuries.[4] One reason the Subalternists have written better history is because they have cast a wider net: apart from a more critical use of conventional sources (records of the Home Department and of the All India Congress Committee), they have made more extensive use of materials in Indian languages, utilized neglected series of official documents (e.g. forest, medical, and judicial records), conducted fieldwork, and on the whole shown a greater sensitivity to local variations in class and culture. At the same time, their studies have substantially drawn upon the work of sociologists and anthropologists in combating the excessively empiricist orientation of Indian history.

While placing my work in the context of the debates which the Subaltern Studies project has given rise to, I find myself both an insider and an outsider to what more than one Subalternist has referred to as their 'collective odysssey'. While sharing their concern for a more interpretive understanding of lower-class resistance, my own intellectual background diverges in at least two ways.

First, I have tried to bring an ecological dimension to the study of agrarian history and peasant resistance. The relationship between colonialism and ecological decline is one neglected by historians of modern India, who have been rather more aware of the social and political consequences of British rule. However, in Uttarakhand by far the most important consequence of colonial rule was the system of commercial forestry it introduced. Yet the conflict between state forestry and the peasantry, while perhaps at its most intense in Uttarakhand, was played out (with variations) in other forest regions of the subcontinent as well. Its origins were as much ideological as economic: for peasant use and state use were embedded in very different understandings of the social role of the forests. I argue, therefore, that ecological history cannot merely be the history of changes in the landscape; it must link environmental changes with changing, and competing, human perceptions of the 'uses' of nature.

[4] See Ranajit Guha (ed.), *Subaltern Studies: Writings on South Asian History and Society*, volumes I to IV (1982–5); David Hardiman, *Peasant Nationalists of Gujarat* (1981); David Hardiman, *The Coming of the Devi* (1987); Gyanendra Pandey, *The Ascendancy of the Congress in Uttar Pradesh* (1978); Ranajit Guha, *Elementary Aspects of Peasant Insurgency in Colonial India* (1983), all published by Oxford University Press, New Delhi.

Second, I am not a historian but a sociologist trying to write history. This is a work of historical sociology, in which I am, as compared to most historians, more consciously theoretical and comparative in my approach. Here I am on slippery ground, for historians have in general a sharp scepticism of the pretensions of sociologists. E. P. Thompson, for example, rarely misses an opportunity to side-swipe at the sociologist's penchant for arid abstraction. Twenty years ago John Womack prefaced his great study of the peasantry in the Mexican Revolution with these words, in which he made clear his relative evaluation of the two disciplines:

> [T]his is a work not in historical sociology but in social history. It is not an analysis but a story because the truth of the revolution in Morelos is in the feeling of it, which I could not convey through defining its factors but only through telling of it. The analysis that I thought pertinent I have tried to weave into the narrative, so that it would issue at the moment right for understanding it.[5]

Around the same time, but probably unknown to Womack, an Indonesian historian was completing his own opus on peasant movements against the Dutch in Java, a magisterial study which deserves to be much better known in ex-colonial countries like India. Sartono Kartodirdjo could not have disagreed more with Womack for, he wrote, 'the one subject matter which certainly does exhibit the actual or potential interdependence of history and sociology is the social movement.'[6] While appreciating Womack's reservations—and which sociologist will deny that historians write with so much more feeling?—I am, like Kartodirdjo, more hopeful of a potential union, provided sociologists stop waiting for historians to provide them 'data' from which to generalize and learn the tools of historical research themselves. It seems to have escaped most historically-minded sociologists that generalizations are far more convincing when based on more, not less, primary data. As things stand, 'primary' data usually passes through several hands, and several interpretations, before it reaches the generalizing sociologist. It is well to remember that those two masters of historical sociology, Marx and Weber, were often wildly off

[5] John Womack, *Zapata and the Mexican Revolution* (New York, 1969), p. x.

[6] Sartono Kartodirdjo, *The Peasants' Revolt in Banten in 1988* (The Hague, 1966), p. 12.

the mark in their assessments of Indian society not only because of their strong prejudices about non-European cultures in general, but also because they relied exclusively on other peoples' already loaded interpretations of an alien culture. At the same time, by rejecting the historian's obsession with the accumulation of certified facts, Marx and Weber did provide an array of sociological concepts that have scarcely outlived their usefulness—concepts that have found their way into the work of even the most atheoretical historian.[7] As far as the study of peasant resistance is concerned, the work of James Scott, Teodor Shanin, and Barrington Moore Jr—to name only three sociologists—and of Ranajit Guha, Sartono Kartodirdjo, and E. P. Thompson—to mention but three historians—is ample proof of the potential interdependence, one denied by historians even as they practise it, of sociology and history.

[7] A comparative work spanning several continents and several centuries may of course have to rely exclusively on secondary sources; yet it is the sociologist (like Marx and Weber) with some experience of doing primary research who is more likely to carry off a large-scale work of synthesis.

Acknowledgements

Having accumulated an unusually large number of debts for a work of this kind, I can do no better than start in chronological order.

C. S. Venkatachar, possessed of a scholarly detachment quite remarkable in a former civil servant of the Raj, first evoked an interest in the study of Indian society. My first teachers in sociology, Anjan Ghosh and Kamini Adhikari, encouraged me to take up what was for sociologists uncharted territory, even as they insisted I locate my empirical findings in wider theoretical debates. Two scholars with an unrivalled knowledge of Uttarakhand, Shekhar Pathak and Thakur Shoorbeer Singh Panwar, were always forthcoming with advice and encouragement. Anil Agarwal, Acharya Gopeshwar Narain Kothiyal, Paripurnanand Painuli, Thakur Sarop Singh, and Smt. Lalita Devi Vaishnav gave me ready access to valuable source material in their possession. I am greatly indebted to the many scholars who commented on the manuscript in whole or in part: Kamini Adhikari, Anjan Ghosh, David Hardiman, Louise Fortmann, Rukun Advani, Michael Adas, James Scott, John Richards, Dharma Kumar, K. Sivaramakrishnan, and an anonymous reader for the University of California Press. I owe a special debt to Jim Scott for introducing me to a wide range of comparative work on peasant protest in Europe and Asia.

I am grateful to the staff of the following institutions for their help in locating documents for this study: Forest Research Institute Library, Dehradun; National Archives of India, New Delhi; National Library, Calcutta; Uttar Pradesh State Archives, Lucknow; Regional Archives, Dehradun and Nainital; and Nehru Memorial Museum and Library, New Delhi. Two of my previous employers, the Centre for Studies in Social Sciences, Calcutta, and the Centre for Ecological Sciences, Indian Institute of Science, Bangalore, provided a congenial atmosphere for the completion of this work.

Among the many other individuals who provided help of various kinds, I must especially mention the following: Sunderlal Bahuguna, Jayanta Bandyopadhyay, Chandi Prasad Bhatt, Bill Burch, Partha Chatterjee, Robi Chatterji, J. C. Das, Bernard d'Mello, Madhav Gadgil, Jean Claude Galey, Vinay Gidwani, Sumit Guha, Ashis Nandy, Gyan Pandey, K. S. Pundir, Ajay Rawat, Satish Saberwal, Atul Saklani, Hari Sen, and Shiv Visvanathan.

My parents and my wife followed the course of this work with interest and a growing exasperation. Their support at all times has been critical.

Finally, I should note that earlier versions of chapters 3 and 5 respectively were published in the *Economic and Political Weekly*, special number, 1985, and in Ranajit Guha (ed.), *Subaltern Studies IV* (New Delhi: Oxford University Press, 1985).

Glossary

andolan	popular movement
bandh	general strike (see *hartal*)
banj	oak
bardaish	supply of provisions
begar, utar, coolie utar	forced labour
chaukidar	watchman
chir	long-leaved pine
darbar, dirbar, durbar	royal court
deodar	cedar
dewan, diwan	chief minister
gaddi	throne
ghar	house
gherao	to surround
hartal	general strike (see *bandh*)
hookah	pipe
kand	firing
kisan	peasant
kisan andolan	peasant movement
jati	caste
jath	country fair
jatha	group
lakh	one hundred thousand
malikhana	rent
padayatra	walking tour
padhan, pradhan	headman
pahari, paharee	hillman
panchayat	village council
pargana	county

patti	a group of villages
patwari	revenue official in charge of a patti
praja	citizens, subjects
praja mandal	citizens' forum
quintal	one hundred kilograms
raja	king
rawal	head priest
sabha	association
sarvodaya	(here) belonging to the Gandhian movement

Abbreviations

F&P	Foreign and Political Department
F.D.	Forest Department
For. Div.	Forest Division
GAD	General Administration Department
GRH	*Garhwali*
IF	*Indian Forester*
ISR	*Indian States Reformer*
NAI	National Archives of India
NMML	Nehru Memorial Museum and Library
RAD	Regional Archives, Dehradun
RAN	Regional Archives, Nainital
UPSA	Uttar Pradesh State Archives, Lucknow
WP	Working Plan
YV	*Yugvani*

UTTARAKHAND
1815 - 1949
TIBET
TIBET
NEPAL
NEPAL
TEHRI GARHWAL STATE
SIMLA HILL STATES (Himachal Pradesh)
R. Bhagirathi
R. Alakananda
Uttarkashi
Badrinath
Tehri
Gopeshwar
Dehradun
Narendra nagar
Srinagar
Rudraprayag
Pauri
BRITISH GARHWAL DISTT
ALMORA DISTT
Hardwar
Lansdowne
Bageshwar
Ranikhet
KUMAUN DIVISION
Almora
Pithoragarh
Nainital
Bhawali
NAINITAL DISTT
Haldwani
ROHILKHAND
Scale : 1 : 1 000 000

CHAPTER 1

A Sociology of Domination and Resistance

> [The] peasantry is a class neglected by the throng of writers in quest of new subjects. This neglect, it may be, is simple prudence in days when the working class have fallen heir to the courtiers and flatterers of kings, when the criminal is the hero of romance, the herdsman is sentimentally interesting, and we behold something like an apotheosis of the proletariat. Sects have arisen among us, every pen among them swells the chorus of 'Workers arise!' even as once the Third Estate was bidden to 'Arise'! It is pretty plain that no Herostratus among them has had the courage to go forth into remote country districts to study the phenomena of a permanent conspiracy of those whom we call 'the weak' against those who imagine themselves to be the 'strong'—of the Peasantry against the Rich.
>
> —Balzac

TWO APPROACHES TO THE STUDY OF LOWER-CLASS PROTEST

The historical and sociological study of lower-class protest is a relatively recent phenomenon. As a separate field it emerged only after World War II. Among a host of factors, the growing influence of academic Marxism in Europe and the rise of anti-colonial movements in Asia and Africa were particularly important in initiating a reappraisal of the two fundamental projects of modernity: the rise of capitalism in Europe, and its transplantation, in the form of colonialism, in non-European territories. Challenging the view that these processes of social change were by and large harmonious, historians were able to document the deep-rooted and endemic opposition to the economic and political changes initiated by capitalism and colonialism. As part of a larger movement from 'consensus' to 'conflict' approaches in sociology, and from 'top down' to 'bottom up' in history, these works have firmly placed the study of lower-class resistance on the scholarly agenda.

It would serve little purpose here to review the voluminous literature on peasant and working class movements that has accumulated in the past decades.[1] While the field's importance has been widely commented upon, what is less apparent is the emergence of two distinct approaches in the literature. As I believe this divergence to be of methodological and theoretical significance for future work in the field, I have attempted, in what follows, to characterize these two trends.

The first approach, which I call the Structural–Organizational (S–O) paradigm, is concerned with analysing large-scale historical processes—e.g. capitalism, imperialism, and the rise of the nation-state—what Charles Tilly, one of its most influential practitioners, has called the 'master processes' of social change.[2] It investigates the impact of these changes on different social classes, identifying those classes likely to be adversely affected, and among these the classes likely to revolt against their superiors. It is keenly interested in the role of political parties (whether regional, nationalist or communist) in organizing the disaffected, in the role of the state as a mechanism of repression, and finally in the historical outcome of movements of social protest.

The second approach, termed here the Political–Cultural (P–C) paradigm, accepts the importance of large-scale economic change. It argues, however, that if economics is the only important determinant of collective action, many peasants and labourers living at the margins of subsistence would be rebelling all the time. Crucial to a fuller understanding of resistance

[1] Even the major studies are too numerous to be listed here. A partial listing of works in English could include: Barrington Moore, *Social Origins of Dictatorship and Democracy* (Harmondsworth, 1966); Eric Wolf, *Peasant Wars of the Twentieth Century* (New York, 1969); Rodney Hilton, *Bond Men Made Free* (London, 1973); Eric Hobsbawm, *Primitive Rebels* (Manchester, 1959); George Rudé, *The Crowd in History* (New York, 1964); Hobsbawm and Rudé, *Captain Swing* (Harmondsworth, 1969); E. P. Thompson, *The Making of the English Working Class* (Harmondsworth, 1963); Sartono Kartodirdjo, *The Peasant Revolt in Banten in 1886* (The Hague, 1966); J. C. Scott, *The Moral Economy of the Peasant* (New Haven, 1976); Ranajit Guha, *Elementary Aspects of Peasant Insurgency in Colonial India* (New Delhi, 1983).

[2] Charles Tilly, *Big Structures, Large Processes, Huge Comparisons* (New York, 1985).

are systems of political legitimacy and the interplay between ideologies of domination and subordination. Looking more closely at local class relations and their cultural idiom, the P–C paradigm asks—how is legitimacy claimed by the superordinate classes, how is it granted, and when does it break down? While accepting that economic deprivation is often a necessary condition for resistance, it suggests that protest will take place only when there is a perceived erosion, whether partial or total, of patterns of legitimate authority. Lastly, this approach has a more sophisticated view of the role of political organizations, arguing that the rank and file, far from uncritically accepting the ideology of the leadership, often reshape and rework it to suit their own purposes.[3]

Flowing from these theoretical differences are certain methodological preferences. The S–O paradigm is prone to view protest as instrumental, oriented towards specific economic and political goals. Here, success is the gauge by which the significance of protest is measured. By contrast, the P–C paradigm is more likely to emphasize the expressive dimensions of social protest—its cultural and religious idioms. The significance of lower-class resistance, it argues, consists not merely in what the rebels accomplish or fail to accomplish, but also in the language in which social actors express their discontent with the prevailing arrangements. Second, implicit in the S–O paradigm is a unilinear progression from 'spontaneous' to 'organized' forms of protest, with individual action at one end of the scale and organized party activity at the other. The P–C approach, on the other hand, distinguishes between different mechanisms of protest, relating specific actions to specific systems of domination. While accepting that certain forms of protest are likely to predominate in particular societies and historical periods, it does not accept the historical inevitability of a progression from unorganized to organized forms. For most rebels have available a wide range of protest mechanisms, with the use of one tactic (e.g. organized revolt) not precluding the use of another, ostensibly more 'primitive', tactic (e.g. arson) at a later date.[4]

[3] Cf. J. C. Scott, 'From Protest to Profanation: Agrarian Revolt and the Little Tradition', *Theory and Society*, vol. 4, 1977.

[4] See, in this connection, Michael Adas, 'From Footdragging to Flight: The

In sum, the practitioners of the S–O approach look for underlying regularities, draw large generalizations, and adhere to strict notions of causality in analysing social protest: they are closer to the 'science' end of the social-science spectrum. The P–C approach, on the other hand, stresses differences in the language and mechanisms of protest, relating these differences to particular cultural contexts: thus it is closer to the 'interpretive' end of the spectrum. The S–O paradigm stands at the confluence of structural Marxism and organizational sociology, a meeting captured in Charles Tilly's organizing trinity of concepts, 'interest, organization, and opportunity'.[5] Among the major works in this genre are those by Eric Wolf and Charles Tilly, and Barrington Moore's classic on dictatorship and democracy.[6] The P–C paradigm consists of a more eclectic brew, drawing selectively on Marxism, Weber, and the interpretive turn in social science. Perhaps its most influential Western exponent is James Scott, while in India the pathbreaking studies of the Subaltern Studies school come within its ambit.[7] The division also mirrors the schism emerging in the sociology of social movements, with the P–C paradigm standing close to the Collective Behaviour school, the S–O paradigm to Resource Mobilization theory.[8]

Evasive History of Peasant Avoidance Protest in South and South-east Asia', *Journal of Peasant Studies*, vol. 13, no. 2, 1986.

[5] Charles Tilly, *From Mobilization to Revolution* (Reading, Mass., 1978); *idem*, *The Contentious French* (Cambridge, Mass., 1986). See also George Rudé's review of the latter work in *Times Literary Supplement*, 4 April 1986.

[6] Wolf, *Peasant Wars*; Tilly, *The Contentious French*; Barrington Moore, *Social Origins*.

[7] J. C. Scott, *Weapons of the Weak: Everyday Forms of Peasant Resistance* (New Haven, 1986); Ranajit Guha, *Subaltern Studies: Writings on South Asian History and Society*, volumes I to IV (New Delhi, 1982–5). Cf. also Richard Cobb, *The Police and the People: French Popular Protest, 1769–1820* (Oxford, 1970).

It is difficult to place the pioneering works of Hobsbawm and Rudé in either category. While their interest in the culture of resistance draws them close to the P–C approach, their 'progressive' view of history and faith in the Leninist party as the perfect embodiment of the aspirations of the oppressed classes are more typical of the S–O school. The other distinguished British Marxist historian of lower-class protest, E. P. Thompson, can be more easily placed in the P–C camp.

[8] J. Craig Jenkins, 'Resource Mobilization Theory and the Study of Social Movements', *Annual Review of Sociology*, no. 9, 1983; J. R. Gusfield, 'Social Move-

THE LANDSCAPE OF RESISTANCE

While the orientation of this work places it within the P–C paradigm, both the approaches described above have their distinctive strengths and weaknesses. While the S–O framework may be particularly suited to studying Tilly's master processes of social change, case studies of the cultural idiom of resistance would draw largely upon the organizing concepts of the P–C school. Here, two caveats are in order. First, a close attention to the language of domination and subordination in any one society does not preclude either the use of theoretical concepts drawn from the social sciences or the formulation of generalizations based on the careful comparative analysis of protest in different conjunctures.[9] Second, one must be wary of the pitfalls of an exclusively 'interpretive' approach—namely the downplaying of the material basis of human society so characteristic of anthropological attempts to analyse a culture from within and on its own terms.[10]

In this work the material structure of Uttarakhand society serves as the 'landscape of resistance'.[11] Following Marx's postulate that social being conditions social consciousness, I argue that the social relations and forces of production set certain limits to the forms a culture (and within it, resistance) may take. However, a truly materialist approach would begin not with the economic landscape but with the natural setting in which the economy is embedded. For if production relations sharply define the boundaries of political structures and cultural-symbolic systems, they in turn are limited by the eco-

---

ments and Social Change: Perspectives of Linearity and Fluidity', in Louis Kriesberg (ed.), *Research in Social Movements, Conflict and Change*, vol. 4 (Greenwich, Conn., 1981).

[9] This is exemplified by a culturally sensitive work pitched at an extremely high level of generality, Barrington Moore's *Injustice*. Interestingly, while his earlier work (*Social Origins*)—a vastly influential study in the S–O genre—is quite deaf to the cultural idiom of protest, *Injustice* is a major contribution to a culturally rooted political sociology.

[10] This neglect of structure is quite apparent in the later works of the cult figure of interpretive anthropology, Clifford Geertz. See especially his *The Interpretation of Cultures* (New York, 1973), and *Local Knowledge* (New York, 1980).

[11] I owe this term to James Scott, *Weapons of the Weak*. My usage is somewhat different from Scott's.

logical characteristics—the flora, fauna, topography, and climate—of the society in which they are placed.

It is not my intention to substitute, for explanations based exclusively on economic and social factors, an equally uncritical ecological determinism.[12] Yet I would emphasize that in a region so markedly influenced by its ecological setting as the Indian Himalaya, a study of processes of social change would be seriously flawed unless set in the context of simultaneous processes of environmental change. Thus the 'ecological landscape of resistance', outlined in the following two chapters, will incorporate the linkages between forests and agriculture, the management of forests in the indigenous system, the specific forms of state intervention and the changes it induced, and of course the agrarian relations of production normally regarded as the material base. Once this landscape has been set in place, we can turn to the study's major concern: the nature and form of social protest movements asserting traditional claims over the forest. In this manner the book spans the gap between two distinct scholarly traditions: the sociology of lower-class protest and the ecologically oriented study of history.

The fusion of these hitherto parallel discourses will hopefully help move the study of popular opposition to colonial rule in India beyond the current preoccupation with the role of the Congress party. Until the recent advent of the Subaltern Studies school, historical research on Indian nationalism was located firmly in the S–O genre: in focusing on the part played by the Congress party in organizing the peasantry, it had little time for what one critic has called the 'internal face' of Indian nationalism.[13] Consequently, we have as yet a very primitive understanding of the social composition, culture and ideology of many of the tribal and peasant movements in twentieth-century India. A second area of neglect germane to this work is the study of the often considerable impact of colonial forest/environmental policies on agrarian economy and peasant protest. For, by looking only at social conflicts around land and within the workplace, historians have for the most part been

[12] The best-known example of which is, of course, Marvin Harris, *Cows, Pigs, Wars, and Witches: The Riddles of Culture* (New York, 1974).

[13] Gyanendra Pandey, *The Ascendancy of the Congress in Uttar Pradesh* (New Delhi, 1978), p. 215.

curiously unaware of the equally bitter conflicts concerned with the control and utilization of forests, water and other natural resources.[14] Much work on social movements has, moreover, been marked by provincialism; very rarely are Indian developments located or analysed in a wider comparative framework.

In trying to overcome these limitations this book has three major aims. Its primary focus is on the links between structures of domination and the idioms of social protest. Here Uttarakhand is a fascinating case study, for between 1815 and 1949 it was divided into two distinct socio-political systems—the princely state of Tehri Garhwal and the colonial territory of Kumaun. While the region was quite homogeneous in terms of economy and culture, during this period the structure of the state, and especially the style of rule, differed substantially in the two domains. The ruler of Tehri Garhwal, representative of a dynasty that stretched back 1200 years and that was perhaps the oldest in north India, could also call upon his symbolic status as the head of the Badrinath temple—one of the holiest in Hinduism—in pursuance of his claims of legitimate authority. Of much more recent origin, the colonial government of Kumaun was also separated from its subjects by a gulf of race and language. Consequently, the structure of authority was quite different in the two contexts, one approximating Weber's 'traditional' authority, the other 'bureaucratic' authority.[15] At the same time, the peasantry in both territories was subject to virtually identical processes of ecological change. An elaboration of these similarities and differences will help us appreciate the interplay between structures of domination and styles of protest. We shall also see how these distinct socio-political systems and histories of protest influence the trajectory

[14] Cf. Ramachandra Guha and Madhav Gadgil, 'State Forestry and Social Conflict in British India', *Past and Present*, no. 123, May 1989.

[15] Max Weber, *Economy and Society*, translated by Guenther Roth and Claus Wittich (Berkeley, 1968). Weber is not concerned with the colonial situation, in which bureaucratic authority does not have the positive features he sometimes associates it with. Colonial bureaucratic structures have no popular sanction; they are legitimized only by the superior force of alien rulers. The two elements in Weber's treatment relevant here are the impersonal character of authority in bureaucracies (as opposed to the personalized systems of traditional authority), and his conception of bureaucracy as the most efficient way of exercising authority over human beings.

of a contemporary social movement, the Chipko Andolan.

The second major focus is on the links between competing systems of forest use and management, ecological decline, and agrarian protest. There are voluminous histories of Indian forestry written by forest officials.[16] Set in a region whose forests were among the most intensively worked in the subcontinent, this book traces a different path, directing attention away from the perceptions of the forest department towards the perceptions of the villagers of Uttarakhand affected by its policies.[17] In contrast to other regions, where peasant subsistence was not so closely interwoven with the forests, in Uttarakhand the ecological dimension is crucial to a fuller understanding of the social idiom of popular protest.

Finally, while the book's core consists of a comparative analysis of social protest in Tehri Garhwal and Kumaun divisions, it also attempts three additional kinds of comparison. First, I use the Tehri Garhwal case to develop a theory of customary rebellions in traditional monarchies which takes issue with Max Gluckman's germinal treatment of the subject.[18] Second, I use the Kumaun case to make a larger critique of party-centred histories of nationalism, arguing that the connections between the peasantry and 'organized' politics are more complex and more surprising than has hitherto been supposed. Third, in the concluding chapter I compare movements in twentieth-century Uttarakhand with movements in defence of forest rights in early-capitalist Europe. The persistence of forest conflicts in the one case, and their diminution and eventual disappearance in the other, is, I suggest, indicative of the ecological limits to full-blown industrialization on the Western model in ex-colonial countries. The union of history and ecology is therefore not merely a methodological imperative; it is also an invaluable guide to the understanding of contemporary social concerns.

[16] Especially E. P. Stebbing, *The Forests of India*, three volumes (London, 1922–7).

[17] For a more detailed study, at an all-India level, see Madhav Gadgil and Ramachandra Guha, *This Fissured Land: Humans and Nature in the Indian Subcontinent*, forthcoming (Oxford University Press, New Delhi).

[18] Max Gluckman, *Order and Rebellion in Tribal Africa* (London, 1963).

CHAPTER 2

The Mountains and Their People

> We entered an enchanted garden, where the produce of Europe and Asia—indeed of every quarter of the world—was blended together. Apples, pears and pomegranates, plantains, figs and mulberry trees, grew in the greatest quantity, and with the most luxuriant hue. Blackberries and raspberries, hung temptingly from the brows of the broken crags, while our path was strewed with strawberries. In every direction, were blooming heather—violets and jasmine, with innumerable 'rose trees in full bearing' . . . I have beheld nearly all the celebrated scenery of Europe, which poets and painters have immortalized, and of which all the tourists in the world are enamoured; but I have seen it surpassed in these . . . unknown regions [of the Himalaya.]
>
> — Thomas Skinner, *Excursions in India, Including a Walk over the Himalaya to the Source of the Jumna and the Ganges* (1832)

Through most of recorded history the Indo-Gangetic plain, a vast unbroken territory extending westwards to the Arabian Sea and eastwards to the Bay of Bengal, has been the political 'core' of India, the epicentre of the great kingdoms that have risen and fallen with the centuries. Rising sharply from this plain the Himalaya, source of the holy rivers of Hinduism, has loomed large in the spiritual and religious life of the subcontinent. The transition from this plain to the Himalaya is achieved via the Siwaliks, a line of hills fifteen to fifty kilometres in breadth and from a few hundred to a few thousand feet in elevation, that run along the southern edge of the Himalaya. Separating these outer hills from the fertile plain is a band of swamp and forest called the Terai. Inhabited only by a few hunting and gathering communities, and highly malarial, the Terai formed an effective barrier to the penetration of large armies from the plains.

The Himalayan region proper, lying a few kilometres north

of the Siwaliks, rises quickly to an average elevation of 7000 feet. The inner hills extend a hundred kilometres to the north, culminating in the great snowy peaks that surpass in elevation all other parts of the world. The hills are criss-crossed by river valleys, resembling gigantic ravines carved out of hillsides. At the bottom of each valley flows the river with narrow strips of cultivable land adjoining it. Alongside the river are steeply sloping hills, rising up to 9000 feet. It is this ecological region, lying between the snowy peaks and the outer hills, that is the focus of this study.

Political history

Garhwal and Kumaun refer to the two kingdoms that ruled Uttarakhand through much of the medieval period. At one stage both territories were under the sway of one dynasty, the Katyuris. The Katyuris ruled for several centuries, first from Joshimath in the Alakananda valley and later from the Katyur valley in present-day Almora district.[1]

Following the decline of the centralized political authority of the Katyuris, which cannot be dated with certainty, the area broke up into many small principalities. The independent chiefdoms of Garhwal were first subjugated by Ajaypal Panwar in the thirteenth century, while the unification of Kumaun took place under Som Chand around AD 960.[2] 'Kshatriyas' from Malwa (Gujarat) and Rajputana respectively, the Panwars and the Chands soon consolidated their rule. In this they were helped by the isolated nature of their territories, bounded on the north by the Greater Himalaya and separated from the Indo-Gangetic plain in the south by the Siwalik hills. Thus they neither came under the sway of the Mughals nor were they subject to invasion from the north. They were seriously threatened only after the unification of Nepal in 1768 under the Gurkha chief Prithvinarayan Sah. After repeated attempts the Gurkhas conquered Kumaun in 1790 and Garhwal in 1804.

The Gurkhas introduced certain changes in the agrarian

[1] See L. D. Joshi, *The Khasa Family Law* (London, 1929), pp. 28–9.

[2] These dates are currently the subject of controversy amongst historians of Uttarakhand. They were first put forward by E. T. Atkinson in his massive work, *The Himalayan Districts of the North-western Provinces of India*, 3 volumes, (Allahabad, 1882–6).

structure—built around strong village communities, with most members enjoying a vested interest in land—via the system of military assignments. Their rule was, however, short-lived. When the Anglo-Gurkha wars culminated in the treaty of 1815, the East India Company had annexed both Kumaun and Garhwal. Retaining Kumaun and eastern Garhwal (now known together as Kumaun division), the British restored the western portion—known as Tehri Garhwal after the new capital—to the son of the last Garhwali ruler.

The boundaries of the treaty of 1815 were fixed with a view to controlling the route to Tibet and the passes used for trade. It was the prospect of commercial intercourse with Tibet, and not considerations of revenue, that induced Lord Hastings to embark on the hill campaign. While Kumaun bordered Nepal in the east, both northern Almora and British Garhwal had important trade routes to Tibet.[3] Its location, strategic from the viewpoints of both defensive security and trade, played an important part in the evolution of British land policy in Kumaun.[4]

The boundaries of Kumaun division coincided with well defined physical features. The river Kali separated it from Nepal in the east; the Himalaya separated it from Tibet in the north; in the west it was divided from the state of Tehri Garhwal by the Alakananda and Mandakini rivers; in the south the outer hills demarcated it from the adjoining division of Rohilkhand. Tehri Garhwal, likewise bounded in the south and north by the Siwalik hills and Tibet respectively, was separated from Dehradun district by the Tons and Yamuna rivers in the west.

SOCIAL STRUCTURE

Caste[5]

The social structures of Kumaun and Garhwal share marked similarities. The largest ethnic stratum is made up of the Khasa

[3] British Garhwal refers to the portion of Garhwal now constituted as a British district. Along with Nainital and Almora it formed 'Kumaun division'.

[4] John Pemble, *The Invasion of Nepal* (London, 1971), chapter III, 'The Matter of Himalayan Trade'. Cf. also B. P. Saksena (ed.), *Historical Papers Relating to Kumaun, 1809–1842* (Allahabad, 1956).

[5] This section draws on the following works: R. D. Sanwal, 'Social Stratifica-

or Khasiya which comprise the traditional peasantry, while the next largest stratum consists of the Doms serving the cultivating body as artisans and farm servants. Numerically the smallest but ritually the highest are the Thuljat—Brahmins and Rajputs claiming to be descendants of later immigrants from the plains.[6]

Most writers adhere to a 'conquest' theory whereby the Doms are viewed as the original inhabitants who were conquered and enslaved by the Khasas. While the Khasas were a widespread race in prehistoric Asia, the origins of the hill Khasas is obscure. They have, however, adhered to a Vedantic form of Hinduism at least since the eighth century.[7] The Khasas in turn were subjugated by later immigrants from the plains who came to hold both political power and ritual status.

This three-tiered structure—Thuljat/Khasa/Dom—emerged, then, out of what were originally distinctions between ruler and ruled. The structure can be conceptualized as a series of binary distinctions, of which the two basic oppositions were (*i*) Bith (clean) *vs.* Dom (unclean); (*ii*) within Bith, Thuljat (immigrant) *vs.* Khasa (indigenous). While both Thuljat and Khasa had Brahmin and Kshatriya segments, Thuljat as a whole ranked higher than Khasa; for example, a Thuljat Kshatriya was considered superior to a Khasa Brahmin. These distinctions can be pictorially represented, as in the following chart:

---

tion in the Hill Region of Uttar Pradesh', in Indian Institute of Advanced Study, *Urgent Research in Social Anthropology* (Simla, 1969); *idem*, *Social Stratification in Rural Kumaun* (Delhi, 1976); G. D. Berreman, *Hindus of the Himalayas* (Berkeley, 1973); Pannalal, *Hindu Customary Law in Kumaun* (1921; rpt. Allahabad, 1942); A. C. Turner, 'Caste in the Kumaun Division and Tehri Garhwal State', *Census of India*, 1931, vol. 18, pt 1; E. H. H. Eyde, 'The Depressed Classes of the Kumaun Hills', *Census of India*, 1921, vol. 16, pt 1, appendix C.

[6] An analysis of the 1931 census data from UP showed Kumaun and Garhwal as being 'a highly distinctive caste region that also has a high degree of homogeneity'. While the index of dissimilarity for Almora and Garhwal, 0.08, was 'considerably lower than the value for any pair of contiguous plains districts', the index reached its highest value, 0.81, across the mountain/plain boundary between Garhwal and Bijnor districts. See D. E. Sopher, 'Rohilkhand and Oudh: An Exploration of Social Gradients across a Political Barrier', in R. G. Fox (ed.), *Realm and Region in Traditional India* (Delhi, 1977), p. 289.

[7] That is, following the advent of Adi Sankaracharya in the hills. Prior to this Buddhism exercised a vigorous influence that can still be discerned in the iconography of hill temples.

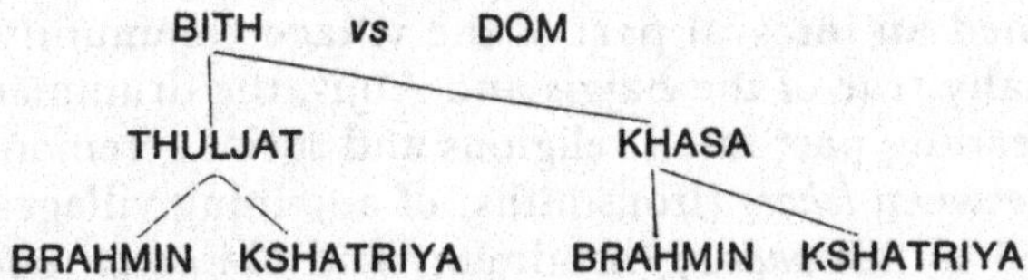

SOURCE: After R. D. Sanwal, *Social Stratification in Rural Kumaun* (Delhi, 1976).

The geographical isolation of the hill tracts fostered an ambiguous relation with the so-called 'Great Tradition' of Hinduism. On the one hand, contact with plains Hinduism was maintained through the pilgrims who came annually to visit the famous temples in the hills. As a result, one finds little evidence of an 'almost universal antipathy' which hillmen are believed to feel towards the inhabitants of the plains.[8] On the other hand, caste restrictions and other rules of orthodox Hinduism were singularly lax. Brahmins customarily used the plough and ate meat, while there was a great deal of informal interaction between high and low castes, especially on festive occasions. And as the opening out of the economy under British rule facilitated status mobility, over time the Khasa merged with the Thuljat.

With reference to the untouchable Doms, ritual rules of purity and pollution were not defined as exclusively as in the plains.[9] While each village had two water sources, one for the Bith, the other for the Dom, the Dom could smoke from the same pipe as the Khas–Rajput (the dominant peasant caste) and touch without polluting food not cooked or mixed with water (e.g. fruit and grain). Mostly artisans and tenants, the

[8] David Arnold, 'Rebellious Hillmen: The Gudem Rampa Risings, 1839–1924', in Ranajit Guha (ed.), *Subaltern Studies I* (Delhi, 1982), p. 13.

[9] According to the 1921 census the population of Doms was as follows:

District	Total population	Population of depressed classes
Nainital	276,875	32,970
Almora	530,338	108,659
British Garhwal	485,186	77,334
Tehri Garhwal	318,414	54,325

Doms formed an integral part of the village community. This was especially true of the Bajgis and Aujis, the drummers who played a leading part in all religious and social ceremonies. In conflicts between *lohars* (ironsmiths) of adjoining villages, each was backed by his *padhan* (headman) and *panchayat* (council). On occasions when the artisan was fined, the people of his village collectively paid up on his behalf. Commercialization of the economy, by giving artisans outside employment as masons, carpenters, etc., also helped mitigate the iniquities of the system.

Agrarian relations

Social anthropologists studying ritual hierarchy in Garhwal and Kumaun have stressed the similarities between hill society and the rest of India, seeing the former as a variant of the pan-Indian trend.[10] While this may be true in so far as caste is concerned, there are significant differences in terms of control over land and in political structure. The (attenuated) presence of caste notwithstanding, hill society exhibits an absence of sharp class divisions. Viewed along with the presence of strong communal traditions, this makes Uttarakhand a fascinating exception which one is unable to fit into existing conceptualizations of social hierarchy in India. This distinctive agrarian structure, described below, is germane to the specific forms taken by the movements of social protest that are the subject of this study.[11]

The Central Himalaya are composed of two distinct ecological zones: the monsoon-affected middle and low altitude areas, and the high valleys of the north, inhabited by the Bhotiya herdsmen who had until 1962 carried out the centuries-old trade with Tibet.[12] Along the river valleys cultivation was carried out, limited only by the steepness of land and more frequently by the difficulty of irrigation. Two and sometimes

[10] The standard works are those by Berreman and Sanwal.

[11] Cf. chapters 4 and 5, where the democratic nature of the village community and its communal traditions are seen to play an important role in shaping the idiom of protest.

[12] The Bhotiyas, who are peripheral to this study, have been described in R. P. Srivastava, 'Tribe/Caste Mobility in India and the Case of Kumaun Bhotias', in C. von Fürer Haimendorf (ed.), *Caste and Kin in Nepal, India and Ceylon* (Bombay, 1966).

three harvests were possible throughout the last century, wheat, rice, and millets being the chief cereals grown. The system of tillage and methods of crop rotation bore the mark of the hillfolk's natural environment. With production oriented towards subsistence needs, which were comfortably met, there remained a surplus of grain for export to Tibet and southwards to the plains. Usually having six months' stock of grain in hand, and with their diet supplemented by fish, fruit, vegetable, and animal flesh, the hill cultivators were described by Henry Ramsay, commissioner from 1856 to 1884, as 'probably better off than any peasantry in India'.[13]

Through the nineteenth century European travellers and officials were frequently given to lyrical descriptions of peasant life in the Himalaya, comparing it favourably not merely to social conditions in the adjoining Indo-Gangetic plain but also to the everyday existence of British and Irish villagers. One official, returning from a trip to Tibet, compared the 'homely sight' of the 'pretty hamlets nestling in [the] fertile valleys' of Almora district with the 'barren wilderness' and 'treeless landscape' characteristic of life on the other side of the Himalaya.[14] That grain production easily exceeded subsistence was testified to by various mountaineering expeditions, who welcomed climbing in Upper Garhwal because the surplus produce of the interior villages made it 'very easy to live off the country'.[15] Perhaps the most evocative picture was drawn by the military adventurer Thomas Skinner, whose description of a scene in the Yamuna valley begins this chapter. Skinner marvelled at the 'remarkably clean' and 'well cultivated' villages whose 'terraces are bound by hedges, and neatly kept as they would be in England'. Apologizing for talking too much of 'green fields', he explains that he has only tried to 'convey as truly as I can, a

[13] H. G. Walton, *Almora: A Gazetteer* (Allahabad, 1911), pp. 57–9; S. D. Pant, *The Social Economy of the Himalayans* (London, 1935), p. 137; 'Correspondence Relating to the Scarcity in Kumaun and Garhwal in 1890', in *British Parliamentary Papers*, vol. 59 (1890–2).

[14] C. A. Sherring, *Western Tibet and the Indian Borderland* (1916; rpt. New Delhi, 1974), pp. 366–7.

[15] Eric Shipton, 'More Explorations round Nanda Devi', *The Geographical Journal*, vol. 90, no. 2, August 1937, p. 104; F. S. Smythe, 'Explorations in Garhwal around Kamet', *The Geographical Journal*, vol. 79, no. 1, January 1932, p. 3.

picture of the most delightful scenery, and most lovely spots on the face of the earth'. Coming across a shepherd boy playing his pipe, he comments that 'the notes were sweet and simple, and in such a situation, among such scenes, could not fail to bring to the mind an Arcadian picture.' Clearly, Skinner's evocation of mountain landscape is the more effusive for his having spent many years in the plains of India. At the same time, it is noteworthy that his Himalayan Arcadia is not an uninhabited wilderness but a composite picture of fields, houses, woods, fruit trees, birds, and streams.[16]

The hill land-tenure system inherited by the British differed no less strikingly from that in the plains. The first commissioner, G. W. Traill, observed that at least three-fourths of the villages were *hissedari*—i.e. wholly cultivated by the actual proprietors of the land, from whom the revenue demand was perforce restricted to their respective shares of the village assessment. The remaining villages were divided into (*i*) those in which the right of property was recognized in earlier recipients of land grants (many dating only from the period of Gurkha rule), while the hereditary right of cultivation remained with the original occupants (called *khaikar*); (*ii*) a handful of villages owned by a single individual. Here too, individual tenants (called *khurnee*) were able to wrest easy terms owing to the favourable land–man ratio.[17] As even the most important landowners depended not on any legal right but on the actual influence they exercised over village communities, there was not one estate which could be termed 'pure zamindari'. Government revenue and certain customary fees were collected by the *elected* village padhan, who reported in turn to a higher revenue official called the *patwari* (in charge of a *patti* or group of villages) who was entrusted with police duties and the responsibility of collecting statutory labour for public works.[18] While over time much of the class of khurnee merged with that

[16] Thomas Skinner, *Excursions in India, Including a Walk over the Himalaya Mountain to the Sources of the Jumna and the Ganges*, two volumes (London, 1832), I, pp. 223, 242, 246–7, 260, 268, etc.

[17] G. W. Traill, 'Statistical Sketch of Kumaun', in *Asiatic Researches*, vol. 16 (1828; rpt. Delhi, 1980).

[18] J. H. Batten, 'Report on the Settlement of the District of Garhwal' (1842); *idem*, 'Final Report on the Settlement of Kumaun', both in Batten (ed.), *Official Reports on the Province of Kumaun* (1851; rpt. Calcutta, 1878). The extent of land

of khaikar, the latter differed from the hissedar only in that he could not transfer land and had to pay a fixed sum as *mali-khana* to the proprietor. This sum represented the conversion into a cash payment of various cesses and perquisites earlier levied. But, by the end of the century, fully nine-tenths of all hillmen were estimated to be hissedars, cultivating proprietors with full ownership rights.[19]

Some evidence from census returns is given in Table 2.1. Not strictly comparable with the other mountainous districts, Nainital comprised a few hill pattis and a large area of the Terai which had begun to be settled by the end of the nineteenth century.[20] Within the hill districts proper, one observes that around 60 per cent of the agrarian population were owner-cultivators. Having already noted the position of *khaikhari* tenures, we can conclude that around 80 per cent of the total population farmed largely with the help of family labour. The extraordinarily low proportion of agricultural labour confirms

---

cultivated and share of gross produce retained by different classes of cultivators as estimated by Batten were:

Class	Per cent share of gross produce	Per cent of land cultivated
Cultivating proprietors (hissedar)	80	60
Original occupants reduced to occupancy tenants (khaikhar)	70–5	20
Tenants settled by proprietor (khurnee)	66	20
Non-resident tenants	NA	

Under the earlier rulers 'the agricultural assessment originally fixed was extremely light, and its rate and amount would appear to have been very rarely revised.' Traill, quoted in E. K. Pauw, *Report on the Tenth Settlement of the Garhwal District* (Allahabad, 1896), p. 53.

[19] B. H. Baden-Powell, *The Land Systems of British India* (1892; rpt. Delhi, 1974), vol. II, pp. 308–15; V. A. Stowell, *A Manual of the Land Tenures of the Kumaun Division* (1907; rpt. Allahabad, 1937). The latter statement, attributed to Pauw, is obviously an overestimate, but significant in so far as it reflects a strongly perceived contrast with the land systems of the plains.

[20] See B. K. Joshi, 'Underdevelopment of Hill Areas of UP', GIDS, Lucknow, mimeo, 1983, for the distinction between hill and terai.

TABLE 2.1

Occupational Classification of Agricultural Households in Kumaun, 1911–1921 (Workers and Dependants)

Category	DISTRICT					
	Nainital		Almora		British Garhwal	
	1911	1921	1911	1921	1911	1921
Those whose income is						
I. Primarily from rent:						
(*a*) landlords	3,023		681		102	
(*b*) occupancy tenants	5,025		21		2	
(*c*) ordinary tenants	15,199		22		17	
Total class I	23,247 (9.89)	722 (0.35)	724 (0.15)	530 (0.11)	121 (0.03)	155 (0.03)
II. From cultivation of their holdings						
(*a*) landlords	48,887 (20.80)		287,952 (59.31)		292,649 (66.60)	
(*b*) occupancy tenants	22,449 (9.55)		107,519 (22.15)		104,793 (23.85)	
(*c*) ordinary tenants	118,411 (50.38)		88,337 (17.16)		34,799 (7.92)	
Total class II	189,747 (80.73)	184,276 (89.15)	478,808 (98.62)	486,776 (98.04)	432,241 (98.37)	448,649 (99.11)

III. Farm servants and field labourers	14,212 (6.05)	15,261 (7.38)	1,771 (0.36)	2,411 (0.49)	3,917 (0.89)	1.744 (0.39)
IV. Goatherds, shepherds and herdsmen	4,886 (2.07)	3,741 (1.81)	3,151 (0.65)	6,035 (1.21)	1,507 (0.34)	642 (0.14)
V. Others (including forestry)	2,956 (1.26)	2,698 (1.31)	1,053 (0.22)	763 (0.15)	1,609 (0.37)	642 (0.14)
VI. Agriculture and pasture (total)	235,428	206,698	485,507	496,515	439,395	451,832
VII. Total population	323,519	276,875	525,104	530,338	480,167	485,186
VIII. VI as % of VII	72.65	74.65	92.46	93.62	91.51	93.30

NOTE: (*i*) A simpler classification was adopted in 1921 owing to the non-co-operation movement.
(*ii*) Figures in parentheses denote percentage of agricultural population (VI).

SOURCE: *Census of India*, 1911 and 1921.

the picture of an egalitarian peasant community, a picture used more often as an analytical construct than believed to exist in reality.[21]

The land system of Tehri Garhwal differed only in that theoretically all land vested in the sovereign. While landlords could not alienate their holdings, land was hereditary and could be gifted to religious endowments or leased out to tenants. Except for the *muafi* (revenue-free holding) of Saklana, there were few large landowners. As in Kumaun division, the agrarian system was dominated by peasants cultivating their holdings with the help of family labour. This is corroborated by the census figures.

TABLE 2.2

Land Holdings in Tehri Garhwal[1]

	1911	1921
Total population	300,819	318,414
Occupancy tenants	251,722	300,365[2]
Ordinary tenants	22,503	—
Rentiers	747	133
Farm servants and field labourers	1,799	922

[1] All figures for workers and dependants
[2] Includes ordinary tenants

SOURCE: As in Table 2.1.

Thus, over 80 per cent of the population corresponded to the category of hissedar in Kumaun division, except that they enjoyed hereditary rights of usufruct and not of ownership. Land revenue, paid directly to the king, was collected by patwaris who, along with the padhans, got a fixed share of the revenue as well as certain customary fees from the villagers. The kinsmen of the raja were, however, exempt from revenue. An indication of the dominance of small peasant production is given by the land revenue figures of 1910. Of the Rs 115,000 collected as revenue, 96,100 (or about 84 per cent) was col-

[21] Cf. D. Thorner, 'Peasant Economy as a Category in Economic History', in T. Shanin (ed.), *Peasants and Peasant Societies* (Harmondsworth, 1972).

lected as *khalsa*, i.e. revenue paid directly by the cultivator, and 18,900 as paid by *jagirs*, muafi and *gunth* (temples).[22]

Community traditions

The absence of sharp inequalities in land ownership within the body of cultivating proprietors—who formed the bulk of the population—was the basis for the sense of solidarity within the village community. Exhibiting a strong sense of clanship, peasants often derived their caste name from the village they inhabited. The institutional expression of this solidarity was the village panchayat. With every adult member of the 'clean' castes having a voice, the hill panchayat differed markedly from the caste panchayat of the plains. While not accorded formal rights, the Doms could also invoke the authority of the panchayat to settle their affairs.

Covering a wide range of activities, the panchayat dealt not only with social and religious matters but with judicial questions as well. Well after the establishment of colonial law in Kumaun, panchayats frequently continued to deal internally with matters technically under the jurisdiction of civil and criminal courts. In Tehri Garhwal, although the state had taken over some of its duties, the panchayats continued to be very powerful. While there was virtually no crime, Tehri peasants rarely ventured to the monarch's court, preferring to settle disputes amongst themselves.[23]

Role of women

A peculiar characteristic of hill agriculture—prevalent from Kashmir in the west to Arunachal in the east—is the important role assigned to women. In the difficult terrain no single economic activity can sustain the household. Typically, there is a 'basket' of economic pursuits—cultivation, cattle rearing, outside employment, perhaps some trade—that requires the equal participation of women. Thus,

> the women of the house are also equal partners in the struggle to achieve economic security. Their labour is in no way less valued than

[22] Based on H. K. Raturi, *Garhwal Varnan* (Bombay, 1910); *idem*, *Garhwal ka Itihas* (1928; rpt. Tehri, 1980); and conversations with Acharya G. N. Kothiyal.

[23] Joshi, *Khasa Family Law*, pp. 34, 194–9; Turner, 'Caste System', pp. 559–60; E. A. Blunt, *The Caste System of Northern India* (1931; rpt. Delhi, 1969), p. 145; Skinner, *Excursions in India*, vol. II, pp. 16–17.

that of the male members. They work equally with men in the fields, help them in looking after domestic animals and, of course, take physical care of husband and children. Except ploughing, a wife does virtually everything to help her husband in cultivation, which [elsewhere] are the men's task.[24]

Here the disproportionate role played by women in cultivation is ascribed to the imperatives of economic security in an inhospitable environment. Other writers, notably S. D. Pant in his pioneering work on Kumaun,[25] have tended to see in this unnatural division of labour incipient signs of sexual oppression. It may be pointed out that apart from her contribution to the tasks of cultivation, the woman of the household is exclusively responsible for household chores (cooking, cleaning, etc.), the rearing of children, and the collection of fuel, fodder and water. Foreign travellers were invariably struck by the importance of women in economic life, in stark contrast to male-dominated European agriculture.[26] These chores often involved 16 to 18 hours of hard work, and the husband was prone to chastise and even beat his wife when the tasks were not performed to his satisfaction. Reformers hoped that the spread of education, if it took women into its fold, would go a long way towards mitigating these evils.[27] Others commented more sharply on the disproportionate share of farm and family labour borne by women, and visualized a rebellion that 'has been lacking so far, but discontent is daily increasing and a change may occur any time.'[28]

State and society

Its isolated position and, later, its status as a recruiting ground for army personnel were reflected in the administrative policies

[24] Ramesh Chandra, 'Sex Role Arrangements to Achieve Economic Security in Northwest Himalayas', in C. von Fürer Haimendorf (ed.), *Asian Highland Societies in Anthropological Perspective* (New Delhi, 1981), p. 209.

[25] Pant, *Social Economy*.

[26] 'Mountaineer', *A Summer Ramble in the Himalayas* (London, 1860), p. 207; James Kennedy, *Life and Work in Benares and Kumaun 1839–1877* (London, 1884), p. 239.

[27] See *Garhwali* (Dehradun), 5 May 1928, 22 September 1928, etc.

[28] See Pant, *Social Economy*, p. 192. While this revolt may have been delayed, the participation of women in contemporary social movements (cf. chapter 7) bears witness to this prophetic statement.

followed in Kumaun division. While the 'peculiar circumstances of Kalee [i.e. Eastern] Kumaun and its position on the borders of the Nepal territory render a moderate [revenue] demand especially expedient', in Garhwal too the settlement officer was advised 'to form the settlement on the same principles of moderate demand . . .'[29] That these instructions were faithfully adhered to is borne out by Table 2.3.

TABLE 2.3

Land Revenue in Kumaun and British Garhwal, 1848

	Kumaun			British Garhwal			Average for province		
	Rs	a.	p.	Rs	a.	p.	Rs	a.	p.
Rate/acre/ total area	NA			NA			0	14	1
Rate/acre/ total Malguzaree	0	7	3	0	12	14	1	3	8
Rate/acre/ total cultivation	0	12	9	1	1	2	1	12	1

SOURCE: R. A. Shakespear, *Memoir on the Statistics of the North Western Provinces of the Bengal Presidency* (Calcutta, 1848).

Army recruitment had started by the mid nineteenth century, with both Kumauni and Garhwali soldiers being drafted into Gurkha units. The Garhwali Regiment, with headquarters at Lansdowne in the outer hills, was formed in 1890, becoming the 39th Garhwal Rifles in 1901. Essentially peasant farmers who returned to cultivate their holdings upon retirement, hill soldiers enjoyed an enviable record for their bravery.[30] In these circumstances, British land-revenue assessment was extraordinarily light—around Rs 3 per family—and

[29] R. Alexander, asst secretary to the comm., 3rd Div., Sudder Board, Camp Futtegurh, 7 February 1837, in Saksena (ed.), *Historical Papers*, pp. 233–4.

[30] A. L. Mumm, *Five Months in the Himalayas* (London, 1909), pp. 13–15; J. C. G. Lewer, *The Sowar and the Jawan* (Ilfracombe, Devon, 1981), pp. 46–50; P. Mason, *A Matter of Honour* (London, 1975), pp. 384–92. Garhwalis won three out of the five Victoria Crosses awarded to Indians during World War I, and were to win

its revision barely kept up with the increase in population. A rapid expansion of cultivated area was watched over by a highly personalized administration exemplified in the person of Henry Ramsay,[31] whom fellow Englishmen hailed as the uncrowned king of Kumaun.[32]

At one stage the hills had afforded distinct possibilities of tea cultivation. In 1862–3 over 35,000 pounds of tea was produced in Dehradun and Kumaun, and an estimate of waste land fitted for tea cultivation revealed that it was feasible to match the entire export trade of China from this region alone. As the climate, elevation and variety of vegetative types all suited Europeans, some officials strongly recommended large-scale colonization by white settlers. Holding out the 'certain prospect of comfort', colonization would be a 'perfect god-send to the starving peasantry of Ireland and of the Scotch Highlands'.[33] The refusal of the hill peasant to shed his subsistence orientation, and the opposition anticipated at the introduction of white settlers, led to these plans being shelved.[34] In fact, in the odd year when the monsoon failed, grain was imported by the authorities and sold at remunerative prices—a measure, it was stressed, necessitated not by the poverty of the population (who could well afford to buy grain) but by the inaccessibility of many villages and the lack of markets in an economy characterized by an absence of traders in food grains. Such measures may help explain the absence of any revenue-based agitations in either the nineteenth or the twentieth century.[35]

---

undying fame when they refused to fire at a crowd of Khudai Khitmatgars at Peshawar in 1930. For the latter episode, see Shekhar Pathak, *Peshawar Kand ki Yad* (Almora, 1982).

[31] Pant, *Social Economy*, p. 88; H. Ramsay, comm., KD, to secy, Sudder Board of Revenue, NWP & O, no. 147, 14 July 1856, in file no. 2, pre-Mutiny records, Regional Archives, Dehradun.

[32] See Jim Corbett, *My India* (Bombay, 1952), chapter IV, 'Pre-Red-Tape Days'.

[33] B. H. Hodgson, 'On the Colonialization of the Himalaya by Europeans' (1856), in his *Essays on the Languages, Literature and Religion of Nepal and Tibet* (1874; rpt. Varanasi, 1971), pt II, pp. 83–9.

[34] 'Reports on Tea Plantations', in *Selections from the Records of Government of the North Western Provinces*, vol. V (Allahabad, 1869); Walton, *British Garhwal*, pp. 37–9.

[35] Census of India, 1891, vol. 16, pt I, NWP & O (general report); A. S. Rawat, 'Administration of Land Revenue in British Garhwal (1856–1900)', in

If anything, state interference in the everyday world of peasant agriculture was even less in Tehri Garhwal. Not only was land revenue pitched lower than in the adjoining British territory, at marginally above Rs 2 per family in the early decades of this century,[36] but cultivators were also allowed to bring uncultivated land under the plough between two settlements without incurring any liability to enhanced assessment. And as income from forests came to constitute a major proportion of the king's revenue (chapter 3), there was little incentive to induce peasants to change their subsistence mode towards a market-oriented agriculture. The opening out of Tehri Garhwal was a slow process, hastened only after the world wars and the recruitment of Tehri peasants into the British Indian army. It was only in the last decade of the Tehri raj that the advent of a more revenue-oriented administration and radical revisions of the land settlement led to transformations in peasant society (chapter 5), whose scale far exceeded the gradual social changes of the preceding century and a half.

The 'begar' system

If land policy in British Kumaun did not quite exhibit the revenue orientation of colonial governance in other parts of India, Tehri Garhwal too resembled the archetypal 'feudal' princely state more in the breach. Indeed, the only major intrusion by the state in the life of the peasant before its takeover of the forests was the system of forced labour. Known by various names during the colonial period (*coolie utar*, *bardaish*, *begar*, *godam*), it has been the subject of a fine recent study.[37] The British operated the system, a legacy of the petty hill chiefs who preceded them, from Darjeeling to Simla, on grounds of administrative convenience in tracts whose physical situation made both commercial transport and boarding houses economically unattractive. As embodied in their settle-

---

Quarterly Review of Historical Studies (Calcutta), vol. 21, nos. 2 and 3, pp. 36–40 (1981–2).

[36] For details see the various annual reports of Tehri Garhwal deposited at the National Archives.

[37] Shekhar Pathak, 'Uttarakhand mein Coolie Begar Pratha: 1815–1949', unpublished Ph.D. thesis, Department of History, Kumaun University, 1980; this has now been published as a book by Radhakrishnan Publishers, Delhi.

ment agreements,[38] landholders were required to provide, for all government officials on tour and for white travellers (e.g. shikaris and mountaineers), several distinct sets of services. The most common of these involved carrying loads and building *chappars* (temporary rest huts), and the supply of provisions (bardaish) such as milk, food, grass, wood and cooking vessels. The actual operations, governed by custom, were far more complex than those sanctioned by custom. Although only hissedars and khaikars were technically liable to be called upon to provide coolie-bardaish, *sirtans* (tenants at will) were also held liable 'as a matter of custom and convenience'. Other forms of statutory labour included the collection of material and levelling of sites for building, roads and other public works, transporting the luggage of regiments moving from Lansdowne, and the carrying of iron and wood for the building of bridges in the interior. Old men and widows were exempt from these burdens at the discretion of the DC (district collector); otherwise remissions were rarely granted. According to the settlement villagers were to be reimbursed for these services, but in actual fact they were often rendered free.[39] While convinced of the 'inequity of the practice' as early as 1850, the government concluded after an enquiry that there existed no available substitute.[40]

In Tehri the different kinds of unpaid labour which could be requisitioned by the state, in addition to bardaish (provisions), were as follows: *gaon begar*, where villagers had to carry the luggage of subordinate officials; *manzil begar*, where villagers had to supply labour for the convenience of higher officials travelling on duty, for guests of the state, or for the carriage of

[38] As Taradutt Gairola argued, the Allahabad high court had passed judgments that the practice was in fact illegal. See his speech in the UP Legislative Council, 16 December 1918, in file no. 21 of 1918–19, dept xv, Regional Archives, Nainital.

[39] Note by D. A. Barker on '*quli-bardaish*', 13 April 1915, in GAD file 398/1913, UPSA ('Begar System in the Kumaun Division'); Shekhar Pathak, 'Kumaun mein Begar Anmulan Andolan', paper presented at seminar on peasant movements in UP, at Jawaharlal Nehru University, on 19 and 20 October 1982, pp. 1–2.

[40] NWP, Board of Revenue Proceedings, vol. 491, cons. 97, pro. 289, 'Forced Labour in Kumaun and Garhwal', India Office Library, London (notes collected by Shri Dharampal).

building materials which could not be transported by mules; *benth*, where labour was supplied for the construction of important buildings or for state occasions (e.g. royal marriages). While the extent of the household's contribution was proportional to the land revenue it paid, remissions were usually granted to village headmen, old men, widows and the handful of jagirdars and muafidars.[41]

THE CULTURAL ECOLOGY OF THE HIMALAYANS

With land revenue fixed at a comparatively low level, in both Tehri Garhwal and Kumaun divisions the begar system constituted the one major intervention by the state in the day-to-day life of the village. The absence of a class of 'feudal' intermediaries further reinforces the image of an independent peasantry firmly in command of its resources. As compared to the sharply stratified villages of the Indo-Gangetic plain, Uttarakhand came much closer to realizing the peasant political ideal of 'a popular monarchy, a state without nobles, perhaps without churchmen, in which the peasantry and their kings are the only social forces'.[42]

It has been suggested that this relative autonomy came about only through a long drawn out process of struggle between the peasantry and the overlord.[43] The absence of sharp class cleavages *within* village society, however, clearly owes its origins to the ecological characteristics of mountain society. Whereas the possibilities of 'extensive' agriculture were limited by the extent of culturable land and the paucity of irrigation, 'intensive' agriculture for the market was severely hampered by the fragility of the soils and poor communications. There

[41] 'Note on the Employment of Unpaid Labour in the Tehri Garhwal State' (prepared by Tehri durbar), enclosed with no. 1885, XVI-63, 17 January 1914, from P. Wyndham, comm., KD, to CSG, UP, in GAD file 398/1913.

[42] Rodney Hilton, *The English Peasantry in the Later Middle Ages* (Oxford, 1975), p. 15, quoted in Rosamund Faith, 'The Great Rumour of 1377 and Peasant Ideology', in T. H. Ashton and R. H. Hilton (eds), *The English Rising of 1381* (Cambridge, 1984), p. 63.

[43] Cf. Joshi, *Khasa Family Law*. For a theoretical exposition of the conflict between 'feudal' and 'communal' modes of power, see Partha Chatterji, 'More on Modes of Power and the Peasantry', in Ranajit Guha (ed.), *Subaltern Studies II* (Delhi, 1982).

have always existed major ecological constraints to the generation of surplus and consequently to the emergence of social classes in hill societies. In Uttarakhand, as in the Alps, Andes, and other comparable ecosystems, agrarian society has had a more or less uniform class structure, composed almost wholly of small peasant proprietors, and with a marginal incidence of big landlords and agricultural labourers. This distinctive class structure meshed nicely with the other ecologically determined hallmark of mountain society, the close integration of agriculture with forests and pasture.

Forests and social institutions in the indigenous system

The best class of cultivation in these mountains was to be found in villages between three and five thousand feet above sea level, having access on the one hand to good forest and grazing ground, and on the other to riparian fields in the depths of the valley. Village sites were usually chosen halfway up the spur, below oak forests and the perennial springs associated with them, and above the cultivated fields along the river bed. In such a situation all crops could be 'raised to perfection', a healthy elevated site was available for houses, and herds of cattle could be comfortably maintained. Until 1910 most villages came close to this ideal.[44]

With animal husbandry being as important to their economy as grain cultivation, the hillfolk and their cattle migrated annually to the grass-rich areas of the forest. Temporary cattle sheds (*kharaks*) were constructed and the cultivation of small patches carried out. In localities where sheep and goats were reared, they were taken to the alpine pastures above the tree line where they stayed till the first autumn snows.

In the permanent hamlets oak forests provided both fodder and fertilizer. Green and dry leaves, which served the cattle as litter, were mixed with grass and the excreta of the animals and fermented to give manure to the fields. In winter manure was moulded from dry leaves and subjected to rot. Thus the forest augmented the nutritive value of the fields, directly through its foliage and indirectly through the excreta of the cattle fed with

[44] Walton, *Almora*, pp. 47–8; *idem*, *British Garhwal: A Gazetteer* (Allahabad, 1911), p. 167.

fodder leaves and forest grass. Broad-leaved trees also provided the villagers with fuel and agricultural implements.[45]

In the lower hills the extensive *chir* forests served for pasture. Every year the dry grass and pine needle litter in the chir forest was burnt to make room for a fresh crop of luxuriant grass. Simultaneously, the needle litter, whose slippery surface endangered the otherwise sure-footed hill cattle, was destroyed. Very resistant to fire, chir was used for building houses and as torch-wood. In certain parts where pasture was scarce, trees were grown and preserved for fodder.[46]

In such multifarious ways the extensive forests were central to the successful practice of agriculture and animal husbandry. In addition, they were the prime source of medicinal herbs, and in times of dearth, of food as well. Indeed, the hillman was 'especially blessed by the presence in almost every jungle of fruit, vegetables or roots to help him over a period of moderate scarcity'.[47]

This dependence of the hill peasant on forest resources was institutionalized through a variety of social and cultural mechanisms. Through religion, folklore and tradition the village communities had drawn a protective ring around the forests. Across the region covered by this study there existed a highly sophisticated system of conservancy that took various forms. Often, hilltops were dedicated to local deities and the trees around the spot regarded with great respect. Many wooded areas were not of spontaneous growth and bore marks of the hillfolk's instinct for the plantation and preservation of the forest; indeed 'the spacious wooded areas extending over the mountain ranges and hill sides [bore] testimony to the care bestowed upon them by the successive generations of the Kumaunies.'[48] With villages usually sited halfway up the spur,

[45] This paragraph is drawn from Franz Heske, 'Problem der Walderhaltung in Himalaya' (Problems of Forest Conservation in the Himalaya; hereafter referred to as 'Problem'), *Tharandter Forstlichien Jahrbuch*, vol. 82, no. 8, 1931. I am grateful to Professor S. R. D. Guha for translating from the German. See also Patiram, *Garhwal: Ancient and Modern* (Simla, 1916), pp. 53–4; E. C. Mobbs, 'Life in a Himalayan Valley', in four parts, *Indian Forester*, vol. 60, nos. 10, 11 and 12; and vol. 61, no. 1 (1934–5).

[46] Heske, 'Problem', pp. 555, 564–5; Pauw, *Garhwal*, pp. 23, 47.

[47] Walton, *Almora*, p. 59.

[48] G. B. Pant, *The Forest Problem in Kumaun* (Allahabad, 1922), pp. 30–1.

sacred groves had an obvious functional role in stabilizing water flows and preventing landslides. Particularly in eastern Kumaun and around temples, *deodar* plantations had become naturalized, some way east of the trees' natural habitat. Temple groves of deodar varied in extent from a few trees to woods of several hundred acres.[49] This magnificent tree, one surveyor remarked, is 'frequently planted by the Hindus in all parts of the mountains, and attains a gigantic size'.[50] As late as 1953 it was reported that the finest stands of deodar were found near temples, venerated and protected from injury.[51] Commenting on the numerous sacred places in deodar forests, an official observed that 'such spots are frequently prominent places where a good view is obtained, or a beautiful glade in the forest, or where there is some unusual natural phenomena, as a large rock split with a tree growing between the two halves.' Sacred spots were normally marked with cloth or coins.[52] Nor was tree worship restricted to the deodar; a Swiss geologist expedition found, in a village in the Upper Dhauli valley in Garhwal, a sacred birch tree remarkable in its size: with a spread of eighty feet and a double trunk ten feet in diameter.[53] In such sacred groves, the 'traditional form of forest preservation', and one found all over India, no villager would injure the vegetation in any way.[54] In fact, the planting of a grove was regarded as 'as a work of great religious merit'.[55] In parts of Tehri, even today, leaves are offered to a goddess known as Patna Devi (goddess of leaves), this being only one of several

[49] S. B. Bhatia, *WP for the East Almora Forest Division, UP, 1924–25 to 1933–34* (Allahabad, 1926), pp. 13, 32. (WP stands for 'Working Plan'. I use the abbreviation even within monograph titles.)

[50] R. Strachey, 'On the Physical Geography of the Provinces of Kumaun and Garhwal in the Himalaya', *Journal of the Royal Geographical Society*, vol. 21, 1851, p. 76.

[51] N. L. Bor, *Manual of Indian Forest Botany* (Delhi, 1953), p. 18.

[52] E. C. Mobbs, 'Life in a Himalayan Valley', pt IV, *Indian Forester* (IF), vol. 61 (1935), pp. 1–8.

[53] A. Heim and A. Gansser, *The Throne of the Gods: An Account of the First Swiss Expedition to the Himalayas*, translated by Eden and Cedar Paul (London, 1939), p. 116.

[54] D. Brandis, *Indian Forestry* (Woking, 1897), p. 12.

[55] S. M. Edwardes, 'Tree Worship in India', *Empire Forestry*, vol. 1, no. 1 (March 1922), pp. 78–80.

examples of the association of plants with gods.[56] Cases were not unknown of open land being left uncultivated that were dedicated to fairies of the forests, who were believed to come there at night to play.[57] In the Tons valley, tubers and roots—the peasantry's food during times of scarcity—are used only during culturally specified times to inhibit overexploitation.[58]

While sacred groves testified to the role played by traditional religious beliefs in the preservation of nature, in other instances it was informal management practices that regulated the utilization of forest produce by the community. A civilian newly posted to the hills in the 1920s was struck by the way communal action continued to survive in the considerable areas serving as village grazing ground, and by fuel and fodder reserves walled in and well looked after. Despite official apathy the old customary restrictions on the use of the forests operated 'over large areas'; while no formal management existed, practical protection was secured by customary limitations on users. In many patches of oak forest there were rules that prohibited the lopping off of leaves in the hot weather, while the grass cut by each family was strictly regulated. The penalty for the infringement of these rules included boycott and/or the exclusion from the forest of the offender.[59] Traditionally, many villages had fuel reserves even on *gaon sanjait* (common land) measured by government, which the villagers cut over in regular rotation by common consent. With the planting of timber trees a fairly common phenomenon, the jungles preserved within their boundaries were zealously guarded by villages nearby. Thus, Tehri officials observed that peasants strongly asserted their claim to species like *bhimal*, a valuable fodder tree usually found near habitations.[60] In British Garhwal, Chaundkot *pargana* was singled out for its oak forests within village boundaries, called *bani* or *banjanis*, where branches of trees were cut only at specified times, and then with the permission of the entire village

[56] R. K. Gupta, *The Living Himalayas: Volume 1: Aspects of Environment and Resource Ecology of Garhwal* (Delhi, 1983), p. 295.

[57] Mobbs, 'Himalayan Valley', pp. 10–11.

[58] Sunderlal Bahuguna, personal communication.

[59] Note by J. K. Pearson, December 1926, in FD file 83/1909, UPSA.

[60] H. K. Raturi, *Garhwal Varnan* (Bombay, 1910), p. 36.

community.[61] In remote areas, untouched by commercial exploitation of forests, one can still come across well maintained banjanis containing oak trees of a quality rarely observed elsewhere.[62]

Undoubtedly, this situation was facilitated by the near-total control exercised by villages over their forest habitat. As 'the waste and forest lands never attracted the attention of former [i.e. pre-British] governments',[63] the peasant communities enjoyed the untrammelled use of their produce. While the native kings did subject the produce of the forests, such as medicinal herbs, to a small cess as and when they were exported, the products of the forests consumed by the people themselves were not taken into account.[64] In such circumstances, where they exercised full control over their forest habitat, co-operation of a high order was exhibited by adjoining villages. Every village in the hills had fixed boundaries, existing from the time of the pre-Gurkha rulers, and recognized by G. W. Traill in the Kumaun settlement of 1823 (the so-called *san assi* boundaries). Within these limits the inhabitants of each village exercised various proprietary and other rights of grazing and fuel, secured by long usage and custom.[65] Quite remarkably, this co-operation existed even across political boundaries; thus, the adjoining villages in Tehri and Bashar state amicably grazed their flocks and fetched wood from common forest and pasture land without any kind of dispute.[66]

Although the above account consists largely of fragments reconstituted from official discourse, it is apparent that the role of forests in hill life was highlighted by the existence of social and cultural institutions which enabled the peasantry to re-

[61] Note by V. A. Stowell, D. C. Garhwal, n.d., probably 1907; note of August 1910 by Dharmanand Joshi, the late deputy collector, Garhwal, both in FD file 83/1909.

[62] Observations in villages of Pithoragarh district, October 1983.

[63] E. K. Pauw, *Report*, p. 53.

[64] See E. T. Atkinson, *The Himalayan Districts of the North Western Provinces*, vol. 1 (Allahabad, 1884).

[65] T. D. Gairola, *Selected Revenue Decisions of Kumaun* (Allahabad, 1936), p. 209.

[66] Joint Report, 26 October 1910, of Mr Darling, political assistant commissioner, Simla, and Dharmanand Joshi, retired deputy collector on special duty, in file no. 210/1910, political department, UPSA.

produce its existence—this notwithstanding the later construction of an ideology which viewed the usurpation of state monopoly over forests as a logical corollary of the lack of 'scientific' management practices among the original inhabitants of forest areas.[67] The 'intimate and reverential attitude toward the land', which Robert Redfield regards as being a core value of peasant society, seems to have incorporated, in Uttarakhand, a reverential attitude towards the forest as well.[68] In other parts of India where forests are closely interwoven with material life, we observe very similar patterns of cultural restraints on resource utilization. Thus, in tribal India even today, 'it is striking to see how in many of the myths and legends the deep sense of identity with the forest is emphasized.'[69] In such forest areas not only did the forests have a tremendous influence in moulding religious and spiritual life,[70] the inhabitants also exhibited a deep love of vegetation, often acting 'entirely from a sense of responsibility towards future generations' by planting species whose span of maturity exceeded a human lifetime.[71]

As this description of traditional conservation systems suggests, these hardy peasant communities had been primed for collective action. The absence of serious economic differences greatly facilitated social solidarity, as did the ties of kinship and caste shared by villagers. In its democratic characteristics and reliance on natural resources Uttarakhand is representative of mountain societies in general, in which ecological constraints to the intensification and expansion of agriculture have historically resulted in an emphasis on the close regulation of the common property resources so crucial for the subsistence of individual households. Tailored 'to the characteristics of the community's own environment and population', the detailed rules for the management and utilization of forests and pasture

[67] See Ramachandra Guha, 'Forestry in British and Post-British India: A Historical Analysis', in two parts, *Economic and Political Weekly*, 29 October and 5–12 November 1983.

[68] Robert Redfield, *Peasant Society and Culture* (Chicago, 1961), pp. 19, 63–4.

[69] *Report of the Scheduled Areas and Scheduled Tribes Commission, Volume I, 1960–61* (Delhi, 1967), p. 125.

[70] See M. K. Raha, 'Forest in Tribal Life', *Bulletin of the Cultural Research Institute*, vol. 2, no. 1, 1963.

[71] C. von Fürer Haimendorf, *Himalayan Barbary* (London, 1955), pp. 62–3.

account in large measure for the stability and persistence of many mountain communities.[72] Lucien Febvre's description of Andorran highlanders applies quite beautifully to Uttarakhand —namely that there was an 'effective solidarity among them and a special development of certain rules in their scheme of government, especially those which relate to common property and grazing rights'.[73] As Uttarakhand was virtually unaffected by external political forces in the millennia before the Gurkha invasion, these systems of resource use had become an integral, seemingly permanent part of the social fabric. They were superseded by another system of forest management, propelled by powerful economic and political forces, which rested on a radically different set of priorities. The socio-ecological characteristics of this new system, and its impact on traditional patterns of resource use, are spelt out in the next chapter.

[72] See Robert Netting, *Balancing on an Alp* (Cambridge, 1981), chapter III, 'Strategies of Alpine Land Use'.

[73] Lucien Febvre, *A Geographical Introduction to History* (1925: rpt. London, 1925), translated by E. G. Mountford and J. H. Paxton, p. 176 f.

CHAPTER 3
Scientific Forestry and Social Change

> Then began a life of guerilla warfare for [head forester] Michaud, his three foresters, and Groison. Unweariedly they tramped through the woods, lay out in them of nights, and set themselves to acquire that intimate knowledge which is the forest-keeper's science, and economizes his time. They watched the outlets, grew familiar with the localities of the timber, trained their ears to detect the meaning of every crash of boughs, of every different forest sound. Then they studied all the faces of the neighbourhood, the different families of the various villages were all passed in review, the habits and characters of the different individuals were noted, together with the ways in which they worked for a living. And all this was a harder task than you may imagine. The peasants who lived on the Aigues, seeing how carefully these measures had been concerted, opposed a dumb resistance, a feint of acquiescence which baffled this intelligent police supervision.
>
> — Balzac, *The Peasantry*

THE FORESTS OF UTTARAKHAND

Early travellers were impressed by the extent and density of the Himalayan forests. In 1793 a visitor to the court of the king of undivided Garhwal proclaimed that 'the forests of oak, fir, and boorans [rhododendron] are here more extensive and the trees of greater magnitude, than any I have ever seen.'[1] An early commissioner of Kumaun, investigating sources of fuel for a proposed iron mine, was bold enough 'to declare that the forests of Kumaun and Garhwal are boundless and, to all appearances, inexhaustible'.[2] Almost a century later two Swiss

[1] T. Hardwicke, 'Narrative of a Journey to Srinagar', *Asiatic Researches*, vol. 6 (1809; rpt. Delhi, 1979), p. 327.

[2] J. H. Batten, comm., KD, to W. Muir, secy to govt, NWP, 6 August 1855, in 'Papers regarding the Forests and Iron Mines in Kumaun', in *Selections from the Records of the Government of India (Home Department)*, supplement no. VIII (Calcutta, 1855), pp. 6–7.

geologists were likewise 'surprised at the vast extension of the wooded ranges in the lower Himalaya'.[3]

The varied conditions of topography and altitude in Uttarakhand had given rise to a wide variety of forest types. While a detailed description would be out of place here, a brief statement of the forest types is given in Table 3.1.[4]

TABLE 3.1

Distribution of Vegetation by Altitude in the Central Himalaya

Altitude (in feet)	Characteristic vegetation
13,000	Vegetation entirely ceases
12,000	Birch and blue pine
11,000	Fir, spruce, yew, cypress and bush
10,000	Rhododendron and chestnut limit; grassy slopes begin
9,000	Higher level oaks (*tilonj* and *kharsu*) chiefly occur
8,000	*Banj* oak limit
7,000	Blue and chir pine limit; banj oak and rhododendron in abundance
6,000	Deodar begins; banj and rhododendron begin to give way to pine
5,000	Chir pine in abundance
4,000	*Sal* limit; *haldu* and *tun*

SOURCE: Adapted from S. D. Pant, *Social Economy of the Himalayans* (London, 1935).

The major division is between the conifers and the broadleaved species. Within this division the most important and common species, especially in the altitudes inhabited by human populations, are the banj or *ban* oak (*Quercus incana*) and the chir or *chil* pine (*Pinus roxburghii*). In general, the species distribution reflects the process of *ecological succession* whereby stable forest cover is established on any terrain. This succession can generally be divided into three stages:[5] (*i*) the initial stage,

[3] A Heim and A. Gansser, *Central Himalaya* (1939; rpt. Delhi, 1975), p. 229.

[4] This is dealt with exhaustively in the working plans for each forest division.

[5] Based on R. S. Troup, *Silviculture of Indian Trees* (Oxford, 1921), Introduction and *passim*.

in which certain species of trees, usually with small or light seeds, take possession of newly exposed ground; (*ii*) the transitional stages, in which changes take place on ground already clothed with some vegetative cover; (*iii*) the climax stage, which represents the farthest advance towards a hygrophilous (i.e. adapted to plentiful water supply) type of vegetation which the locality is capable of supporting. While it could be said that in the Himalaya the oaks and other broad-leaved species represent stage (*iii*) and the conifers stage (*ii*), in the days before forest management mixed forests were the norm. In general, the more favourable the locality is for vegetation the greater the number of species struggling for existence in it.

Two points are noteworthy. While the oaks (and other broad-leaved species) are more valuable for hill agriculture, on both ecological and economic grounds the conifers have had, since the inception of 'scientific' management, a variety of commercial uses. Second, while 'progressive' succession—from stage (*i*) to (*iii*)—occurs in nature, 'retrogressive' succession—from stage (*iii*) to (*ii*) to (*i*)—can be caused by the hand of man, either accidentally or deliberately. Foresters are cautioned that in many cases 'the natural trend of this succession may be diametrically opposed to what is desirable from an economic point of view.'[6] This disjunction between the natural trend of ecological succession—whereby oak is the climactic stage—and the imperatives of commercial forestry—which favoured the extension of conifers—has had a major influence on the development of scientific forestry in Uttarakhand.

THE GROWTH AND DEVELOPMENT OF STATE FORESTRY IN UTTARAKHAND

The landmark in the history of Indian forestry is undoubtedly the building of the railway network. The large-scale destruction of accessible forests in the early years of railway expansion led to the hasty creation of a forest department, set up with the help of German experts in 1864. The first task before the new department was to identify the sources of supply of strong and durable timbers—such as sal, teak and deodar—which could be used as railway sleepers. With sal and teak being very heavily

[6] Ibid., pp. iv–v.

worked out,[7] search parties were sent to explore the deodar forests of the Sutlej and Yamuna valleys.[8] Intensive felling in these forests forced the government to rely on the import of wood from Europe. But with emphasis placed on substituting indigenous sleepers for imported ones, particularly in the inland districts of northern India, the department considered the utilization of the Himalayan pines if they responded adequately to antiseptic treatment.[9]

Successful forest administration required checking the deforestation of past decades,[10] and for this the assertion of state monopoly right was considered essential. A prolonged debate within the colonial bureaucracy on whether to treat the customary use of forests as based on 'right' or on 'privilege' was settled by the selective use of precedent and the principle that 'the right of conquest is the strongest of all rights—it is a right against which there is no appeal.'[11] An initial attempt at asserting state monopoly through the forest act of 1865 having been found wanting, a comprehensive all-India act was drafted thirteen years later. This act of 1878 provided for the constitution of 'reserved' or closed forests, divested of existing rights of user to enable sustained timber production. The act also provided for an elaborate procedure of forest settlement to deal with all claims of user, which, if upheld, could be transferred to a second class of forest designated as 'protected'.[12] While the

[7] Thus, by 1869, the sal forests of the outer hills were all 'felled in even to desolation'. See G. F. Pearson, 'Sub Himalayan Forests of Kumaun and Garhwal', in *Selections from the Records of the Government of the North Western Provinces*, 2nd series, vol. 2 (Allahabad, 1869), p. 132 (hereafter *Selections*).

[8] See G. P. Paul, *Felling Timber in the Himalayas* (Lahore, 1871).

[9] D. Brandis, 'Memorandum on the Supply of Railway Sleepers of the Himalayan Pines Impregnated in India', IF, vol. 4 (1879), pp. 365–85.

[10] A vivid account of the official measures that induced this deforestation can be found in E. P. Stebbing, *The Forests of India*, 3 volumes (London, 1922–7), 1, pp. 36–62, 288–9, 505–9, 523–30, etc. By 'successful' forest administration I mean successful from the viewpoint of strategic imperial needs.

[11] C. F. Amery, 'On Forest Rights in India', in D. Brandis and A. Smythies (eds), *Report of the Proceedings of the Forest Conference held at Simla, October 1875* (Calcutta, 1876), p. 27.

[12] For the 1878 act which, apart from minor modifications continues to be in operation, the basic documents are: B. H. Baden-Powell, 'On the Defects of the Existing Forest Law (Act VII of 1865) and Proposals for a New Forest Act', in B. H. Baden-Powell and J. S. Gamble (eds), *Report of the Proceedings of the Forest*

burden of proof to establish 'legally established rights' was on the people, the state could grant both 'non-established rights' and 'terminable concessions' at its discretion.[13]

State forestry in Tehri Garhwal

The commercial exploitation of the forests of Tehri Garhwal predates similar operations in the British territory. The Yamuna valley, particularly, harboured the finest stands of deodar found anywhere, with the tree's resilient wood being in great demand for railway sleepers. In fact, around 1850 an intrepid Englishman named Wilson had leased the state's forests for a paltry sum of Rs 400 per annum and pioneered the water transport of timber. On the expiry of Wilson's lease in 1865 the government of the North Western Provinces, well aware that 'the importance of adding as much as possible to the limited area of forest now capable of yielding large timber is very great',[14] successfully negotiated a twenty-year lease of all forests in the state for Rs 10,000 per annum. Clearly, strategic imperial needs, and not disinterested motives of forest preservation, led the British to enter into this contract.[15] In April 1885 the lease was renegotiated whereby the chir forests of the Tons valley reverted to state control, the deodar forests remaining with the Imperial Forest Department. Although the lease was renewed for a further twenty-year period in 1905, from 1902 'as an act of grace' the raja was paid 80 per cent of net profits in lieu of an annual rental.[16]

The leased forests were divested of existing rights of user enjoyed by the surrounding population and worked for the extraction of railway sleepers. Preliminary surveys, which

---

Conference, 1873–74 (Calcutta, 1874), pp. 3–30; D. Brandis, *Memorandum on the Forest Legislation Proposed for British India* (*Other than the Presidencies of Madras and Bombay*) (Simla, 1875).

[13] 'Instructions for Forest Settlement Officers in the NWP & O', no. 682/XIV, 328–63, dated 29 May 1897, in file no. 279, dept IV A, list no. 2, post-Mutiny records, RAD.

[14] Col. R. Strachey, secy, GOI, to secy to govt, NWP, in the PWD, 29 March 1864, foreign dept, revenue B prog., May 1864, no. 10, NAI.

[15] P. D. Raturi, *WP for the Jamuna For. Div., Tehri Garhwal State 1932–33 to 1952–53* (Tehri, 1932), p. 49.

[16] J. C. Tulloch, *WP for the Leased Deodar Forests in Tehri Garhwal* (Allahabad, 1907), pp. 1–5.

identified the nature of timber growth in the different forest zones, established beyond doubt that the property acquired at a nominal lease would 'yield a fine yearly revenue, besides supplying the wants of both government and the railways for timber'.[17] The forests were then brought under working plans that regulated the yearly extraction and prescribed appropriate silvicultural practices to enable adequate reproduction of species like čhir and deodar. Forming 'perhaps the largest and most compact deodar forest in the world', the Yamuna woods exported 6,500,000 deodar sleepers in the period 1869–85.[18] At the time when the rate of forest destruction imperilled further railway expansion, the forests of Tehri Garhwal proved a strategically valuable resource for British colonialism.

Meanwhile the raja had constituted a skeletal forest staff in 1885 and, twelve years later, Pandit Keshavanand Mamgain, a native Garhwali, was deputed from the forest department of the North Western Provinces. Keshavanand, who began the work of demarcating the forests, was succeeded as conservator of forests by Sadanand Gairola in 1905. In 1907 Rama Dutt Raturi took over the post and demarcated the forests and waste land into three classes: (*i*) the first class or reserved forests; (*ii*) the second class, intended for the exercise of forest concessions; and (*iii*) a class for the constitution of village forests.

While the third class remained largely inoperative, over time the distinction between the first two classes was abolished. As the 'legal' property right in the forest was claimed by the sovereign, the peasantry was only allowed to exercise certain 'concessions' notified by the durbar. Regulations fixed the amount of building timber allotted to households, while free grazing was allowed in the second and third class forests within a five-mile radius of each village. Villagers could also collect dry fallen wood and cut grass in specified areas. In return the peasants were to help in extinguishing forest fires as and when

[17] G. F. Pearson, 'Forests in the Bhageerathi Valley', in *Selections*, vol. 2, p. 121. Also *idem*, 'Report on the Bhageerathi Valley Forests', in *Selections*, vol. 3 (Allahabad, 1870), pp. 106–16.

[18] N. Hearle, *WP for the Tehri Garhwal Leased Forest, Jaunsar For. Div.* (Allahabad, 1888), pp. 1–16.

these occurred. In addition, a tax of half a *seer* of ghee was levied on every buffalo possessed by a state subject.[19]

TABLE 3.2

Durbar Revenue from Leased Forests, 1909–1924

Average for period	Raja's share of surplus (in lakhs)
1909–10 to 1911–12	0.96
1912–13 to 1914–15	1.52
1915–16 to 1917–18	1.72
1918–19 to 1920–21	2.03
1921–22 to 1923–24	1.45

SOURCE: Computed from E. C. Mobbs, *WP for the Tons For. Div., T.G. State, 1925–46* (Allahabad, 1926).

As Table 3.2 indicates, British management demonstrated the commercial value of the Tehri forests, and in common with other native chiefs the raja became 'generally very much alive' to the value of his forest property.[20] On the leased forests reverting totally to state control in 1925, the durbar invited Dr Franz Heske, a renowned German expert, to survey the forests and advise on their systematic working. Based on Heske's recommendations, forest settlement operations were embarked upon during 1929–31, and officers sent to the Forest Research Institute to undergo training.[21] Several new forest divisions were constituted, and gradually the entire forests of the state came to be managed under working plans.[22] Under state management the revenue orientation became more marked

[19] M. N. Bahuguna, *WP for the Tehri For. Div., Tehri Garhwal State, 1939–40 to 1969–70* (Tehri, 1941); Tehri durbar circular no. 21 of 1930, reproduced in V. P. S. Verma, *WP for the Tehri For. Div., Garhwal Circle, UP, 1973–74 to 1982–83* (Nainital, 1973), appendix, pp. 580–4.

[20] E. A. Smythies, *India's Forest Wealth* (London, 1925), p. 27.

[21] *Garhwali* (hereafter GRH), 20 October 1928; file no. 730–1/26, F. and P. dept, NAI.

[22] Four new divisions were constituted: Tehri, Uttarakashi, Yamuna and Tons.

(Table 3.3). While exact figures are unobtainable, the extraction of timber was considerable, especially during World War II. In the first three years of the war, over 1.4 million cubic feet—double the average extraction in normal years—of timber was exported for use on the front. Over 20,000 trees were

TABLE 3.3

Revenue and Surplus of Tons Forest Division, Tehri Durbar, 1925–1945

(in lakhs)

Year	Gross revenue	Net revenue (surplus)
1925–26	3.01	2.41
1926–27	4.20	3.55
1927–28	2.81	2.43
1928–29	2.49	1.79
1929–30	2.31	1.89
1930–31*	1.31	0.53
1931–32*	1.82	0.53
1932–33*	1.01	0.50
1933–34*	1.77	0.80
1934–35	1.99	1.31
1935–36*	1.24	1.09
1936–37	0.92	0.73
1937–38	1.10	0.50
1938–39	1.64	1.41
1939–40	4.16	3.94
1940–41	3.12	2.87
1941–42	2.30	2.08
1942–43	6.04	5.83
1943–44	4.02	3.80
1944–45	3.49	3.39

* Does not include revenue from departmental timber operations.

SOURCE: K. P. Pant, *WP for the Tons For. Div. (leased forests), T.G. State, 1945–6 to 1964–5* (Dehradun, 1948).

exported annually from the Tons valley alone.[23] Over time, forests came to constitute the largest single item of revenue for the durbar, a far cry from the days when the king had leased out a seemingly valueless property for a pittance. In 1935–6, for example, forests accounted for 7.3 lakhs out of a total of 17.94 lakhs that accrued to the exchequer on all heads.[24] As the state took greater interest in the commercial management of its woodland, village access to the forests was correspondingly reduced.

Forestry in Kumaun division

The systematic management of the Kumaun hill forests commenced with the constitution of small blocks of reserved forests to furnish a permanent supply of fuel and timber to the administrative centres of Nainital and Almora and the cantonment town of Ranikhet.[25] A survey was commissioned to report on the detailed composition of the hill forests, particularly those within 'reasonable distance' of land and water, and select sites for roads and saw mills.[26] This was followed in 1893 by the declaration of all unmeasured land in Kumaun division as 'district protected forest' (DPF)—what was thought 'of primary importance was to assert the proprietary right of Government in these forests' and lay down certain limits to the hitherto unregulated access of rightholders.[27] Official interest in these forests, dominated by the long-leaved or chir pine, quickened further with two important scientific developments being reported by Indian forest officials. The tapping of chir pine for oleo-resin had been started on an experimental basis in the 1890s. By 1912 methods of distillation had been evolved which would enable the products to compete with the American and French varieties that had hitherto ruled the market. At the same time, fifty years of experimentation on a process to pro-

[23] See P. D. Raturi, 'War Effort of Tehri Garhwal State Forest Department (1939–42)', IF, vol. 68 (1942), pp. 631–4.

[24] See *Annual Administrative Report of the Tehri Garhwal State, 1936–37* (Tehri, 1937).

[25] D. Brandis, *Suggestions Regarding Forest Administration in the Northwestern Provinces and Oudh* (Calcutta, 1882).

[26] T. W. Webber, *The Forests of Upper India* (London, 1902), pp. 38–43.

[27] Note by J. S. Campbell, Kumaun division, 6 July 1910, in FD file no. 83/1909, UPSA.

long the life of certain Indian woods for use as railway sleepers through chemical treatment finally bore fruit. Of the timbers successfully treated the chir and blue pines were both found suitable and available in substantial quantities, and could be marketed at a sufficiently low price.[28]

Four distinct phases, representing the progressive diminution of villagers' rights in the forests of Kumaun, can be distinguished:[29]

(*i*) Between 1815 and 1878 the state concentrated on the submontane sal forests of the foothills, while the forests of Kumaun proper were left untouched. However, the forests around Nainital were demarcated in the 1850s and those around Ranikhet and Almora in 1873 and 1875, respectively.

(*ii*) Between 1878 and 1893 these forests were notified as reserved under the 1878 act, while grants of forest made to iron companies and several other tracts in Almora and Garhwal districts were declared reserved or protected forests.

(*iii*) On 17 October 1893 all waste land not forming part of the measured area of villages or of the forests earlier reserved was declared to be DPF under the act, although the necessary enquiry (vide section 28) had not been made. Thus, DPF comprised, apart from tree-covered lands, snow-clad peaks, ridges and cliffs, river beds, lakes, buildings, temple lands, camping and pasture grounds, and roads and shops.[30] A skeletal forest

[28] Puran Singh, 'Note on the Distillation and Composition of Turpentine Oil from the Chir Resin and the Clarification of Indian Resin', *Indian Forest Records* (IFR), vol. IV, pt I (Calcutta, 1912); R. S. Pearson, 'Note on the Antiseptic Treatment of Timber in India, with Special Reference to Railway Sleepers', IFR, vol. II, pt I (Calcutta, 1912). Also *idem*, 'A Further Note on the Antiseptic Treatment of Timber, with Results Obtaining from Past Experiments', IFR, vol. VI, pt IX (Calcutta, 1918). These two sets of findings finally led to the constitution of the Kumaun circle on 2 October 1912, and forest settlements being undertaken in the three districts.

The two chief products of oleo-resin, turpentine and rosin, had a wide variety of industrial uses. While resin was used in the manufacture of shellac, soap, paper, oil cloth, linoleum, sealing wax, printing inks, electric installations, and gramophone records, turpentine was the chief thinner and solvent used in the manufacture of paint and varnish, the basis of synthetic camphor, and an ingredient of boot-polish and liniments. See Smythies, *India's Forest Wealth*, p. 80.

[29] Following Pant, *Forest Problem*, pp. 6–26.

[30] As I have noted, this proclamation was made with a view to asserting proprietary right in these lands.

staff was constituted and on 24 October 1894 eight types of tree—including deodar, chir and sal—were reserved. Rules were framed for regulating the lopping of trees for fuel and fodder and claims for timber, while trade by villagers in any form of forest product was prohibited. On 5 April 1903 the Kumaun DPF were divided into two classes: closed civil forests, which the state considered necessary for reproduction or protection; and open civil forests, where villagers could exercise their rights subject to the rules prescribed in 1894.

(iv) All these cumulative incursions culminated in 1911 with the decision to carve extensive reserves out of the DPF. Forest settlements carried out in the three districts between 1911 and 1917 resulted in the constitution of almost 3000 square miles of reserved forest in Kumaun division. Elaborate rules were framed for the exercise of rights, specifying the number of cattle to be grazed and amount of timber and fuelwood allotted to each rightholder. Villagers had to indent in advance for timber for construction of houses and for agricultural implements, which would be supplied by the divisional forest officer (DFO) from a notified list of species. The annual practice of burning the forest floor for a fresh crop of grass was banned within one mile of reserved forests. As this excluded few habitations in these heavily forested hills, the prohibition virtually made the practice illegal.[31]

Within a few years of commercial working the Kumaun forests had become a paying proposition. When one full fifteen-year cycle (1896–1911) had revealed that resin tapping did not permanently harm trees, attempts were made to 'develop the resin industry as completely and rapidly as possible'.[32] Between 1910 and 1920 the number of resin channels tapped rose from 260,000 to 2,135,000,[33] a rate of increase matched by the production of rosin and turpentine (Table 3.4). When the construction of a new factory at Bareilly was completed in 1920—

[31] Details of these rules can be found in A. E. Osmaston, *WP for the North Garhwal For. Div., 1921–22 to 1930–31* (Allahabad, 1921), appendix.

[32] E. A. Smythies, 'The Resin Industry in Kumaun', *Forest Bulletin No. 26* (Calcutta, 1914), p. 3. Cf. also R. G. Marriot, *The Resin Industry in Kumaun, Compiled in the Kumaun Circle*, bulletin no. 9, United Provinces forest department (Allahabad, 1936).

[33] Stebbing, III, p 660. The work was done by small contractors (practically all from outside Kumaun), under the supervision of the forest department.

TABLE 3.4

Imports into and Production in India of Rosin and Turpentine, 1907–1923

Year	Rosin			Turpentine		
April to March	Imports	Indian production	Total (cwts)	Imports	Indian production	Total (gallons)
1907–8	76,200	4,845	81,045	225,560	16,086	241,646
1910–11	41,600	6,625	48,225	197,720	17,051	214,771
1913–14	45,769	20,100	65,869	193,937	58,803	252,740
1916–17	18,760	43,500	62,260	80,000	125,663	205,663
1919–20	13,855	46,700	60,555	113,638	148,680	262,318
1921–22	10,602	57,200	67,802	70,369	163,151	233,520
1922–23*	18,037	82,000	100,037	90,364	279,100	369,464

* Calendar year 1922.

NOTE: Until 1920 two factories accounted for total production—Bhowali (UP) accounted for roughly 60 per cent and Jalloo (Punjab) for the rest.

SOURCE: E. A. Smythies, *India's Forest Wealth* (London, 1925).

with a rated capacity of 64,000 cwts of rosin and 240,000 gallons of turpentine, a capacity that could be easily expanded fourfold—production was outstripping Indian demand. This put under active consideration proposals for the export of resin and turpentine to the United Kingdom and the Far East.[34] Indeed, the only impediment to increased production was the lack of adequate means of communication. The extensive pine forests in the interior had to remain untapped, with extraction restricted to areas well served by mule tracks and sufficiently close to railroads.[35]

The war provided a fillip, as well, to the production of chir sleepers. The cessation of antiseptic imports proved a 'blessing in disguise' when the Munitions Board requisitioned untreated sleepers.[36] In 1914 three large antiseptic treatment centres were established at Tanakpur, Hardwar and Kathgodam respectively, where the Sarda, Ganga and Gaula rivers debouched onto the plains.[37] Almost four lakh sleepers were supplied during 1916–18, and the Kumaun circle began to show a financial surplus for the first time, with all stocks being cleared. The government saw-mill was unable to deal with all the indents it received. Nevertheless, over 5000 chir trees were felled and sawn annually. For the forest department its activities during the war were adequate justification for the recent and controversial forest settlement in the hills.[38]

[34] Imperial Institute, Indian Trade Enquiry, *Report on Lac, Turpentine and Resin* (London, 1922), esp. pp. 29–51. India was the only source of oleo-resin within the British dominions.

[35] The available technology of transportation crucially affected the working of these forests. Coniferous timber could be floated out to railheads by water. The oaks, though durable, were too heavy and consequently did not merit commercial exploitation. All attempts to float resin in cans having remained unsuccessful, the pine forests of Almora and Nainital, at a lesser distance from the plains, were tapped earlier than those in Garhwal. While proposals for building a railway line through the Alakananda valley up to Karanprayag were mooted at various times, in the latter forests resin-tapping on a large scale had to await the construction of motor roads after 1947. See R. N. Brahmawar, *WP for the Garhwal For. Div., 1930–31 to 1939–40* (Allahabad, 1932), p. 138 and *passim*.

[36] Stebbing, III, pp. 658–9.

[37] J. E. C. Turner, 'Antiseptic Treatment of Chir Pine Sleepers in the Kumaun Circle, UP', IF, vol. 40 (1914), pp. 427–9.

[38] *Annual Progress Report of Forest Administration in the United Provinces for the Forest Year 1916–17* (hereafter APFD) (Allahabad, 1918), pp. 20, 38, 45; APFD,

After the forest movement of 1921 (see chapter 5) the Kumaun Forest Grievances Committee (KFGC), in a bid to allay the discontent with forest regulations, constituted the so-called class I forests. These forests were handed over to the district administration and the remaining forests—called class II reserves—continued to be vested directly with the forest department, the principle of demarcation being that all forests not considered of commercial importance were to be excluded from the class II reserves. Thus a large proportion of the class I forests consisted of high-level fir, spruce and oak forests.[39]

Although the recommendations of the KFGC withdrew the forest department's jurisdiction over large areas, the class II reserves continued to be worked, on a sustained basis, for both timber and resin. Operations were considerably stepped up during World War II, when 'fellings and sawings were pushed into the remotest forests of the Himalayas . . .' In 1940–1 alone, 440,000 sleepers were supplied to the railways, mostly of chir pine.[40] The recorded figures show an increase (at an all-India level) over pre-war outturn of about 65 per cent. In the hills, working-plan prescriptions were considerably upset by war requirements, the excess fellings being estimated at as much as six annual yields.[41] As at the time of the expansion of the railway network, the Kumaun forests proved to be an important resource for British colonialism during the two world wars.

SCIENTIFIC FORESTRY AND SOCIAL CONTROL

Aiming at a radical reorientation of existing patterns of resource utilization, commercial forestry was to initiate a major transformation in agrarian relations. In the years following the introduction of forest management, protest at the onerous regulations was a recurrent feature in Uttarakhand. Apart from

1917–18, pp. 22–3. I have estimated the number of trees felled from figures (pertaining to recorded fellings only) given in different working plans.

[39] See C. M. Johri, *WP for the Garhwal For. Div., Kumaun Circle, UP, 1940–41 to 1954–55* (Allahabad, 1940), esp. the attached map.

[40] H. G. Champion and F. C. Osmaston, *E. P. Stebbing's Forests of India*, vol. IV (Oxford, 1962), chapter IX.

[41] Ministry of Agriculture, *India's Forests and the War* (Delhi, 1948), pp. 107–11.

social movements (cf. chapters 4 and 5) which occurred at regular intervals, the contravention of forest laws represented the most tangible evidence of such protest. While the trajectory of social protest is described more fully in later chapters, it suffices to say here that breaches of the forest law led to the evolution of management strategies of considerable sophistication which could ensure the sustained output of commercially valued timber species.

The mechanisms of protest—the contravention of rules concerning the lopping of trees and grazing, and the burning of the forest floor for a fresh crop of grass—were in effect an assertion of traditional rights whose exercise was now circumscribed by the imperatives of scientific forestry. By its very nature commercial forestry—which divides the forests into blocks which are completely closed after the trees are felled—disrupts existing patterns of resource utilization. In order to enable regeneration to take place in the logged areas, closure to humans and cattle is essential. Likewise, in the areas under reproduction fire is to be avoided as hazardous to young saplings. Thus the continuance of customary patterns of forest use represented a major threat to commercial timber operations. This was especially true of the firing of the forest, in contravention of the forest act, which sometimes resulted in a total annihilation of recent regeneration.

Faced with recurrent and widespread protest, forest officials in Uttarakhand had to develop and perfect a set of silvicultural strategies which could simultaneously exercise control over the customary use of the forest and enable the reproduction of favoured species of trees. In the circumstances, an earlier emphasis on ensuring regeneration and enforcing control over large areas of forest came under close scrutiny. A change of focus, from extensive to intensive methods of forest management, was advocated as the only solution. Drawing on the lessons gleaned from a tour of European forests, an eminent silviculturist observed:

> everything points to the concentration rather than to diffusion of work as the ground-work of successful forest management in India. Concentration implies more efficient and economical work on natural and artificial regeneration with subsequent tending operations, more economical and thorough exploitation under a definite system of roads

or other export works, the possibility of using fire in effecting regeneration, the conduct of special fire protective measures in definite areas where protection is most urgently required, a more economical use of the staff and better supervision over it, a more workable arrangement as regarded to closure to grazing, and, what is of great importance in the mixed forests of India, special facilities for regulating the proportion of valuable species to what is economically and silviculturally desirable.[42]

In Uttarakhand three elements in the customary use of the forest—grazing, lopping and the burning of the forest floor—constituted the most serious threat to rationalized timber production. However, the changeover from extensive to intensive operations enabled silviculturists to successfully manipulate these practices to subserve the ends of commercial forestry. Thus grazing, far from being an unmitigated evil (as forestry textbooks would have it), in many areas actually helped the reproduction of favoured species like chir and deodar by keeping down the thick undergrowth of grass and brushwood. As one report observed, the concentration of regeneration operations helped divert grazing from areas closed for reproduction and towards the rest of the forest where 'far from being a curse the grazing would in many cases be a blessing in tending to keep down inflammable undergrowth'. However, even where grazing was found beneficial on silvicultural grounds, it would introduce an element of 'insecurity' in forest operations, particularly as 'all forest rights tend to get more onerous'. Officers were therefore cautioned that while allowing grazing under favourable silvicultural conditions, it must be strictly regulated: villagers were to be told unambiguously that grazing was being allowed as a favour and could not be claimed as a matter of right.[43]

Lopping, likewise, was skilfully used to promote one of the primary aims of forest management: increasing the proportion of the commercially valuable species (chiefly conifers) in the forest crop. Working plans prescribed detailed operations,

[42] R. S. Troup, *A Note on Some European Silvicultural Systems with Suggestions for Improvements in Indian Forest Management* (Calcutta, 1916), pp. 3–4.

[43] Ibid., p. 4; W. F. d'Arcy, 'Grazing Rights in Forests', IF, vol. 9 (1883), pp. 359–61; H. G. Champion, 'The Influence of the Hand of Man on the Distribution of Forest Types in the Kumaun Himalayas', IF, vol. 49 (1923), pp. 131–2.

covering thousands of hectares, that included the felling and girdling of broad-leaved species in order to 'help' the conifers 'in their struggle' with other species. In addition, villagers were allowed unrestricted access to oak and other broad-leaved species, it being later reported with satisfaction that this selective lopping and girdling was likely to transform mixed forests into pure stands of chir pine.[44]

Perhaps the most important management innovation, however, was designed to combat the centuries-old custom of burning the chir forests for pasture. The needles of chir falling on to the forest floor both suppressed the grass and rendered the hillside dangerous for cattle. Thus, in late April or early May, villagers resorted to the time-honoured remedy of fire to obtain a fresh crop of grass, and, 'when no restrictions exist burning [was] resorted to everywhere at this season.'[45] Although mature chir trees are remarkably resistant to fire, continuous reproduction in areas of commercial logging operations rendered the young growth particularly vulnerable to fire. Fire protection was at once 'the most important as well as the most difficult question concerned with the management of our [forest department's] chir forests', more particularly as villagers were 'very averse to this measure'.[46] Not accustomed to any interference with their customary practices, it was evident that for the peasants universal fire protection would 'always be a source of complaint'.[47] The resolution of this problem assumed a growing importance with the growth of the resin industry and the perfection of antiseptic treatment of railway sleepers. Initially, foresters tried to completely ban the practice of annual firing by placing large tracts of forests under protective measures. These operations enjoyed mixed success in the early years of forest administration. The figures given in Table 3.5 highlight the fluctuating rates of success in the Kumaun circle. Both 1916 and 1921 were exceptionally dry fire seasons,

[44] Brahmawar, *Garhwal WP*, p. 57. Cf. also R. S. Troup, *The Silviculture of Indian Trees*, p. 1123, and Tullock, *Tehri Garhwal WP*, p. 7.

[45] See C. G. Trevor and E. A. Smythies, *Practical Forest Management* (Allahabad, 1923), pp. ix–xi.

[46] N. Hearle, *WP for the Deoban Range, Jaunsar For. Div., NWP* (Allahabad, 1889), p. 22.

[47] E. A. Smythies, 'Some Aspects of Fire Protection in Chir Forests', IF, vol. 37 (1911), p. 59.

TABLE 3.5

*Fire Protection in Kumaun Circle 1901–1921**

Year	Area attempted (acre)	Area burnt	Success (per cent)
1909–10	186,117	49,008	73.67
1910–11	247,637	479	99.81
1911–12	269,772	6,179	97.71
1912–13	330,770	4,830	98.45
1913–14	397,409	7,800	98.04
1914–15	375,187	9,567	97.45
1915–16	533,638	192,400	63.95
1916–17	371,113	239	99.94
1917–18	377,263	1,484	99.61
1918–19	395,660	3,673	99.07
1919–20	401,451	33,769	91.59
1920–21	404,455	272,865	32.54

*Kumaun Circle did not exactly correspond with Kumaun Civil Division.

SOURCE: Computed from C. G. Trevor and E. A. Smythies, *Practical Forest Management* (Lucknow, 1923).

coinciding with outbreaks of 'planned incendiarism'.[48]

The major disasters of 1916 and 1921 led to considerable rethinking among scientific forestry experts on the desirability of extensive fire-protection measures. Incendiarism 'left a deep and lasting impression on the mind of the silviculturist, compelling him to think on new lines about ways and means of preventing the recurrence of such wholesale destruction, past methods of placing excessive trust in the people having conspicuously failed.'[49] In Kumaun fire protection was verily 'the stumbling block of [forest] management'.[50] Areas that had been protected for many years accumulated much grass and

[48] For details see chapter 5. Arson was usually directed at carefully chosen targets, e.g. chir forests worked for commercial purposes and resin depots.

[49] J. E. C. Turner, 'Slash in Chir Pine Forests: Causes of Formation, Its Influence and Treatment', IFR, vol. XIII, pt VII (Calcutta, 1928), pp. 22–3.

[50] See review of APFD, 1922–3, in IF, vol. 50 (1924), pp. 265–6.

debris; here, regeneration was totally wiped out by unforeseen outbreaks of fire. And where trees were being tapped for resin, fire ignited the open resin channels and consequently the tree itself.[51] An additional fire hazard was the large amounts of waste wood that accumulated in forests newly felled for railway sleepers.[52] Several years earlier, similar operations in the foothills of Punjab had conclusively proved that the

> Forest Department is quite helpless to cope with a serious outbreak of incendiarism. Fire lines, fire guards, special night patrols, etc. have been tried in vain and there is no doubt that once the villagers have made up their minds to burn the forests the Forest Department is powerless to prevent them.[53]

As a result, the inspector-general of forests and other senior foresters convened several meetings that investigated proposals for the firing of forests by the agency of the department itself, combined with regeneration operations which could be concentrated in specific areas—to aid protection—rather than widely dispersed.

The results of these investigations were summarized in a lengthy monograph authored by R. S. Troup. Troup's proposals showed a remarkable grasp not merely of silviculture but of the social and cultural environment in which the workings of colonial forestry science were predicated. Departmental firing, he pointed out, was advocated not 'as a measure directly beneficial to the forests, but as the lesser of two evils, in cases where universal fire protection endangers the area under regeneration' —indeed, 'regulated burning may be absolutely necessary to save the area under regeneration.'[54] Troup's detailed prescriptions, which are widely in operation even today, envisaged a system of controlled burning. Thus, areas under regeneration were divided into blocks and separated from the rest of the forest by 'fire lines' of a width of up to 100 feet. These lines were cleared of tree growth and burned annually, under depart-

[51] H. G. Champion, 'Observations on Some Effects of Fires in the Chir Forests of the West Almora Division', IF, vol. 45 (1919), pp. 353–63.

[52] See Turner, *Slash in Chir Pine Forests*, for details.

[53] H. M. Glover, 'Departmental Firing in Chir Forests in the Rawalpindi Division, Punjab', IF, vol. 39 (1913), pp. 568–71.

[54] R. S. Troup, '*Pinus longifolia roxb*: A Silvicultural Study', *The Indian Forest Memoirs*, silvicultural series, vol. 1, pt 1 (Calcutta, 1916), p. 72.

mental control, during winter or early spring, preferably after a spell of rain. When this had been successfully accomplished, villagers were allowed to burn the rest of the open forest—subject to certain controls—before the end of March and the onset of summer. Occasionally, supplementary narrow lines of up to 15 to 20 feet in width were cleared of grass; in the event of a fire these were employed as bases for counter-firing. The size of the fire lines and the blocks which they protected would, Troup emphasized, have to vary with local conditions; for 'where incendiarism is common, broad cleared lines merely reduce the forest area without affording any real safeguard; under such conditions narrow lines as counter-firing bases are equally effective.'[55]

These proposals soon gained acceptance among foresters. Departmental burning which 'reduced the damage done to forests . . . and rendered the villagers more contented with forest management' spread to Tehri Garhwal and is in fact widely in operation even today.[56] Troup's manual on fire protection strikingly reflected the environment of popular resistance in which colonial forestry operated, and which it tried with varying success to overcome. Before outlining the prescribed techniques, which embodied decades of research in the hill forests of Punjab and Uttar Pradesh, Troup observes: 'In forest administration generally, and in fire protective operations in particular, the value of enlisting the sympathies of the local population and the undesirability of imposing irksome restrictions of an unnecessary character are matters of common knowledge.' In districts

> where the population is particularly truculent, any degree of success in universal fire protection is now recognized after years of fruitless endeavour, to be unattainable, and the concentration of protective measures on blocks under regeneration, with careful annual or periodic burning of the remaining areas, is considered to be the only possible means of effecting successful reproduction.[57]

Clearly, the concentration of regeneration operations and adoption of a flexible attitude towards grazing, lopping and fire protection were informed by the silviculturist's perennial fear of popular protest. At the level of forestry ideology 'grazing and

[55] Ibid., p. 73. [56] Bahuguna, *Tehri WP*, p. 61. [57] Troup, *Pinus*.

lopping are declared enemies of the forest'.[58] Working among a peasant population implacably opposed to commercial forestry, colonial silviculturists quickly rejected a total ban on customary use, adopting instead strategies of manipulation and control which minimized the threat to rationalized timber production. Summarizing the experience of a century, the official manual of silviculture remarks that foresters have, over time, learnt 'to turn to good effect the various destructive [*sic*] influences threatening the forest', the essential point 'being that the silviculturist shall have them under his control instead of having to fight them as declared enemies'.[59]

Alienation of humans from nature

What, one may now ask, was the cumulative impact of these strategies of management and control on the relationship between humans and forest in Uttarakhand? At the most obvious level the reservation of large tracts of forest meant an effective loss of control over their habitat for forest-based communities. Inevitably, an increased pressure was felt on the forests that did remain open to villagers, in many cases hastening their destruction.

A more fundamental change was the reorientation in agrarian relations induced by scientific forestry. In response to peasant protest, state forestry evolved a set of strategies, described earlier, that could manipulate the customary use of the forest in order to enable sustained timber production. An underlying principle of these techniques was that individual use of the forest represented a lesser threat to commercial forestry than the collective use sanctioned by custom. Accordingly, and through the mechanisms of the forest act, the state preferred to deal directly with individual households rather than with village communities as such.

This transition from collective to individual use of the forest bespoke a fundamental change in the agrarian life of Uttarakhand. For the loss of community ownership had effectively broken the link between humans and the forest. Although the government had, in certain areas, made over limited tracts of

[58] F. C. Ford Robertson, *Our Forests* (Allahabad, 1936), p. 28.

[59] H. G. Champion and S. K. Seth, *A General Silviculture for India* (New Delhi, 1968), pp. xix–xx.

forests to the villages (the so-called 'third class' or 'village' forests) the proviso in the forest act that these forests must first be declared 'reserved' strengthened suspicion of the state's true intentions.[60] Many officials were convinced that if villagers were assigned a proper legal title to forest land and assured both of the products grown and the management, they would continue to preserve tree growth as zealously as before.[61] In the absence of such assurances Garhwali peasants, apprehensive that the demarcation of reserved forests would be followed by the government taking away other wooded areas from their control, were in certain cases deforesting woodland.[62] In the ecologically comparable pargana of Jaunar Bawar which bordered Tehri Garhwal on the west, a similar process followed settlement operations. Thus, 'not altogether without reason, the villagers believe that any self-denial or trouble they may exercise in preserving and improving their third class forests will end in appropriation of the forests by the [forest] department as soon as they become commercially valuable.'[63]

The erosion of the social bonds which had regulated the customary use of the forests thus led to what can be described as an alienation of humans from nature. The concept of alienation used here draws directly from the work of Marx on the alienation of the worker under conditions of industrial capitalism.[64] While the application of Marx's theory, formulated in an entirely different context, must be done with some degree of caution, I would argue that in both instances we are dealing with the growth of a social system (industrial capitalism/colonialism) that replaced another (craft production/subsistence agriculture) whose social relations did not produce conditions of alienation and estrangement.[65]

[60] See B. Ribbentrop, *Forestry in British India* (Calcutta, 1900), p. 126.

[61] W. H. Lovegrove, 'The Formation of Communal Forests', IF, vol. 34 (1908), pp. 590–1; notes by J. K. Pearson and V. A. Stowell in FD file 83/1909, UPSA.

[62] T. D. Gairola to secy to govt, UP, 8 January 1918, in FD file 83/1909, UPSA.

[63] Supdt, Dehradun, to comm., Meerut division, dated 22 May 1897, in file no. 244, list no. 2, RAD.

[64] The classic text is Karl Marx, 'Economic and Philosophical Manuscripts' (hereafter EPM), in Lucio Colletti (ed.), *Karl Marx: Early Writings* (Harmondsworth, 1975), pp. 280–400.

[65] Cf. Lewis Feuer, 'What is Alienation? The Career of a Concept', in Maurice Stein and Arthur Vidich (ed.), *Sociology on Trial* (Englewood Cliffs, 1963).

Capitalism produces an atomized society, one that is in conflict with communal activity and communal consumption—defined by Marx as 'activity and consumption that confirm themselves directly in *real association* with other men'.[66] By analogy, state control was a negation of the communal appropriation of nature in Uttarakhand. Not only did forests constitute an important means of subsistence, but their products were treated, as in other peasant societies, as a free gift of nature to which all had equal access. The assertion of state monopoly ran contrary to traditional management practices. These practices were at once an affirmation of communal action oriented towards production and of the unity between humans and nature. Colonial forest law, which recognized only individual rights of user (this was true of Tehri Garhwal as well), initiated the fragmentation of the community and erosion of social bonds, processes hastened by the commercialization and capitalist penetration of later years. Further, the produce of the forests no longer belonged to the hill villagers but was appropriated by the state for the use of the classes it represented. Despite the spatial gulf, the interests of these classses were sharply opposed to those of a peasantry alienated from the forest growth it had helped to nurture.

Other writers have, in different cultural and historical contexts, commented on similar processes of the alienation of humans from nature. Verrier Elwin has talked of the 'melancholy' effect forest reservation had on the tribals of Central India, for whom nothing aroused more resentment than the taking away of the forests they regarded as 'their own property'.[67] Indeed, the Gonds, although they possessed an extensive medical tradition, were convinced that these remedies did not operate in this age of darkness, Kalyug, which began when the government took away their forests.[68] In Europe, too, the takeover of woodland for hunting or for timber production was deeply resented by the peasantry, for whom 'the law, almost any law but forest legislation particularly, appeared alien and destructive'. Resorting to extensive forest fires at state incursion into their rights, the French peasantry 'had come to hate the

[66] Marx, EPM, p. 350.

[67] V. Elwin, *A Philosophy for NEFA* (Delhi, 1960), pp. 86 f.

[68] V. Elwin, *Leaves in the Jungle* (1936; rpt. London, 1968), p. 57.

forests themselves, and hoped that if they ravaged them enough they would get rid of their oppressors.'[69]

As this last citation makes evident, in its extreme form alienation occasionally forced peasants to degrade the surroundings with which they once lived in symbiosis. The lack of interest that has, at times, been exhibited by forest communities in preserving vegetation on land that is no longer vested in them may be traced to the loss of community control consequent on state intervention. In Uttarakhand such alienation took various forms. In eastern Kumaun the reservation of large tracts of forests adjoining cultivation, and the constant harassment by forest patrols, had even led to villagers losing interest in their cultivation.[70] Elsewhere, forest reservation evoked a fear that if the villagers looked after the forests as of yore, 'a passing forest official will say—here is a promising bit of forest—government ought to reserve it. If on the other hand, they ruin their civil forest, they feel free from such reservation.'[71] Today, in an ironic but entirely predictable development, villagers in parts of Garhwal look upon the reserved forest as their main enemy, harbouring the wild animals that destroy their crops.[72] This is of course a classic form of alienation wherein the forest now appears as an entity *opposed* to the villager. Above all, alienation signifies a mode of life in which circumstances distort the innate qualities of human beings, compelling them to act in a self-destructive fashion.[73]

[69] Eugene Weber, *Peasants into Frenchmen* (Stanford, 1976), pp. 59–60. Cf. George Perkins Marsh on the period immediately following the French revolution: 'In the popular mind, the forest was associated with all the abuses of feudalism, and the evils the peasantry had suffered from the legislation which protected both it and the game it sheltered blinded them to the still greater physical mischiefs which its destruction was to entail upon them. No longer protected by the law the crown forests and those of the great lords were attacked with relentless fury, unscrupulously plundered and wantonly laid waste, and even the rights of property in small private woods were no longer respected.' David Lowenthal (ed.), *Man and Nature* (1864; rpt. Cambridge, Mass., 1967), p. 244.

[70] S. D. Pant, *Social Economy of the Himalayans* (London, 1935), p. 86.

[71] Note by H. S. Crosthwaite, secy to govt, to governor, UP, 2 April 1922, in FD file 109/1921, UPSA.

[72] P. H. Gross, *Birth, Death and Migration in the Himalaya* (Delhi, 1982), pp. 174–5.

[73] Feuer, 'What is Alienation?', p. 131. As an indication of how far alienation has proceeded in some areas, I recall a conversation with the Chipko leader Chandi Prasad Bhatt in October 1983. When I told him that colonial administrators in the

THE AGENDA OF SCIENTIFIC FORESTRY

The analysis of scientific forestry presented in this chapter points to its context-laden character. Predicated on the ideological setting in which they operate, the techniques of scientific forestry are, as it were, designed to reorder both nature and customary use in its own image. Clearly, the need to develop such strategies arose from the historical circumstances in which state forestry was first imposed on Uttarakhand. Having disrupted traditional forms of resource utilization, scientific forestry had to contend with the simmering discontent, occasionally breaking out into open revolt, that accompanied the takeover of the Himalayan forests. In the event, both legislation and silvicultural technique were designed to facilitate social control. Here, the evolution of colonial silviculture mirrored the history of German forestry, from which it claimed a direct lineage, where the 'development of scientific sylviculture and of positivist criminology were two sides of the same coin: one studying sustained yield and the other the endemic ('moral' as they would say) obstacles to that yield.'[74]

The silvicultural agenda of colonial foresters working in the Himalaya was the transformation of mixed forests of conifers and broad-leaved species into pure stands of commercially valuable conifers. This manipulation of a delicate and imperfectly understood ecosystem was further complicated by the competing demands exercised on the forest by the peasantry. Even if the usurpation of the forests by the state redefined customary use as forest 'crime', it could not, within the framework of colonial administration, completely eliminate 'illegal' use by peasants. Like their German counterparts, colonial foresters had therefore to overcome the social obstacles to sustained yield. Faced with a set of constraints that were both eco-

1920s had singled out Chaundkot pargana for its well-tended oak groves, he remarked that this part of southern Garhwal was now notable only for its lack of tree cover.

[74] Peter Linebaugh, 'Karl Marx, the Theft of Wood, and Working Class Composition: A Contribution to the Current Debate', *Crime and Social Justice*, no. 6, Fall–Winter 1976, p. 14. On the worldwide influence of German forestry, see Bernard Fernow, *A History of Forestry* (Toronto, 1902), and Franz Heske, *German Forestry* (New Haven, 1937).

logical as well as social, British foresters arrived at two mutually reinforcing solutions. At an instrumental level they carefully regulated peasant access by restricting it to areas of forest not deemed commercially profitable. While completely forbidden to enter areas under commercial working, peasants were by no means at liberty to use the rest of the forest at will. The detailed provisions of the 1878 act sharply defined (and delimited) the amount of fuel, fodder, etc. each family was allowed to take from the forest. At the same time, the punitive sanctions of the act were a strong deterrent to its transgression. At a deeper epistemic level the language of scientific forestry worked to justify the shift towards commercial working. The terms 'valuable' and 'desirable' and the prefix 'inferior', used mainly to refer to oaks, bear no relation to the ecological and other functions the species thus described may perform for the surrounding countryside. By a similar act of redefinition, one that rested on a prior usurpation of 'legal' rights of ownership by the state, many users of the forest were designated its enemies. Thus the management profile of each forest division, the so-called 'working plans', while indicating possible sources of injury to the forest crop, includes men in the same category as natural hazards and wild animals.

These strategies were developed to enable the sustained reproduction of favoured species of trees while minimizing the threat to state monopoly that peasant protest entailed, ends which could be achieved only through the skilful manipulation and redefinition of customary practices of forest use. In the application of these techniques, considerations of control were paramount. The strategies forged by forestry science and legislation manipulated agrarian practices by carefully regulating the intrusion and exclusion of 'man', classified in the terminology of forestry science as one of the 'enemies' of the forest. Not surprisingly, the dislocation of agrarian practices that followed the imposition of state monopoly was to have far-reaching consequences.

This manipulation of ecological systems and human beings was deemed necessary to maintain a permanent supply of marketable forest produce. Given its poor statistical base and scanty knowledge of the Himalayan ecosystem, 'scientific' forestry was not able to fulfil even its primary objective. Recent research by Indian ecologists—ironically enough, commissioned by the forest department—has clearly demonstrated the yawning gulf between, on the one hand, the ideology of 'sustained yield' that is the *sine qua non* of scientific forestry, and, on the other, the actual operations of timber harvesting wherein the output of logged material often exceeds the increment to forest stock.[75] What is more relevant to our concerns, however, are the processes of social change that came in the wake of the commercialization of the forest. By introducing a radical shift in the management priorities of the Himalayan ecosystem, commercial forestry came into sharp conflict with a system of management that pre-dated it by several centuries, and whose priorities could hardly have been more dissimilar. It is to this conflict, between the imperatives of scientific forestry and the economic and cultural values of the hill peasantry, that we shall now turn.

[75] M. Gadgil, R. Ali and S. N. Prasad, 'Forest Management and Forest Policy in India: A Critical Review', *Social Action*, vol. 27, no. 2, 1983.

CHAPTER 4

Rebellion as Custom

> The institution of monarchy seemed to satisfy certain eternal needs in the societies of old, needs which were entirely real and essentially human. The societies of today are equally aware of [these needs] yet are usually content to satisfy them in other ways. But in the eyes of his faithful subjects, a king was, after all, something very different from a mere high official. He was surrounded by a 'veneration', which did not simply originate in the services he performed. How can we understand this feeling of loyalty which was so strong and so specific at certain periods in our history, if, from the outset, we refuse to see the supernatural aura which surrounded these crowned heads?
>
> —Marc Bloch

> [Hegemony] does not entail any acceptance by the poor of the gentry's paternalism upon the gentry's own terms or in their approved self-image. The poor might be willing to award their deference to the gentry but only for a price. The price was substantial. And the deference was often without the slightest illusion: it could be seen from below as being one part necessary self-preservation, one part the calculated extraction of whatever could be extracted. Seen in this way, the poor imposed upon the rich some of the duties and functions of paternalism just as much as deference was in turn imposed upon them. Both parties to the equation were constrained within a common field of force.
>
> —E. P. Thompson

RAJA AND PRAJA IN TEHRI

The peasant political ideal, in which the peasantry and the king are the only social forces, came as close as is historically possible to being realized in Tehri Garhwal. Here the social structure was polarized between the raja (king) on the one hand, and his *praja* (citizenry), organized in strong and remarkably egalitarian village communities, on the other. Although the unification of Garhwal was completed only in the fourteenth century, the ruling dynasty could trace its lineage to Kanak Pal, a

Panwar Rajput of Malwa who took over the throne of Garhwal around AD 688. With the ruling dynasty having enjoyed over 1200 years of continuous rule, broken only by the eleven-year Gurkha interregnum, the kingdom of Garhwal was by far the oldest in north India. Its isolated status and secure boundaries undoubtedly helped the maintenance of Panwar rule. According to the Mughal historian Ferishta, the ruler of Garhwal 'commanded great respect from the emperors of Delhi'.[1]

Although in theory the sovereign possessed proprietary rights in the soil, the cultivating body which formed the bulk of the population enjoyed all privileges of ownership except for the right to alienate land (cf. chapter 2). Even artisan castes often cultivated a portion of land which yielded enough for their subsistence.[2] This relative autonomy (and prosperity) was strengthened by several factors, chief among which was the absence, over most of the kingdom, of an intermediary rentier class between the peasantry and the monarch. Land revenue demand, too, was extraordinarily light, lower than in the neighbouring British territory. Cultivators had the right to extend their fields during the period intervening between two successive land-revenue settlements without incurring the liability of enhanced assessment.[3] British travellers were apt to comment on the low incidence of land revenue, one 'wholly disproportionate to the extent of the [Tehri] Raj'.[4] As in other agrarian societies largely governed by customary law, the monarch would grant remission of revenue in years of distress. Occasionally, when crops failed, substantial amounts of money were advanced for the procurement of grain.[5]

The king as 'Bolanda' Badrinath

The exalted status of the monarch may be viewed in the context of these two factors, namely the durability of the Garhwal

[1] Quoted in S. S. Panwar, 'Garhwalis: The Warrior Race of the North', *The Commentator* (Dehradun), 16 August 1971.

[2] 'Mountaineer', *A Summer Ramble in the Himalaya* (London, 1860), p. 165.

[3] No. 1885/XVI-63, 17 January 1914, from comm., KD, to CSG, UP, in GAD 398/1913, UPSA.

[4] W. Moorcroft and G. Trebeck, *Travels in Hindusthan* (1837; rpt. Delhi, 1971), p. 15.

[5] See, for example, T-G Report, 1892–3, in nos. 267–9, Progs, January 1894, Internal B, foreign dept, NAI.

kingdom and the comparative autonomy enjoyed by the agrarian population—the latter a consequence of the low level of revenue demand imposed by the state. This was strengthened by the quasi-divine status enjoyed by the king in the eyes of his subjects, which stemmed from the historical connection between the throne of Garhwal and the sacred shrine of Badrinath. Located in the interior hills a few miles from the source of the Alakananda (one of the two rivers that form the Ganga), the Badrinath temple is perhaps the holiest shrine for Hindus. It is believed that Kanak Pal helped Adi Shankara in expelling Buddhism from the hills and in erecting the Badrinath temple. His successors assumed the responsibility for the management of the temple, endowing it with the revenue of a large number of villages (*gunth*) to meet its expenses. In addition, another set of villages en route was designed as *sada bart* villages, their income set aside to feed and house pilgrims. Over time, the Panwar rulers acquired the title of 'Bolanda Badrinath', i.e. Speaking Badrinath, or the deity personified. The Garhwal rulers enjoyed the religious title of 'Shri 108 Basdrischarayaparayan Garhraj Mahimahendra, Dharmabaibhab, Dharma Rakshak Sirmani', a title used as the form of address in all petitions to the monarch.[6]

The throne (*gaddi*) of Garhwal was commonly referred to—after its ruling deity—as the gaddi of Badrinath, on which state officials would take the oath of office.[7] The raja 'being from time immemorial the *religious* head of the temple',[8] pilgrims traditionally made ritual obeisance to him before proceeding to the shrine, a practice that continued at least until the late nineteenth century.[9] For the peasantry the king was the very

[6] Memorandum to the secretary, Indian States Committee, sd Chakradhar Juyal, home member, in file no. 122-P/1931, F&P dept, NAI. This was a rather modest list when compared to that used by the tsar of Russia, who was at once the 'Emperor and Autocrat of all Russias, Moscow, Kiev, Vladimir and Novgorod, Tsar of Kazan, Tsar of Poland, Tsar of Siberia, Tsar of Kherson in the Tavrida, Tsar of Georgia, Grand Duke of Finland . . .' See Teodor Shanin, *Russia as a 'Developing' Society* (New Haven, 1986), vol. 1, p. 34. (Full citation in Bibliography.)

[7] *Garhwali Visheshank* (special number), 4 October 1919; H. K. Raturi, *Narendra Hindu Law* (Lucknow, 1918), pp. 72–3.

[8] 'Notes on the Badrinath Temple', 6 July 1914, in 'Tour Diary of Pt. Keshavanand Mamgain [forest member, T-G state] for 1914–15', S. S. Panwar collection, emphasis added.

[9] See file no. 306-P of 1931, F&P dept, NAI.

incarnation of the deity, and Garhwali soldiers during the world wars went into battle with the slogans 'Bolanda Badrinath' and 'Jai Badri Vishal' on their lips. The birthday of the raja, 'Shri 108 Maharaj', was celebrated throughout the kingdom at religious shrines, where priests urged devotees to celebrate the birthday of 'their compassionate lord' (*apne dayalu prabhu*) with great gusto.[10]

After the bifurcation of Garhwal in 1815 the Badrinath temple lay in British territory. The Tehri raja, however, continued to be the chairman of its managing committee and the choice of the new *rawal* (head priest) fell to him. Every year a priest was deputed by the king to open the temple gates at the start of the pilgrim season. The exercise of the rawal's authority was subject to the general supervision of the durbar.[11] Like his predecessors, Narendra Shah was aware, none the less, that the lack of territorial control over the shrine undermined the social basis of his legitimacy. Arguing that the temple and the Tehri durbar 'are inseparable' the king offered,[12] in exchange for the four square miles on which the temple stood, to relinquish control over the hill station of Mussoorie (leased to the British) and to forgo the claim to seven hundred square miles of disputed land lying between Garhwal and Tibet.[13] In view of the strategic location of the town of Badrinath, en route to the Niti and Mana passes, and the opposition anticipated from certain Hindu organizations, the request was not acceded to.[14] The persistence with which Narendra Shah pursued the matter underlines the significance of traditional claims to legitimacy exercised by the king of Garhwal.[15]

The motif of the wicked official

A recurring feature of peasant and tribal revolts has been attacks on functionaries of the state. The state, or the monarch, appears as an abstract entity far removed from the scene of

[10] *Garhwali*, hereafter GRH, 25 August 1928.

[11] 'Notes on the Badrinath Temple'.

[12] Maharaja Narendra Shah to pvt. secy to viceroy, 9 December 1930, in file no. 122-P of 1931, F&P dept.

[13] See file no. 102-P of 1933, F&P dept.

[14] File nos 415-P/1933, 556-P/1933, 608-P/1934, all in F&P dept, NAI.

[15] See *Annual Administrative Report of the Tehri Garhwal State for 1935–36* (Tehri, 1936) (hereafter T-G Report), p. 5.

exploitation, while its functionaries become the targets of popular uprisings. The situation of the actual exploiter—the state and the interests which the state represents—is obscured in the minds of rural communities, and surrogate officials are perceived as the true exploiters. The notion of a 'just' government, integral to the Hindu tradition, is another factor which influences popular perceptions; thus, tyrannical officials are seen as breaching the ethical code of justice governing relations between ruler and ruled.[16]

The king's concern for the welfare of his subjects is, therefore, contingent on the degree of competence of his officials. Without competent officials (*yogya karamchari*) the king was helpless. The lofty ideals of Raja Narendra Shah were circumscribed, according to his subjects, by the highhandedness and unconcern of the high officials of the durbar, notably the new dewan (chief minister) Chakradhar Juyal.[17] Juyal, it was alleged, had achieved high office not by virtue of competence but through flattery and other devious machinations.[18] The king was constantly enjoined to be aware of the troubles of his subjects and not place sole faith on officials like the present dewan.[19] His 'duty was to protect his subjects from the oppression and cruelty of his officials.'[20]

The tension to which this relationship was subject was particularly manifest in periods of the king's minority, when administrative responsibility vested exclusively in a council of regency and no direct channel of communication existed between raja and praja. During the minority of Kirti Shah, who took over the gaddi in 1892, the desire was persistently expressed that the councillors should be removed and the young prince left to rule entirely on his own.[21] In the absence of an independent sovereign, complaints against the council were routed by villagers to the British government. The inefficiency and extravagance of the councillors in the period before

[16] Dharampal, *Civil Disobedience and Indian Tradition* (Delhi, 1971), Introduction; S. Devadas Pillai, *Rajas and Prajas* (Bombay, 1976), pp. 36–8.

[17] See letter by 'ek Tehri niwasi' (one resident of Tehri), GRH, 19 May 1928.

[18] GRH, 19 October 1929 and 2 November 1929.

[19] See Nardev Shastri, *Dehradun aur Garhwal mein Rajnaitik Andolan ka Itihas* (Dehradun, 1932).

[20] *Indian States Reformer* (hereafter ISR), 22 February 1932.

[21] Letter from S. C. Ross, comm., KD, and pol. agent to T-G state, 15 July 1887, in reply to petition from Assamees of Patti Ramoli, T-G, S. S. Panwar collection.

Narendra Shah's accession were similarly criticized, and their replacement by the acting maharani urged.[22] On his accession the king promised to 'discard and punish the vicious and immoral and to always have at heart the policy of promoting the happiness and welfare of my people, who were so long naturally anxious to see me invested with ruling powers, which is . . . an unerring indication of their loyal devotion to my house'.[23]

The dhandak

In the ruling ideology of kingship, the harmonious relationship between raja and praja was complicated in this manner by officials to whom the king had delegated administrative powers and the day-to-day functioning of the state. These powers were always liable to be misused. While this was not an infrequent occurrence, there existed in the moral order of society mechanisms whereby the peasantry could draw the attention of the monarch to the wrongdoings of officials.[24] Traditionally, peasant protest in Uttarakhand took the form of individual and collective resistance to tyranny by officials with a simultaneous call to the monarch to restore justice. This form of protest was known as the dhandak, derived from 'dand kiye gi', the admonition used by Garhwali mothers to hush troublesome children.[25] Dhandaks were never directed at the king or at the institution of kingship; rather, they emerged in response to what was perceived as oppression by subordinate officials and/or the introduction of new taxes and regulations. On punishments being inflicted upon the erring officials, the dhandak invariably died down, only to flare up again when fresh cases of tyranny occurred.

The dhandak typically encompassed two major forms of protest. First, peasants refused to co-operate with new rules and the officials who enforced them. Alternatively, when the demands grew excessive and were backed by force, villagers fled to the jungles or across political frontiers into British territory—a classic form of protest.[26] Occasionally, peasants

[22] See file no. 332/1916, GAD, UPSA.

[23] Speech by Narendra Shah on his investiture ceremony, in GRH, 6 December 1919.

[24] Cf. A. M. Hocart, *Kingship* (1927; rpt. Chicago, 1970), *passim.*

[25] Personal communication from S. S. Panwar.

[26] Shekhar Pathak, 'Uttarakhand mein Coolie Begar Pratha: 1815–1949', unpublished Ph.D. thesis, Department of History, Kumaun University, 1980,

caught hold of the offending official, shaved off his hair and moustaches, blackened his face, put him on a donkey with his face towards the tail, and turned him out of the state. Such non-co-operation at a local level was often accompanied by a march to the capital. A mass gathering would be proclaimed by the beating of drums, and peasants from surrounding villages would gather at an appointed spot, often a shrine. Here they would decide not to cultivate their fields or pay revenue and march to the capital demanding an audience with the king. On the king appearing in person and promising redress, the crowd would disperse.[27]

In the dhandak the absence of physical violence, barring isolated attacks on officials, was marked. The moral and cultural idiom of the dhandak was predicated firstly on the traditional relationship between raja and praja, and secondly on the democratic character of these peasant communities. The rebels did not mean any harm to the king, whom they regarded as the embodiment of Badrinath. In fact they actually believed they were helping the king restore justice.[28]

Interestingly, the officials, particularly those deputed from British India, who were often the targets of such revolts were unable to comprehend the social context of the dhandak. They invariably took any large demonstration to be an act of hostile rebellion. Keshavanand Mamgain, financial member of the regency council, viewed articles in the *Garhwali* criticizing the council as having

> for their object the creation of discontent and unrest in the minds of the ill-informed subjects of the state leading ultimately to disturbances and riots (dhandaks) which the malcontents of the town of Tehri have in the past found a ready means of bringing the management into contempt and disrepute.

He went on to compare the impending dhandak with the Sinn Fein movement, then at its height in Ireland.[29] And in 1925

---

appendix III, hereafter Pathak; Tejram Bhatt, 'Tehri Niwasi aur Kranti', *Yugvani* (hereafter YV), 1 September 1947.

[27] J. M Chatterjee, 'Popular "Risings" among Hill Tribes', ISR, 22 March 1931.

[28] 'Mass Demonstrations in the Hills', ISR, 22 March 1931.

[29] Financial member to president, council of regency, 23 May 1916, in GAD, 332/1916. UPSA.

C. D. Juyal described the people of the pargana of Rawain as being able to 'reap the pleasures of Heaven on this earth merely for their extreme religious devotion and unequalled loyalty towards your highness'. But a mere five years later, following the 1930 dhandak in which he figured prominently, Juyal thought the rebels 'a formidable and strongly armed gang of outlaws', and the Rawain people 'professionally freebooters'.[30] Actually Juyal himself, who was later to epitomize the callous and wicked official, had at one time been praised by his fellow hillmen for his administrative abilities in British India.[31] This hiatus between the self-perceptions of dhandakis and the views of targeted functionaries may be traced to the theme of the wicked official as one who disturbs the traditional relationship between raja and praja.

The dhandak essentially represents a right to revolt traditionally sanctioned by custom. Hindu scriptures urged obedience to the sovereign, subject to the right to revolt when the king failed to protect his people.[32] In the trans-Yamuna Simla states a form of protest called the *dum* or *dujam*, not dissimilar to the dhandak, was widely prevalent. Such revolts were not directed at the monarch, the peasantry being convinced of his divine origins. In order to draw the king's attention to some specific grievance the cultivators would abandon work in the fields and march to the capital or to other prominent places. As the suspension of farm work affected revenue collection, the king would usually concede the demands of the striking farmers.[33]

EARLY RESISTANCE TO FOREST MANAGEMENT

The changes in agrarian practices consequent on the imposition of forest management (chapter 3) had far-reaching consequences for the life of the hill peasant. With their traditional rights severely curtailed, the villagers regarded state forestry as

[30] Speech by C. D. Juyal on 15 December 1925, and letter by Juyal, both in ISR, 11 January 1931.

[31] Cf. GRH, 27 March 1920.

[32] K. M. Panikkar, *The Ideas of Sovereignty and State in Indian Political Thought* (Bombay, 1963), pp. 22, 54.

[33] 'Mass Demonstrations in the Hills'; nos. 40–2, Internal A, Progs, March 1908, foreign dept, NAI; Ranbir Sharma, *Party Politics in a Himalayan State* (Delhi, 1977), p. 31 and *passim*.

an incursion not sanctioned by custom or precedent. In the forests leased by the British, where the raja had no control, the 'people [had] become the slaves of the Forest Department, the lowest ranger or patrol having more power for good or evil than the Raja and all his councillors.'[34]

While 'powerless' to stop such oppression, Pratap Shah had taken back part of the leased forests in 1885. However, forest management, whether under the British or the aegis of the raja himself, produces uniform results with regard to peasant access to forest produce and pasture. Rationalized timber production can only be ensured—as the preceding chapter argues—by the regulation of traditionally exercised rights. As over time the greater part of the revenue of the Tehri durbar came to be realized from its rich forests, the raja steadily introduced a policy of stricter forest conservancy modelled on the system prevailing in British territory. This met with stiff resistance from villagers who 'began to look on the demarcation boundary pillars with suspicion often developing into positive hostility'. From its early years forest restrictions were 'much disliked and utterly disregarded by villagers and led to cases of organised resistance against authority'.[35] In response to the difficulties created by the reservation of forests, 2500 people of Rawain—a pargana in the north-western part of the state—marched to Tehri to demand an audience with their sovereign. Meanwhile, Pratap Shah died and, according to one chronicler, the peasants took pity on the widowed maharani. Deeming it unjust to put pressure on her, they returned to their homes.[36] Soon afterwards, during the minority of Kirti Shah, the peasants of Patti Ramoli submitted a long list of grievances to the political agent. These included complaints at the extent of begar taken by officials, restrictions on the collection of grass and leaves, and various other taxes levied on land and buffaloes.[37] Elsewhere, resentment was expressed at the policy of allowing

[34] No. 1139/XXII-29, 25 May 1886, from pol. agent, T-G state, to CSG, foreign dept, in nos. 72–9, Internal A, Progs, September 1886, foreign dept, NAI.

[35] P. D. Raturi, *WP for the Jamuna For. Div., T-G State 1932–33 to 1952–53* (Tehri, 1932), pp. 11, 50.

[36] Shyamcharan Negi, 'Tehri Jan Andolan Zindabad', YV, 11 February 1947.

[37] File no. 332/1916, GAD, UPSA.

Gujars (nomadic graziers) to graze large numbers of buffaloes in forest pastures.[38]

The next recorded dhandak concerning forests occurred around 1904 in the patti of Khujni, lying to the south of the capital, Tehri. This was a consequence of the repeated demands for bardaish made by the conservator of forests, Keshavanand Mamgain, and his staff, and the new taxes levied on cattle for which the forests were the main source of fodder. When villagers refused to meet what they regarded as excessive and unjustified levies, the forest staff entered their homes, broke vessels, and attempted to arrest the strikers. Peasants resisted and beat up Mamgain's men; meanwhile some men fled to Tehri. In an affirmation of solidarity and their democratic spirit, the village councils of Khujni resolved that whosoever did not join the rebels would be expelled from the community.[39] Kirti Shah sent a high minister, Hari Singh, to pacify the rebels, who put him under arrest. Like peasant rebels in Russia seeking the tsar's intervention, they were not satisfied with the king's emissary—they needed an assurance from the monarch himself.[40] Ultimately, the new taxes had to be lifted and Mamgain's men were withdrawn from forest work in Khujni.[41]

The man who succeeded Mamgain as conservator, Pandit Sadanand Gairola, was to suffer a worse fate at the hands of enraged villagers. Gairola was directing forest settlement operations in the patti of Khas. Subsequent developments have been described by the official report on the dhandak:

On December 27th, 1906, the forests surrounding the Chandrabadni temple about 14 miles from Tehri town were being inspected, preparatory to their being demarcated and brought under reservation. It is reported that the villagers both then and previously had taken exception to the reservation of these forests, but it was not supposed that their objections would extend beyond the refusal of supplies and petty obstructions. On the morning of the 28th December, however, about 200 villagers armed with sticks assembled at the camping

[38] P. D. Raturi, *WP for the Uttarakashi For. Div., T-G State 1939–40 to 1959–60* (Tehri, 1938), p. 37.

[39] For similar coercion used by village communities on reluctant rebels in revolutionary France, see Georges Lefebvre, *The Great Fear* (rpt. Princeton, 1982), p. 33.

[40] See Daniel Field, *Rebels in the Name of the Tsar* (Boston, 1976), pp. 46–7.

[41] Pathak, p. 462.

ground where the officials' tents were pitched and objected to *any* state interference with forests over which they claimed *full* and *exclusive* rights. They attacked the Conservator against whom they are alleged to have had a special grudge as a *foreigner* to the state, introducing *unaccustomed* forest customs and regulations. It is reported that they beat him, branded him with a hot iron, tore down his tents, pillaged his baggage and took away and broke his guns. He is represented as having escaped with much difficulty into Tehri.

Next day, the Raja sent out his brother, with an armed force to quell the disturbance and arrest the ringleaders. The attempt failed. The people gathered from the villages over a considerable tract of country to a number reported to be about 3000, opposed the Magistrate and began to collect arms. The Raja thereupon applied to Government for assistance.[42]

Unnerved by the strength of the opposition to forest conservancy, the raja resorted to a show of force and, when that failed, asked the British for assistance. Clearly, the recurring dhandaks had forced the sovereign to consider new methods—apart from those socially sanctioned—to contain discontent.

Two aspects of the repeated protests against state forestry need mention: (*i*) their localized nature, and (*ii*) the total isolation from political developments elsewhere in India.[43] The Khas patti dhandak became especially famous for the act of branding the conservator's face with an iron, an act symbolizing a decisive triumph over the inimical powers of forest officials. The incident has passed into legend and different versions are recounted throughout Garhwal even today. Peasants in the Alakananda valley believe that it occurred during the 1921 forest movement in British Garhwal (chapter 5), the officials involved being the British conservator of forests and the commissioner of Kumaun division, Percy Wyndham.[44]

THE DHANDAK AT RAWAIN, 1930

The decisive breakdown of traditional methods of conflict resolution was yet to come. This followed a dhandak in Rawain

[42] No. 46, 16 January 1907, from CSG, UP, to secy to GOI in the foreign dept, in nos. 37–9, Internal B, Progs, October 1907, foreign dept, NAI ('Report on a disturbance which broke out in December 1906 in the native state of Tehri'), emphasis added.

[43] P. N. Painuli, *Deshi Rajyaun aur Jan Andolan* (Dehradun, 1948), pp. 11–12.

[44] Interview with Alam Singh Rawat, Gopeshwar, May 1982.

in opposition to the revision of the forest settlement based on the recommendations of the German expert Franz Heske. The case has, for various reasons, become a *cause célèbre* in Garhwal. What follows is a reconstruction, based on a variety of sources, of the dhandak and its aftermath. With the interpretations of the conflicting parties widely varying, my account is necessarily selective. It is, however, based on a careful consideration of the available evidence.

The parganas of Rawain and Jaunpur lie at the western extremity of Tehri and share certain distinctive cultural traits. Unlike other parts of Uttarakhand, where the consumption of alcohol was unknown till a few decades ago, here liquor was brewed in every household, a practice that met obvious functional needs in the bitter cold. Home brewing had been banned by Dewan Chakradhar Juyal, when, in a bid to augment the state's coffers, liquor contractors had been asked to open shops.[45] Another measure which evoked resistance was the ban on poppy cultivation, imposed by the British government in accordance with their international obligations.[46]

Nor was the revision of the forest settlement, carried out by Padma Dutt Raturi, taken lightly. Villagers contrasted the restrictions over customary rights in forests with the extravagant spending of the Tehri durbar and its officials.[47] Under the new settlement forest concessions were said to have been considerably reduced. It was rumoured that the prescriptions of the settlement could disallow each family from keeping more than ten heads of sheep, one cow and one buffalo—this in an economy largely dependent on sheep and cattle rearing. Villagers were to be levied taxes on herds exceeding the prescribed limit. Peasants complained, too, that very little waste land had been left outside the reserved forests. They were also no longer allowed to cut or lop *kokat* (hollow) trees without a permit. Villagers sent several representations to the durbar; when these elicited no response they resorted to the time-honoured means of obtaining redress—the dhandak.[48]

[45] GRH, 25 April (?) 1931.

[46] No. 256/C, 19 June 1930, from pol. agent, T-G state, to CSG, UP (hereafter Stiffe's Report), in file no. 458-P/1930, NAI acc. no. 22 (microfilm), Crown Representative Records (CRR), NAI.

[47] GRH, 19 April 1930.

[48] T. D. Gairola, 'The Disturbance in Rawain (Tehri)', *Leader*, 3 August 1930,

The dhandak soon spread from Rawain to the neighbouring pargana of Jaunpur. P. D. Raturi's house was surrounded and a portion of the state reserves set on fire.[49] The resisters sent a telegram demanding the king's personal intervention. As the monarch had gone to Europe, the durbar sent Harikrishna Raturi, the former dewan, 'as the man most likely to establish confidence'.[50] Raturi, an old official of the state who first codified its law, was well acquainted with dhandaks. Apprising the peasants of the king's absence, he asked them to stay quiet till his return. They agreed on condition that the durbar stayed the new forest restrictions in the mean time.[51]

Raturi's agreement was, however, not ratified by the dewan. Instead, Juyal conveyed orders to the local magistrate, Surendra Dutt Nautiyal, to arrest the leaders. Nautiyal asked two of them, Rudra Singh and Jaman Singh, to proceed to Barkot on the banks of the Yamuna, where their grievances were to be heard. In Barkot the two, along with Ramprasad (a prominent shopkeeper of the village) and Dayaram, were handcuffed and sent onwards to Tehri. Nautiyal and P. D. Raturi escorted the prisoners part of the way and then left them in the custody of the police. While returning to Barkot the two officials were accosted by a group of peasants who were taking food for the arrested men. In the ensuing quarrel Raturi fired on the group, killing two men and wounding two others. Mounting a horse, Raturi escaped to Tehri. Meanwhile the police supervisor had released the handcuffed men. Nautiyal was captured and interned in a house by the rebels.[52]

The Padma Dutt Raturi episode provided an additional impetus to the dhandak. It began to spread rapidly. In a manner characteristic of peasant upsurges, rumours circulated

---

on microfilm at Nehru Memorial Museum and Library (NMML); GRH 3 May 1930.

[49] Bhaktdarshan, *Garhwal ke Divangat Vibhutiyan* (Dehradun, 1980), p. 342 (hereafter Bhaktdarshan); GRH; 3 May 1930.

[50] Stiffe's Report. In medieval Europe, too, 'sympathetic' officials were used in the not always successful attempt to pacify lower-class rebels. See Emmanuel Le Roy Ladurie, *Carnival in Romans* (New York, 1980), p. 111, and Lefebvre, *Great Fear*, pp 103–4.

[51] GRH, issues of 10 May and 24 May 1930.

[52] GRH, 31 May 1930; 'Rawain ki Chitti' (letter from Rawain), GRH, 28 June 1930.

to the effect that the raja had not gone to Europe but had been held in internment by the present dewan, a foreigner to the state. The dhandakis appointed Hira Singh, padhan of Nagangaon, as their head. He, along with the shopkeeper Ramprasad and Baijram of Khamundi village, assumed leadership of the movement. Villagers were asked to endorse blank papers called *dharmpattas* affirming their support. Village headmen received notices that unless they joined the dhandak within a specified time they would be robbed and beaten up.[53] As an official, posted immediately afterwards to Rawain, recalled, Hira Singh designated himself prime minister of the 'Shri 108 Sarkar'. The appellation clearly indicates the king's continuing legitimacy in the eyes of his subjects, who believed that through their actions they were helping him regain his lost powers. Meetings of this independent authority or Azad panchayat were convened at Tiladi, a vast expanse of level ground overlooking the Yamuna.[54]

Alarmed at the rapid turn of events, Juyal moved to Nainital to confer with N. C. Stiffe, commissioner of Kumaun division and political agent to Tehri Garhwal state. Undoubtedly influenced by the civil disobedience movement then at its height in British India, Stiffe advised Juyal to take punitive action. Juyal returned to Narendranagar on 26 May and ordered the state forces to march the same day. When the troop commander, Colonel Sunder Singh, refused to march on his kinsmen, the dewan removed him from the post and externed him from the state. Juyal personally assumed charge of the troops and marched to Rawain, covering seventy miles in two and a half days. Hoping to impede the army's progress, villagers dropped logs on the road and set fire to them.[55] The dewan sent two villagers to the dhandakis, asking them to surrender. Their response was that when their president (presumably Hira Singh) returned, he would send a reply if he so wished.[56]

Instead, on the 30th the troops marched to Tiladi, where

[53] Report by dewan, 12 June 1930, addressed to vice-president, executive council (hereafter Juyal's Report), in file no. 458-P/1930, NAI acc. no. 22 (microfilm), CRR, NAI.

[54] Personal communication from S. S. Panwar.

[55] S. C. Dabral, *Uttarakhand ka Itihas* (Dugadda, n.d.) (hereafter Dabral) vol. 8, pt I, p. 235; H. S. Panwar, 'Tiladi ka Hatyakand', YV, 26 May 1949.

[56] Juyal's Report.

the villagers had gathered. Juyal's men fired several rounds and an indeterminate number of peasants was killed (estimates vary from four to two hundred). Others frantically jumped into the Yamuna and were drowned. Many villagers fled to the jungles or into British-ruled Jaunsar Bawar.[57] The army also indulged in looting; 164 people were later arrested and confined in Narendranagar jail. Of these, 80 were freed and the remaining awarded sentences ranging from one day to twelve years in jail.[58] The extent of mass support for the revolt can be judged from the fact that of those who died in the incident and its aftermath, one was a Dom—Bhagirath Mistri—and another a kinsman of the raja, Thakur Gulab Singh, representing the two extremes of the social hierarchy of Garhwal.[59]

In his report the dewan portrayed the striking peasants as a gang of outlaws engaged in dacoities and murders throughout the state. He did not explain how a band of outlaws chose as their rendezvous a virtually defenceless field enclosed on three sides by hills. If the villagers had been as well equipped as Juyal made believe, it is difficult to comprehend how the army did not suffer any casualties. Clearly, the dewan was hoping to gain the support of the higher authorities for his attack on unarmed villagers.[60] But his distortion of events was only in part a wilful one; it was also informed by his lack of acquaintance with the cultural idiom of the dhandak. As a police officer from British India, his training equipped him to view any sign of popular unrest with suspicion. In a fashion typical of functionaries of the raj, Juyal blamed urban politicians for fomenting trouble to undermine his authority. He accused Bishambar Datt Chandola, editor of the *Garhwali*, and Pandit Bhawani Dutt, the ex-dewan, of inciting the 'credulous' Rawain folk.[61] This conspiracy theory was also advanced in the communiqué issued by the Tehri durbar shortly after the incident.[62] Although Chan-

[57] GRH, 2 June 1930.

[58] GRH, 25 July 1931.

[59] Shyamcharan Negi, 'Tehri Garhwal ke Shahid', YV, 23 January 1977.

[60] See the two telegrams sent by Juyal and the villagers, respectively, in DO no. 1159, 9 June 1930, from CSG, UP, to pol. secy, GOI, in file no. 458-P/1930, NAI acc. no. 22 (microfilm), CRR, NAI.

[61] Juyal's Report.

[62] 'Tehri Durbar Communiqué', sd D. D. Raturi, chief secy, T-G state, 23 June 1930, in ISR, 1 February 1931.

dola was in close contact with the peasantry during and after the dhandak and did publish their reports in his paper, there is no evidence that he or Bhawani Dutt actually influenced the course of the dhandak.[63] As Stiffe reported, when 'Swarajists' entered the area the local people had no use for these intruders and 'promptly handed them over to the local magistrate'.[64] Evidently, the rebels believed it to be a personal affair between them and their ruler and would brook no outside interference.

On the king's return from Europe the dewan was able to convince him that the gravity of the situation called for a punitive expedition. Despite several representations, the people of Rawain were unable to acquaint the king with their version of events.[65] Shortly afterwards, Narendra Shah deplored the outbreak, criticizing the Rawain folk for deviating from their peaceful ways. Pinning the blame on 'unworthy' headmen, the sovereign asserted that as villagers were ignorant of forest conservancy, he had called in a foreign expert to advise him. In a conciliatory gesture the king promised to end utar by building better roads.[66] In response, the *Garhwali* agreed that while forest management was necessary the present commercial orientation left the wants of peasants unfulfilled. The continuing burden of utar and the ban on private distillation also came in for criticism.[67]

Narendra Shah's failure to dismiss Juyal and make amends epitomized the changing relations between the peasantry and the monarch. In two earlier dhandaks, H. K. Raturi told Stiffe, the outbreaks had been 'quelled by the personal presence of the then Raja, to whose side most of the people gathered'.[68] Constrained by the imperatives of scientific forestry, and wary of the political movements in British India, the administration of Tehri Garhwal began to exhibit a visible strain: inevitable because an increasingly bureaucratic system impinged on the highly personalized structure of traditional authority. Simultaneously, the continuing protests forced the king to adopt a

[63] Personal communication from Smt. Lalita Devi Vaishnav, daughter of the late B. D. Chandola.

[64] Stiffe's Report.

[65] GRH, 25 April 1931.

[66] Speech by maharaja, reproduced in GRH, 2 May 1931.

[67] Reply to above speech in GRH, issues of 2, 9, 16 and 23 May 1931.

[68] Stiffe's Report.

more autocratic style of rule, one reinforced by his closer contacts with British colonialism. Thus, Raja Narendra Shah's approval of the Rawain firing, it was later alleged, stemmed from a belief that, unlike his predecessors, he saw himself not as one of his people but as 'the *ruler* of the Garhwalis'.[69]

It was, however, the dewan and his rapacious behaviour which figured prominently in the popular consciousness. Wild rumours began to circulate that the all-powerful Juyal had proposed new taxes on women and drinking water and an enhanced tax on potato cultivation.[70] His attack on the Rawain peasant lives on in peasant folksongs which recount the awesome terror of the dewan's rule.[71] As one contemporary observer put it, living in Tehri Garhwal after Rawain *kand* (firing) was like living in a jail.[72]

Unprecedented in the history of the state, the Rawain kand was graphically described as an arrow that pierced the heart of the Garhwali motherland (*gadmata*).[73] One writer, shocked that the house of Bolanda Badrinath could sanction such a gruesome act, asked the king:

> These people [of Rawain] resorted to the only method known to them of making their grievances known to the Ruler, who, to them is the incarnation of Badrinath. Your illustrious ancestors never had to resort to firing on such occasions. Why? They treated them like children. But why red-hot bullets on this occasion?[74]

However, this writer's indignation apart, the breakdown of authority was a partial and fragmented one. Half a century later peasants believed that the raja had appropriately rewarded Chakradhar by gouging out his eyes.[75] While the Panwar house lost only some of its enormous prestige, the Rawain kand does mark an important watershed in the social

[69] T. R. Bhatt, 'Affairs of Tehri (Garhwal)', *National Herald* (AISPC), file no. 165 of 1945–6, NMML.

[70] Juyal's Report.

[71] Cf. D. S. Manral, *Swatantra Sangram mein Kumaun–Garhwal ka Yogadan* (Bareilly, 1978), p. 110.

[72] GRH, 13 June 1931.

[73] Govind Chatak, *Garhwali Lokgeet* (Dehradun, 1956), pp. 266–7.

[74] Open letter to His Highness of Tehri, by J. M. Chatterjee, ISR, 22 February 1931. See also Prayag Joshi, 'Tiladi: Murdon ki Ghati', YV, 28 May 1967.

[75] Interview with Jamansingh, Badyar village, January 1983.

history of Tehri Garhwal. This breakdown of traditional authority—however partial—had important consequences in the peasant movements of the 1940s.

THE KISAN ANDOLAN, 1944–8

These intermittent and localized protests were to crystallize into a widespread movement, engulfing large areas of the state, that culminated in the merger of Tehri Garhwal with the Indian Union. Resembling the archetypal peasant movement far more than the dhandak, the Tehri kisan andolan was nevertheless composed of different strands. On the one hand the spread of the nationalist movement into princely India led to the formation of the Tehri Rajya Praja Mandal at Dehradun in 1939. On the other the growing incorporation of the Tehri peasants into the market economy rendered them more vulnerable to its fluctuations, notably during the depression and World War II. The situation engendered by the loss of control over forests, by now almost complete, was further aggravated by the new taxes the durbar imposed on an unwilling peasantry. The intervention of the Tehri Praja Mandal (itself no replication of the Congress, with its activists rooted in the cultural milieu of the state) was, therefore, mediated through a peasant uprising whose idiom was determined rather more directly by a distinctive social history of protest.

The oppressive forest rules continued to be met with suspicion. The rates at which villagers could buy timber in excess of their allotment far exceeded those at which the durbar sold wood to outside agents. In 1939 the forests between the Bhilagna and Bhageerathi rivers caught fire. Many heads of cattle perished, as did nine peasants who attempted to extinguish the blaze. The durbar refused to award any compensation. Outside the forest restrictions, Juyal had introduced a new tax called *pauntoti*, a form of customs duty levied on the belongings of subjects as and when they entered the state. As a greater number of Garhwalis were now dependent on outside employment, this levy was the cause of much resentment. So was the cess on potatoes, one of the state's chief crops.[76]

[76] Dabral, vol. 8, pt II, pp. 271, 320, etc.; A. S. Rawat, 'Political Movements in Tehri Garhwal State', *Uttarakhand Bharati*, vol. II, no. II, 1977, pp. 31–2.

The Praja Mandal (Citizens' Forum), established on 3 January 1939, took up the issues of begar and pauntoti. Its outstanding leader, Sridev Suman, was born in Jowal village of Baimund patti in 1916. A member of the Congress since his youth, Suman played an important part in the activities of its wing, the All India States People's Conference (AISPC). Determined to set up an organizational forum to mediate between raja and praja, Suman wrote articles and delivered speeches on both local and national struggles. He invoked the spirit of Bhagat Singh and B. K. Dutt, and praised Chandra Singh Garhwali, the hero of the soldiers' mutiny in Peshawar in 1930, as a 'glowing example' of a non-violent revolutionary. In and out of the state Suman had a strong influence on the students of the college in Tehri. In 1940, in an unprecedented act, students went on strike. Several were expelled. They continued to be in close touch with Suman and with Garhwali students at the Banaras Hindu University, whose mentor was the respected socialist and doctor from Badyargarh, Khuslanand Gairola. Postal employees in Tehri, who sympathized with Suman, were able to sabotage the censorship enforced by the authorities. On 21 July 1941 Suman embarked on a hunger strike outside the Tehri police station; this continued for several days, and attracted much attention and support.[77]

Externed from the state, Suman continued his work in British India. On his release from a spell of imprisonment in Agra jail, he re-entered Tehri state and began to tour villages and organize meetings. He was arrested and lodged in Tehri jail. Here he embarked on an indefinite hunger strike, appealing that: (*i*) the Praja Mandal should be recognized and allowed to work in the state; (*ii*) the cases against him should be personally heard by the maharaja; (*iii*) he should be allowed contact with the outside world. When these demands went unheeded, Suman succumbed to pneumonia and heart failure after a fast that lasted eighty-four days.[78]

[77] D.O. no. 433-SC/MISE-13/4, 17 September 1941, from resident, Punjab states (RPS), to secy to crown representative (CR), in file no. 449-P(S)/31, pol. dept, pol. branch, NAI acc. no. 15, CRR, enclosing reports by Suman's agent, NAI.

[78] See fortnightly reports on the political situation in the Punjab states (hereafter FR) for the year 1944, in NAI acc. no. 7, CRR.

Despite being labelled (by the British) a follower of Lenin 'who uses Lenin's method of outwardly constitutional agitation combined with secret revolutionary groups of terrorists', Suman's aims were far more restricted in their scope.[79] According to a close associate, Suman's campaign was directed at the officials of the durbar and not at the king, whom he venerated and respected. His ultimate aim was to reach an agreement between the Praja Mandal and the durbar, whereby the former could engage in constructive work under the guidance of the king. In his last declaration in court Suman averred that opposition to the maharaja, to whom he professed total devotion, ran counter to the principles by which he lived.[80]

Suman's supreme sacrifice (*balidan*) was to be of immense propaganda value in the years to come. In the year of his death the durbar embarked on a fresh land survey and settlement, in revision of the settlement operations of 1917–26. The king hoped to take advantage of the incarceration of Suman and other activists in British India. The resident however prophetically warned him that 'unless he could obtain the services of energetic revenue officers he would be asking for trouble.'[81] The extensive operations, carried out under the supervision of the settlement officer, Ramprasad Dobhal, involved the measurement of land and fixation of the new (enhanced) rates of revenue. Immediately, surveying officials had to contend with non-co-operation by peasants who refused to submit to the survey.[82]

Sustained opposition to the settlement followed the submission of interim reports by the *amins* and patwaris, when the settlement officer himself held court to ratify the survey. Dobhal's large entourage, which included his guests and dancing parties, claimed *bara* (services) and begar as a matter of course. Despite rules prescribing payment for rations and transport, officials were taking services at nominal rates and claiming receipts for the full amount. Complaints were made about

[79] Report by Suman's agent in ibid.

[80] Bhaktdarshan, pp. 255–6, 282.

[81] Note on the visit of RPS to T-G, 21 to 23 March 1944, in file no. 347-P(S)/44, pol. dept, pol. branch, NAI acc. no. 7, CRR.

[82] Personal communication from Acharya Gopeshwar Narain Kothiyal, hereafter Kothiyal.

the arbitrary manner in which *nazrana* (revenue) rates were fixed and impediments put on the breaking of fresh ground for cultivation. Peasants also demanded the right to alienate land enjoyed by their counterparts in British Garhwal. Simultaneously, the forest department's highhandedness came in for sharp criticism. One incident was reported of peasants being tied up and stones loaded on their head when a forest fire occurred in their vicinity. Legitimate requests for building timber went unheeded as well.[83]

The first meeting to oppose the settlement, attended by about a thousand peasants, was held on 21 April 1946. The movement, one largely autonomous of the Praja Mandal, was led by a retired employee of the postal department, Dada Daulatram. It spread rapidly to Barjula, Kadakhot, Dangchaura and Akhri pattis. Refusing to supply bara and begar, peasants forced Dobhal's entourage to cook and clean utensils themselves. Nor could they move camp without hiring costly coolies. Refusing to submit to intimidation, villagers desisted from attending *muqabala* (settlements) in Dobhal's court. Instead, the relevant cases were decided in the village panchayat.[84] In some localities peasants tore up the settlement papers which attempted to codify the state's demands, an action characteristic of rural jacqueries throughout the world.[85] Under Daulatram's leadership a *jatha* (group) of peasants marched to Narendranagar, the new capital, raising slogans against begar and nazrana. Daulatram and his associates were arrested and jailed on 21 July 1946.[86]

On hearing of their leader's arrest another jatha proceeded to Tehri. Led by Lachman Singh Bist, an ex-soldier of the Indian National Army, this party had the object of releasing

[83] Typed report by Jainarayan Vyas (secy, AISPC), on a visit to Garhwal, in AISPC, file no. 165/1945–6.

[84] 'Report on movement against Nazrana and Land Settlement excess in Tehri State', unsigned, undated, in ibid.

[85] Sher Singh Mewar, 'Tehri Garhwal ka Krantikari Itihas' (handwritten manuscript at present in my possession), p. 5. Cf. Le Roy Ladurie on the burning of land registers in sixteenth-century France: 'the land registers represented the intrusion of the written word and modern method of calculation into the casual archaism of the seigneurial system. The peasants considered them efficient, therefore highly dangerous.' *Carnival in Romans*, p. 137.

[86] Bhaktdarshan, pp. 479–83.

the prisoners from jail and proceeding to Narendranagar to celebrate '1942 day' on 9 August. In the ensuing scuffle several peasants were arrested but the rest, including Lachman Singh, evaded arrest. Meanwhile, Daulatram and several colleagues, including the young communist Nagendra Saklani, went on a hunger strike in protest against the durbar's actions.[87]

At this juncture the Congress stepped in to mediate between the peasantry and the durbar. The party's traditional suspicion of peasant movements over which it did not exercise control was perhaps reinforced in this case by the immediacy of the interim government in which it was to hold power.[88] Accordingly, a delegation led by Jainarayan Vyas and Khuslanand Gairola visited Tehri Garhwal between 10 and 20 August. An agreement was reached with the durbar whereby the Praja Mandal was registered and allowed to hold processions and meetings. The pact also envisaged the release of those activists in jail.[89] Under its new constitution the 'ultimate object' of the Praja Mandal was the 'achievement of responsible government under the aegis of His Highness . . . by constitutional, legitimate and peaceful means'.[90] Triumphantly, the resident proclaimed that this article constituted 'a very considerable success for the Darbar'.[91]

The terms of the pact were, however, not adhered to by the durbar. While several prisoners were released on furnishing personal bonds, others including Daulatram and the Praja Mandal president, Paripurnanand Painuli, were still in jail and being tried. Daulatram had also been refused defence counsel. On 13 September Painuli, labelled a 'communist' by the authorities, and several other prisoners commenced an indefinite hunger strike, demanding a repeal of the Registration of Associations act under which the Praja Mandal had been derecognized.[92]

[87] D.O. no. XP G-2-5/46, from RPS to secy to CR, 16 August 1946, in file no. 347-P(S)/44, NAI acc. no. 7, CRR.

[88] Cf. Sumit Sarkar, *Modern India* (Delhi, 1983).

[89] Press statement, 26 August 1946, sd J. N. Vyas, in AISPC, 165/1945-6, NMML.

[90] Article II, constitution of Tehri Rajya Praja Mandal, in ibid.

[91] See file no 347-P(S)/44, NAI acc. no. 7, CRR.

[92] Letters to J. N. Vyas from Praja Mandal Karyalaya, Tehri, 20 October 1946, and from Shyamcharan Negi, 14 October 1946, both in AISPC, 165/1945-6.

In the circumstances, there was a growing perception among the Tehri villagers that the Congress signatories of the pact had 'totally forgotten those leaders of theirs who are rotting in jails for the simple crime that they wanted to establish Prajamandal in the state boundaries'.[93] Strongly protesting the durbar's actions (which included the arrest of Suman's brother) the hero of Peshawar, Chandra Singh Garhwali, accused Jainarayan Vyas of deliberately allowing the durbar to sabotage the pact. A professed anti-communist who had purged the AISPC of leftist elements, Vyas suspected their involvement in the kisan andolan. But, as Garhwali pointed out, the solitary communist involved in the movement was Nagendra Saklani, and in his case too the peasantry was unacquainted with his political beliefs.[94]

In December 1946 Painuli effected a dramatic escape from Tehri jail. Donning the robes of a sadhu, he trekked westwards until he reached the Tons valley and British territory. From there he proceeded to Dehradun. He had been presumed dead by the AISPC, who had passed a condolence resolution following his disappearance.[95] On 9 February 1947 Daulatram and five fellow prisoners went on a fast, demanding that they be re-tried in a British Indian court. Using the occasion of the birth of a son, the maharaja released political prisoners on 23 February. Shortly afterwards, Daulatram was rearrested after an altercation with a police constable.[96]

The Praja Mandal had its first open meeting in Tehri on 26 and 27 May 1947, and Daulatram was chosen its head for the next year. On 14 August Painuli sent a wire to the maharaja, warning him of his intention to enter the state on Independence Day. He was promptly arrested on arrival.[97] Gathering momentum, the movement had spread to Saklana, the only muafi in the state.[98] In Saklana, a major potato pro-

[93] Letter from Dr Gairola to J. N. Vyas, undated, in ibid.

[94] Letter from Chandra Singh Garhwali to J. Nehru, 27 November 1946, in AISPC, file no. 242 of 1946–7, NMML.

[95] Interview with Shri Painuli, Dehradun, May 1983.

[96] See FR for 1947, file no. 5(I)-P(S)/47, pol. dept. NAI.

[97] Ibid.

[98] The Saklana muafidars were responsible for revenue collection and enjoyed IIIrd class magistrate's powers; other affairs of government, including forests, were controlled by the Tehri durbar.

ducing area, peasants had been protesting extortion by the potato 'syndicate' to whom the durbar had accorded sole rights of collection and sale. Muletteers were also desisting from paying the tax levied on transport. When the police arrested striking peasants, the refusal to pay taxes became more widespread. Some villagers fled to Dehradun district. The police also raided houses and beat up the inhabitants. Angered, the kisans encircled durbar officials and forced them to leave Saklana. The *muafidars* voluntarily abdicated and left for Dehradun. In the last week of December victorious peasants formed an *azad* panchayat which abolished taxes and declared that each cultivator had ownership rights.[99]

As news of the development at Saklana spread, azad panchayats were formed in several other pattis.[100] In Badyargarh events took a dramatic turn at the Dhadi Ghandiyal *jath*. At this fair, held every twelve years, peasants paid homage to the local deity of Ghandiyal. Shrewdly utilizing this opportunity, Daulatram and his colleagues arranged to address the crowd on the Saklana and Kadakhot dhandaks. The gathering was informed of the impending march on Kirtinagar, where peasants from different parts of the state were expected to congregate.[101]

Following the Dhadi jath, activists fanned out into the villages. In several places *chowkis* (offices) were captured and their patwaris replaced by men chosen from among the peasantry. Survey officials were made to return bribes extorted from villagers. Occasionally, liquor contractors were beaten up and their stills smashed.[102]

Jathas of around fifty peasants each were rapidly sent onwards to Kirtinagar. On 30 December policemen came searching for Daulatram. The constables were arrested by the villagers and asked by Daulatram to report at the court at Kirtinagar. The next day, when the police fired on a crowd at Jakhni village, angry peasants captured the court and police station at Kirtinagar. The police inspector's house, where the

[99] Girdhar Pandit, 'Saklana Andolan: Tehri Jankranti ka Pratam Charan', *Parvatiya Times* (Annual), 30 March 1983.

[100] YV, 15 January 1948.

[101] Interviews in Badyargarh, January 1983.

[102] Govind Negi, 'Tehri Riyasat Mukti Sangarsh: Ek Romanchkari Adhyay', YV, issues of 15 August, 22 August, 5 September and 12 September 1976. Hereafter G. Negi.

deputy collector was also taking refuge, was surrounded. When the officials refused to surrender, the crowd collected kerosene preparatory to burning the house. The deputy collector was caught while trying to escape and taken across the Alakananda river to Srinagar. The police party who had fired at Jakhni on the 31st were found tied up on the road. They were taken to the office of the District Congress Committee at Pauri and made to sign letters of resignation. In Devprayag, too, the court had been captured by the dhandakis. The same night Daulatram and Painuli were spirited away to Narendranagar for negotiations with the durbar.[103]

Meanwhile, thousands of peasants had collected at Kirtinagar. Daulatram himself returned on 9 January. The town had initially been cleared of all officials and an azad panchayat had been proclaimed.[104] In response, the durbar sent an armed force led by Baldev Singh Panwar, a close kinsman of the raja. This force arranged a meeting with Daulatram in the local court. However, as soon as Daulatram returned, soldiers fired teargas shells and bullets at the waiting crowd. When fire was set to the building, senior officials tried to flee. The crowd chased them, whereupon one officer fired several bullets, killing the young communist Saklani.[105]

The next day the crowd took the bodies of Saklani and Moluram (a peasant killed in the firing outside the court) and proceeded to Tehri via Devprayag. En route the jatha exhibited the corpses in different hamlets. A second jatha, led by Daulatram and including the captured officials, proceeded directly to Tehri. On 14 January the two jathas met and immersed the martyrs in the confluence of the Bhageerathi and Bhilagna rivers. The army having fled, an azad panchayat took over Tehri under its padhan, Virendra Dutt Saklani.[106]

Hoping to win over the people through his presence, the raja rushed to Tehri from Narendranagar. His attempt to enter Tehri was foiled when the bridge across the Bhageerathi was

[103] Balkrishna Bhatt, 'Tehri mein Kya Hua', YV, 15 February 1948; D. Ghildiyal, 'Kirtinagar ka Andolan', YV, 1 March 1948.

[104] Letter from Nagendra Saklana to P. N. Painuli, 10 January 1948, in YV, 11 January 1970.

[105] G. Negi.

[106] Bhaktdarshan, pp. 484–5; YV, 15 January 1948.

shut. The physical gulf that separated him from his people became invested with a deeper meaning: as one peasant recounted, on one bank were the massed subjects, on the other their ruler ('*Us taraf raja, is taraf praja*').[107]

The raja had now lost control. Thousands of peasants from Jaunpur and Rawain gathered at Bhavan and handcuffed police inspector Baijram, the man responsible for Suman's arrest. Functionaries of the police, revenue and forest departments were forced out of the locality and an azad panchayat established.[108] In defeat, the raja called in the Praja Mandal leaders for negotiations. A ministry headed by Dr Gairola was established, which held office till the state's merger with Uttar Pradesh the following year.

Peasants and parties

The kisan andolan differed from the preceding dhandaks in two major respects, one of which was in its spread. The initial confluence of several local movements gained an additional impetus with the Kirtinagar kand (firing) and came to cover much of the state. Secondly, this movement had an organizational forum in the shape of the Praja Mandal. The dyadic relationship between raja and praja was therefore complicated by the presence of Congress-inspired nationalists. The specific linkages between the Praja Mandal and the praja it claimed to represent thus need to be examined.

The relationship between the Praja Mandal and the peasantry can be viewed at several levels, each invested with different layers of meaning. The Praja Mandal's aims initially encompassed the reformation of an administration viewed through the prism of modern nationalism as *samantshahi* (feudal). In fact, in the early part of the movement there were reports that the peasant leader Daulatram had 'been disowned by the Praja Mandal'.[109] As we have seen, the AISPC was keen on a settlement with the raja, bypassing the kisan andolan that had enabled its intervention in the first place.

On assuming power on 15 August 1947 the Congress attitude towards the Tehri movements underwent a major shift.

[107] Interviews in Badyargarh, January 1983.

[108] YV, 21 January 1948.

[109] FR for first half of July 1946, in NAI acc. no. 7, CRR.

The desire to integrate princely states with the Indian Union, coupled with the growing pressure of the peasant movement itself, led the Congress to view Daulatram and his associates in a more favourable light. Now the Praja Mandal agitation imperfectly merged with the kisan andolan in a movement that generated its own dynamic: the outcome perhaps exceeding what either the Praja Mandal or the peasantry had envisaged.

The hiatus between the Praja Mandal and those it professed to represent remained, at the level of perception, a considerable one.[110] As a young activist later recounted, the attempt to popularize the slogan 'Inquilab Zindabad' (associated with the Punjabi revolutionary Bhagat Singh) at village meetings met with a miserable failure. As the slogan was raised along with the national tricolour, peasants interpreted it in a manner more representative of their feelings. They responded by shouting 'Yanno Khala Jandabad' (this is the way we will bring about the rule of the flag). Although the Praja Mandal attempted to explain the original slogan and its significance, the same misperception repeated itself at the next village.[111]

Interestingly, whereas Praja Mandal activists explained the origins of the Kirtinagar 'satyagraha' in terms of India having won freedom while Tehri was in bondage, peasants were emphatic that their struggle was against the oppressive taxes and the settlement operations that came in their wake. But it was not merely at the level of perception that this duality persisted; it was imbricated in the significance attached to different actions. Thus, peasant participants recounted, with evident satisfaction, how patwaris had been overthrown and symbolically replaced by their own men, adding that their nominees continued to hold office for some time. (In using a time of social instability to replace state officials with their own nominees, Garhwali peasants were in honourable company; very similar acts attended the peasant revolutions in Russia in 1905 and Mexico in 1919.[112]) On the other hand, Praja Mandal

[110] It must, however, be added that many of the Tehri Praja Mandal activists had a far more positive view of the kisan andolan than the AISPC bosses.

[111] G. Negi.

[112] Shanin, *Russia as a 'Developing' Society*, II, pp. 108–11; John Womack, *Zapata and the Mexican Revolution* (New York, 1969), p. 225.

activists emphasized the formation of the interim ministry as a major fulfilment of their goals.[113]

Peasants were also insistent that the king did not himself know of the injustice (*anniyayi*) being perpetrated in his name. As the AISPC peace mission observed, 'villagers were not found disloyal to the maharaja or the gaddi and had a feeling that all that was being done was not in the knowledge of the maharaja.' The fear of retribution from the police was adduced as an important factor which dissuaded peasants from approaching the king.[114] For its part, the Praja Mandal had a far more ambivalent attitude. Its eagerness to share power with the durbar was nevertheless accompanied by an ideology which was implicitly anti-monarchical.

ELEMENTARY ASPECTS OF CUSTOMARY REBELLION

'I obey, but do not comply.'

—Puerto Rican peasant saying

As we have seen, in Tehri Garhwal the mechanisms of social protest drew heavily on the indigenous tradition of resistance known as dhandak. Yet, for all its distinctiveness, the dhandak is representative of a type of rebellion widely prevalent in pre-industrial and pre-capitalist monarchies. Variations on the dhandak theme have been reported from other parts of Asia, and Africa and Europe as well. The dhandak is a sub-type of what one might call 'customary' rebellion: a form of rebellion that draws its legitimacy from custom and does not seek to overthrow the social order. As Max Weber commented, here 'opposition is not directed against the system as such—it is a case of "traditional revolution"'[115]—peasants' accusations against the ruler being that he or his officials failed to observe the traditional limits to their power. In the classic formulation of Max Gluckman, custom 'directs and controls the quarrels through conflicts and allegiances so that despite rebellion, the same social system is re-established over wider areas of com-

[113] Interviews in Badyargarh and Dehradun, January and April 1983.

[114] Typed report, untitled, prob. by J.N. Vyas, n.d. (probably June 1916), in AISPC, 265/1945–6.

[115] Max Weber, *Economy and Society*, translated by Guenther Roth and Claus Wittich (Berkeley, 1978), volume II, p. 220.

munal life and through longer periods of time.'[116] In this perspective customary rebellion is seen as central to the coherence and persistence of a society, a functional safety valve that allows for the periodic and constructive release of discontent. While Gluckman's interpretation has been very influential, I believe it is both partial and inadequate. A comparative analysis of the 'elementary aspects' of customary rebellion—with the Tehri Garhwal case very much in the foreground—may help reveal this, as may an alternative interpretation of the significance of customary rebellion as a form of social protest.

Typically, the origins of rebellion in traditional chiefdoms and monarchies stem from a perceived breach of the covenant between ruler and ruled. This covenant between high and low, or patron and client, is normally couched in the idiom of father and son. Being by definition the ruler *par excellence*, the monarch patronizes his subjects not only in the economic sphere but in the socio-political and judicial spheres as well. According to the dominant ideology, the peasantry looks to the king for impartial arbitration and social justice. On his accession to the throne of Garhwal in 1919, the young prince Narendra Shah was exhorted to live up to the traditions of his ancestors: the main elements of princely rule being designated as justice (*nyaya*) and protection of subjects (*praja ki raksha*).[117] When, in 1946, Narendra Shah abdicated for reasons of ill health, he invoked 'the Shastric maxim of Raja and Praja conceived as Pita (father) and Putra (son) [which] has always been the guiding principle of the patriarchs who occupied this gaddi'.[118] The symbolism of father and son well epitomized the essentially patriarchal style of domination, where 'protection' of the peasantry harmonized with the kingly ideal of benevolent rule. A similar idiom was skilfully used by German and British colonialists in Africa, with the all-powerful Kaiser, or the English king, symbolizing the head of a large family,

[116] Max Gluckman, *Custom and Conflict in Africa* (Oxford, 1956), p. 47. Cf. also his *Order and Rebellion in Tribal Africa* (London, 1963), and *The Ideas in Barotse Jurisprudence* (New Haven, 1965).

[117] *Garhwali Visheshank* (special number), 4 October 1919.

[118] Statement by Narendra Shah, addressed to 'my beloved Praja', in file no. 49-P(S)/46, pol. dept, NAI.

consisting of the various nationalities under European domination.[119]

This covenant, while indicating the limits of arbitrary action by both rulers and subjects, is continually under threat. For, intermediate between the king and the peasantry are myriad laws relating to the land, the forests, and the waters of the kingdom, and myriad officials to enforce these laws. And in the eyes of the peasantry officials are invariably tyrannical and high-handed; moreover, they tend to pervert the king's commands and interpret laws in their favour and against the interests of the peasants. 'In its simplest and most common expression', observes Daniel Field in his fine study of customary rebellion in Russia, 'popular monarchism took the form of the adage, "the Tsar wants it, but the boyars resist." '[120] Often ethnically and economically distinct from the peasant masses, these officials are both despised and feared. In times of revolutionary change (e.g. Tehri Garhwal in 1948 or Russia in 1905), peasants seize the opportunity to appoint their own men in place of officials deputed from outside. Yet this opportunity very rarely presents itself: more frequently peasants follow the Russian Peasant Union in petitioning the king to 'free us from officials . . . who cost a lot and do not give us order, only disturb our life and work and offend us daily . . . understanding nothing of our problems.'[121] If these pleas are unheeded, peasants take matters into their own hands, physically attacking officials even as they break the new laws. In this act of trespass peasants could cry, as in nineteenth-century France,

[119] See Terence Ranger, 'The Invention of Tradition in Colonial Africa', in Eric Hobsbawn and Terence Ranger (eds), *The Invention of Tradition* (Cambridge, 1983).

[120] Daniel Field, *Rebels in the Name of the Tsar* (Boston, 1976), p. 14. Cf. also Philip Longworth, 'Peasant Leadership and the Pugachev Revolt', *Journal of Peasant Studies*, vol. 2, no. 2, January 1975, pp. 187–8. A fascinating parallel is found in the slave societies of North America. Here, while plantation owners also used a patriarchal ideology which claimed the slaves as children under their protection, the white overseer who actually supervised day-to-day operations was the obvious target of attack, slaves often complaining of his tyrannies to the master. See Eugene Genovese, *Roll, Jordan Roll: The World the Slaves Made* (New York, 1973).

[121] Quoted in Teodor Shanin, *Russia as a 'Developing' Society* (New Haven, 1986), vol. II, p. 112.

'long live the king, down with the Forest Administration'; or, as Balzac puts it, shout 'long live the king, with enthusiasm, to avoid shouting, "long live the count". '[122] Alternatively, as they sometimes did in Garhwal, they could march to the capital demanding an audience with the king—as did the peasants in early Meiji Japan who went to Tokyo hoping to get justice from the central authority 'because they were unable to get a fair hearing from their prefecture'.[123]

Such appeals to the king were made in the name of 'custom' —namely the argument that the new laws were contravening time-honoured social (and natural) arrangements. Custom, as Marc Bloch observed many years ago, is a 'double-edged sword', serving both peasants and their overlords in turn. If French peasants could claim that enclosure violated their hitherto unrestricted access to common land, their lords could insist on the prompt payment of taxes and tithes even in bad crop years.[124] But in the transition to capitalism it is peasants who have more frequently invoked custom, for it is they who stand to lose most from enclosure, state forest management, or the mechanization of agricultural work. European peasants were known to invent king's charters which variously exonerated them from taxes or gave them the run of forests and pasture; they accused officials of 'concealing the king's orders' while insisting that their own actions were perfectly in accord with the wishes of the monarch.[125] In Tehri Garhwal, several centuries later, custom was often the most effective weapon for a peasantry facing the onslaught of a 'modernizing' state. For, 'the ideological struggle to define the present is a struggle to define the past as well', and, like the poor peasants of the Malay village of Sedaka, those left behind by capitalism have no option but to collectively create a 'remembered village and remembered economy that serve[s] as an effective ideological

[122] John Merriman, 'The Demoiselles of the Ariege, 1829–31', in Merriman (ed.), *1830 in France* (New York, 1975), p. 94; Henri Balzac, *The Peasantry* (New York, 1900), p. 311.

[123] William Kelly, *Deference and Defiance in Nineteenth Century Japan* (Princeton, 1985), pp. 205–6.

[124] Marc Bloch, *French Rural History* (rpt. London, 1978), pp. 70–1.

[125] Ladurie, *Carnival in Romans*, pp. 43–7; Lefebvre, *The Great Fear*, pp. 30 ff., 95–7.

backdrop against which to deplore the present'.[126] Of course in Tehri Garhwal the remembered village and remembered economy were not merely figments of the imagination: things were far better before the coming of the forest department, and to that extent Garhwali peasant appeals to the monarch rested on a solid core of truth.

Yet such invocations are not merely tactical; the opposition to new laws and their enforcing officials has often been strengthened, as in eighteenth-century France, by the 'profound conviction that the king was on their side'.[127] In general, appeals to the monarch rested on two core assumptions: that the king symbolized the spirit of the collectivity and that, as the temporal and spiritual head, he was the very fount of justice.[128] The monarch is the head of an 'imagined community'.[129] Unlike the political overlords of contemporary imagined communities like the nation-state, however, his persona is avowedly sacred, not secular.[130] Traditional societies experience life as an ever-expanding web of connections which reaches beyond local and national communities into the depths of nature. It is the function of the monarch to maintain the harmony of this integration between society and nature, between the microcosmos of human beings and the macrocosmos of gods. As the mediating link between the sacred and the profane, the king takes on

[126] J. C. Scott, *Weapons of the Weak: Everyday Forms of Peasant Resistance* (New Haven, 1986), p. 178.

[127] Lefebvre, *Great Fear*, p. 42.

[128] In some modern societies a supreme religious figure could have a very similar symbolic function. Thus the noted Chilean author Ariel Dorfman, commenting on the sense of anticipation with which his countrymen awaited the visit of the Pope, says: 'The despair has been such that now [Chileans] believe that the Pope will fix everything. He represents a figure from the outside who is pure and immaculate and not part of the everyday bickering and horror.' See *Christian Science Monitor*, 30 March 1987, p. 9.

[129] The phrase is from Benedict Anderson, *Imagined Communities: Reflections on the Origins and Spread of Nationalism* (London, 1985). Anderson sees the nation, replacing societies centred around kingship and religion, as the major form of the imagined community in modern times.

[130] The boundaries of such communities are not geographical—as are those of nation-states—but cultural. Thus, even peasants in the British-ruled portion of Garhwal thought of themselves as 'Garhwalis', acknowledging the Tehri monarch as their temporal and spiritual head.

some of the attributes of the gods: he is quasi-divine:

> Sovereigns are the kinsmen, the homologues or the mediators of the gods. The closeness of the attributes of power and of the sacred indicates the link that has always existed between them—a connection that history has tended to pull apart but has never broken.[131]

The divinity of kingship is further heightened in isolated and protected tracts, such as Garhwal, where the tranquillity of the cosmic order and its integration with society remain relatively undisturbed by cataclysmic social or natural events.[132]

In his mediating role the king must faithfully observe the rituals of investiture, symbolically undertake the first annual ploughing, and enact the other societally varying magico-religious ceremonies which are believed to constitute royal power and assure social harmony. Failure to do so may bring the wrath of his subjects upon him or his office. In the Bemba kingdom of Central Africa the chief was blamed for the economic distress of the 1920s, his subjects believing it to be caused

[131] George Balandier, *Political Anthropology* (London, 1970), p. 99. Evans-Pritchard says: 'In my view kingship everywhere and at all times has been in some degree a sacred office. This is because a king symbolises a whole society and must not be identified with any part of it. He must be in the society and yet stand outside it and this is only possible if his office is raised to a mystical plane.' E. E. Evans-Pritchard, 'The Divine Kingship of the Shilluck of the Nilotic Sudan' (Frazer Lecture, 1948), in his *Social Anthropology and Other Essays* (New York, 1962), p. 210. On divine kingship in Africa, see also the classic collection edited by Meyer Fortes and Evans-Pritchard, *African Political Systems* (London, 1940).

[132] Cf. Henri Frankfort, *Kingship and the Gods* (1948; rpt. Chicago, 1978), Introduction. The divinity of the Panwar kings seriously calls into question the thesis of 'secularization' of Hindu kingship—in which the Brahmin is held to have exclusive control over the sacred realm—advanced by Louis Dumont and Romila Thapar in their enormously influential works. See Dumont, 'The Conception of Kingship in Ancient India', in his *Religion, Politics and History in India* (Paris, 1970); *idem*, *Homo Hierarchicus* (London, 1970); Thapar, *A History of India*, vol. 1 (Harmondsworth, 1966). Derived largely from scriptural sources, the Dumont–Thapar thesis does not stand up to the scrutiny of anthropological studies from different parts of India, which conclusively demonstrate that divinity is intrinsic to the Hindu conception of kingship. See, *inter alia*, Frederique Apffel Marglin, *Wives of the God-King* (Delhi, 1985); R. K. Jain, 'Kingship, Territory and Property in Pre-British Bundelkhand', *Economic and Political Weekly*, 2 June 1979; S. C. Sinha, 'State Formation and Rajput Myth in Rajput Central India', *Man in India*, vol. 42, no. 1, 1982; and, for Nepal, R. Burghart, 'Hierarchical Models of the Hindu Social System', *Man*, n.s., vol. 13, no. 4, December 1978.

by the monarch's failure to build, as custom demanded, a new capital upon his accession.[133] Apart from the correct observance of traditional rituals, the physical presence of the king is required—especially at crucial times like the harvest. In the state of Bastar in Central India peasants revolted in 1876 when the king left the state to pay his respects to the Prince of Wales, 'leaving the ryots to the tender mercies of [cruel officials like] Gopinath and Adit Pershad'.[134] Likewise, the Garhwali king's visit to Europe coincided with the Rawain uprising of 1930; and his physical removal from the scene undoubtedly led to the tragedy whereby a routine dhandak ended in an unprecedented massacre.

As the embodiment of the spirit of the collectivity, the protector of his subjects and the fountain of justice, the monarch is the ultimate court of appeal for rebels claiming the sanction of custom. Here lies one major difference between the idiom of customary rebellion in small, relatively homogeneous and well integrated states like Tehri Gahrwal, and in states organized according to different political and economic principles. In large monarchies, for example, one important variant on the theme of customary rebellion is the appearance of a 'pretender'. This phenomenon normally occurs in the far-flung corners of a huge kingdom, where peasants are far removed from the centre of authority and are unlikely to have ever seen a member of the royal family. A pretender comes among the villagers, claiming to be the true monarch (the just tsar in Russia, Ratu Adil in Java); he asks, and frequently gets, their support in a social movement directed against corrupt officials.[135] The dhandak

[133] Karen Fields, *Revival and Rebellion in Colonial Central Africa* (Princeton, 1985), p. 57. 'A legend recorded in the thirteenth century *Heimskringla*', observes Bloch, 'relates that Halfdan the Black, king of Norway, had been "of all kings the one who had brought most success to the harvests". When he died, instead of burying his corpse entire and in one single piece, his subjects cut it into four pieces, and buried each portion under a mound in each of the four principal districts of the country; for "the possession of the body"—or one of its fragments—"seemed to those who obtained it to give hope of further good harvests".' Marc Bloch, *The Royal Touch: Sacred Monarchy and Scrofula in England and France*, trans. J. E. Anderson (1923; English edition, London, 1973), p. 32.

[134] See foreign dept, pol. agent, Progs, August 1876, nos. 163–72, NAI.

[135] For Russia, see Philip Longworth, 'The Pretender Phenomena in Eighteenth Century Russia', *Past and Present*, no. 66., Feb. 1975; *idem*, ' "The Pugachev Revolt", the Last Great Cossack-Peasant Uprising', in H. A. Landsberger (ed.),

can also be distinguished from the phenomenon of regicide found in the segmentary states of Africa, where disaffected subjects can call upon a chief to replace the incumbent to whose inadequacies are attributed current economic and political tensions.[136] In Tehri Garhwal, loyalty was owed to the person occupying the throne, not simply to the institution of kingship; there was no question of the rebels calling upon another person to replace the one in power.

Paternalism from above and from below

> [T]he slaves found an opportunity to translate paternalism itself into a doctrine different from that understood by their masters and to forge it into a weapon of resistance . . . [T]hey acted consciously and unconsciously to transform paternalism into a doctrine of protection of their own rights.
>
> —Eugene Genovese

The religious idiom of divine kingship tends to obscure the mundane and practical ends to which it was put. As Marc Bloch observes, 'the miraculous power attributed to their kings by the "primitives" is generally conceived as employed for collective ends which are intended to serve the well-being of the whole group . . .'.[137] To an outside observer a peasant rebellion calling upon an omnipotent and quasi-divine monarch may smack of naïvety; yet it is striking how often peasants have used the idiom of divine kingship to advance their own interests. Tehri villagers may have looked upon their monarch as Bolanda Badrinath, the deity personified, but they usually called upon his miraculous powers in support of their traditional rights in the forest and in opposition to increases in land tax. This central feature of customary rebellion is captured well by Daniel Field:

Naïve or not, the peasants professed their faith in the Tsar in forms, and only in those forms, that corresponded to their interests . . . [The]

Rural Protest: Agrarian Movements and Social Change (London, 1974). For the Ratu Adil phenomenon in Java, see Sartono Kartodirdjo, *Protest Movements in Rural Java* (Singapore, 1973).

[136] See the works by Gluckman cited in note 116 above; Evans-Pritchard, 'Divine Kingship', and Gillian Feeley-Harnuk, 'Issues in Divine Kingship', *Annual Review of Anthropology*, vol. 14, 1985.

[137] Bloch, *Royal Touch*, p. 33.

goals peasants pursued under the aegis of the myth [of the divine king] were eminently practical: more land, tax relief, and self-rule. Their means were draped in mystery, but their ends were worldly.[138]

Peasants in Tehri, as in Russia, twisted the myth of divine kingship to serve utterly mundane and practical ends. The abolition of the Panwar monarchy was beyond their powers; in the circumstances the dhandak, like the French Carnival, 'used the most effective or most audible means of agitation possible, considering the culture and psychology of the times',[139] to wrest concessions from their superiors. This suggests that far from being a society's safety valve, a functionalist device to maintain the integration and coherence of a society (as some anthropological accounts suggest), customary rebellion is more appropriately viewed as a shrewd and effective tactic used by peasants to exploit the inherent ambiguities of the dominant ideology. Indeed—

> The most common form of class struggle arises from the failure of a dominant ideology to live up to the implicit promises it necessarily makes. The dominant ideology can be turned against its privileged beneficiaries not only because subordinate groups develop their own interpretations, understandings and readings of its ambiguous terms, but also because of the promises that the dominant classes must make to propagate it in the first place.[140]

And so, through a lengthy detour into the indigenous idiom of domination and resistance, we come back full circle to Weber:

> experience shows that in no instance does domination voluntarily limit itself to the appeal to material, affectual or ideal motives as a basis for its continuance. In addition, every such system attempts to establish and to cultivate the belief in its legitimacy.[141]

Weber yes, but with more than a dash of Marx. For what is viewed from above as a justification of elite domination is

[138] Field, *Rebels*, pp. 209–10.

[139] Le Roy Ladurie, *Carnival in Romans*, p. 321. Cf. Eugene Genovese: 'The practical question facing the slaves was not whether slavery itself was a proper relation but how to survive it with the greatest degree of self-determination'. *Roll, Jordan, Roll*, p. 125.

[140] J. C. Scott, *Weapons of the Weak*, p. 338.

[141] Max Weber, *Economy and Society*, vol. 1, pp. 55, 213.

reinterpreted from below as a mandate to rebel against attempts to change, even in the slightest, the relative balance of power between elite and subaltern classes. Thus the legitimizing belief that underlay the eighteenth-century food riot in England serves just as well in explaining the moral idiom of the dhandak. 'By the notion of legitimation', writes E. P. Thompson,

> I mean that the men and women in the crowd were informed by the belief that they were defending traditional rights and customs, and in general that they were supported by the wider consensus of the community. On occasion this popular consensus was endorsed in some measure by license afforded by the authorities.[142]

The dominant ideology, therefore, while serving in a general way to consolidate elite rule, also constricts in some significant respects its room for manoeuvre, just as it necessarily has within it a certain ambiguity and openness that allow for lower-class resistance. Embedded in every ideology that legitimizes domination there is a sub-text, a legitimizing ideology of resistance. The contradiction between the claims of the ruling ideology and the actual state of affairs in any society is, as Scott implies, a most frequent cause of resistance. The central argument of this work is that forms of domination structure forms of resistance. While protest normally arises in response to domination and attempts to resist it, most forms of domination actually enable resistance. Thus the hiatus between the rhetoric of liberal democracy and living conditions in southern United States produced the civil rights movement, and the denial of workers' rights in an avowedly 'socialist' state led to Solidarity. In the same manner, the failure to meet the promise of protection held out by the quasi-divine monarch enabled peasant rebels in Garhwal to claim the sanctity of custom.

[142] E. P. Thompson, 'The Moral Economy of the English Crowd in the Eighteenth Century', *Past and Present*, no. 50, 1970–1, p. 78.

CHAPTER 5

Rebellion as Confrontation

God sent Gandhi in the form of a Bania [merchant] to conquer Bania government.

—Kumaun peasant leader, 1921

This chapter examines the trajectory of social protest in Kumaun division during the early decades of this century. While the absence of popular protest in the first century of British rule had given rise to the stereotype of the 'simple and law abiding hillman',[1] the reservation of the Kumaun forests between 1911 and 1917 'met with violent and sustained opposition',[2] culminating in 1921 when, within the space of a few months, the administration was paralysed first by a strike against utar (statutory labour) and then through a systematic campaign in which the Himalayan pine forests 'were swept by incendiary fires almost from end to end'.[3]

This transformation in peasant consciousness and peasant revolt was closely related to the more subtle but equally enduring changes in the structure of colonial administration. As chapter 2 documents, in view of the strategic location of Kumaun the demands of the state on the peasantry were extraordinarily light; moreover, the style of rule was a typically paternalist one, exemplified in the person of Henry Ramsay, commissioner from 1856 to 1884. It was the advent of forest management—with the hill conifers being arguably the most valuable forest 'property' in India—that indicated a growing intervention of the state in the day-to-day life of the peasantry. The workings of scientific forestry, in particular, by curtailing

[1] P. Mason, *A Matter of Honour* (London, 1975), p. 451; cf. also T. W. Webber, *The Forests of Upper India and Their Inhabitants* (London, 1902), p. 39.

[2] E. P. Stebbing, *The Forests of India*, 3 volumes (London, 1922–6), III, p. 258.

[3] E. A. Smythies, *India's Forest Wealth* (London, 1925), p. 84.

customary rights, drastically affected the mode of peasant social and economic organization. At the same time, the imperatives of exercising effective control led to a more general bureaucratization of state authority. This transition was succinctly expressed by a district officer in Almora in the late 1930s who recalled Ramsay's rule 'as a benevolent despot who could do as he liked and [which] would always remain an envious [*sic*] example to the present generation of civilians who are so much bound by red tape and the bulky Manual of Government Order'.[4]

The trajectory of social protest in British Kumaun was intimately connected with the changes in administrative structures and styles. The early phase of resistance to forest management and the begar system lay, in various ways, in a direct path of continuity with traditional methods of peasant resistance. As this resistance crystallized into a more widespread movement, it began to use new mechanisms of protest—chiefly in response to forest management—in addition to those traditionally used. These changes in the method of protest were matched by concomitant changes in peasant consciousness, both reflecting the rapidly fading legitimacy of the colonial state. Transformations in peasant ideology and forms of resistance, and their interrelationship with changing structures of power and authority, are vividly illustrated by the history of social protest in colonial Kumaun.

EARLY RESISTANCE TO FORCED LABOUR

The incidence of utar was comparatively slight in the first century of British rule. Nevertheless, its impressment was resisted in various ways. The village *pradhan* (himself exempt) occasionally concealed some of the hissedars in his village;[5] alternatively, travellers who indented for coolies found the headman being 'openly defied' by his villagers, who refused to supply labour or provisions.[6] When census returns from Garhwal reported a large excess of males over females in the ten to

[4] M. S. Randhawa, *The Kumaun Himalayas* (Delhi, 1970), p. 12.

[5] J. H. Batten, 'Final Report on the Settlement of Kumaun', in Batten (ed.), *Official Reports on the Province of Kumaun* (1851; rpt. Calcutta, 1878), p. 270.

[6] 'Mountaineer', *A Summer Ramble in the Himalaya* (London, 1860), p. 167.

fourteen age group, this discrepancy was traced to the age (sixteen years) at which men were called upon to carry loads or furnish bardaish. Thus, all those whose age could possibly be understated were reported to be under sixteen.[7] Officials commented too that the hillman's aversion to being made to work under compulsion had led to his earning an undeserved reputation for indolence. While he worked hard enough in his fields, coolie labour—especially during the agricultural season—was performed in a manner that made his resentment apparent.[8] Travellers and soldiers often found themselves stranded when villagers failed to oblige in carrying their luggage. White mountaineers on expedition found that villagers on begar duty, when pushed too hard, either refused requests to prolong the duration of the expedition or expressed their resentment by taking an 'unconscionable time' over meals.[9] It is reported that Henry Ramsay, the long-time commissioner of Kumaun, had once to levy a fine of Rs 500 on a village near Someshwar in Almora district which struck against utar. Another strike in 1903 led to the imprisonment of fourteen villagers of Khatyadi.[10] Concurrently, opposition to the begar system was expressed in newspapers, edited by nationalists of the Gokhale school, from Almora, Nainital and Dehradun. The Kumaun Parishad, based in Almora, took up both the begar and forest issues, asking the forest department to hire its own coolies and build more roads.[11]

With the advent of the forest department the burden of these services on the Kumaun villager dramatically increased. The reservation of the forests and their future supervision

[7] Census of India, 1891, vol. 16, pt 1, NWP & O, General Report, pp. 29–30.

[8] V. A. Stowell, *A Manual of the Land Tenures of the Kumaun Division* (1907; rpt. Allahabad, 1937), pp. 150–6; H. G. Walton, *British Garhwal: A Gazetteer* (Allahabad, 1911), pp. 68–9.

[9] Thomas Skinner, *Excursions in India, Including a Walk over the Himalaya Mountain to the Sources of the Jumna and Ganges* (London, 1832), volume 1, p. 307; A. M. Kellas, 'The Mountains of Northern Sikkim and Garhwal', *The Geographical Journal*, vol. 40, no. 3, September 1912, p. 257.

[10] See Shekhar Pathak, 'Uttarakhand mein Coolie Begar Pratha: 1815–1949', unpublished Ph.D. thesis, Kumaun University, 1980; *idem*, 'Kumaun mein Begar Annulan Andolan', paper presented at Jawaharlal Nehru University, October 1982, pp. 4–14. Hereafter Pathak (1) and (2).

[11] See letter from comm., KD, to chief secretary, UP, 18 September 1916, in FD file 164/1916, UPSA.

involved extensive touring by forest officials who took utar and bardaish as a matter of course. Coming close on the heels of the demarcation of the forest, the additional burdens which the new department had created evoked a predictable response. Forest officers touring in the interior of Garhwal were unable to obtain grain as villagers, even where they had surplus stock, refused to supply to a department they regarded 'as disagreeable interlopers to be thwarted if possible'.[12] Utar, in the words of the Kumaun Forest Grievances Committee, was 'one of the greatest grievances which the residents of Kumaun had against the forest settlement'.[13] When coupled with the abbreviation of customary access to the forest, it represented an intervention unprecedented in its scope and swiftness. Villagers looked back, not altogether without justification, to a 'golden age' when they had full freedom to roam over their forest habitat, and state interference was at its minimum. These emotions were poignantly expressed by a government clerk who applied for exemption from begar and bardaish:

> In days gone by every necessities of life were in abundance to villagers than to others [and] there were no such government laws and regulations prohibiting the free use of unsurveyed land and forest by them as they have now. The time itself has now become very hard and it has been made still harder by the imposition of different laws, regulations, and taxes on them and by increasing the land revenue. Now the village life has been shadowed by all the miseries and inconveniences of the present day laws and regulations. They are not allowed to fell down a tree to get fuels from it for their daily use and they cannot cut leaves of trees beyond certain portion of them for fodder to their animals. But the touring officials still view the present situation with an eye of the past and press them to supply good grass for themselves and their [retinue] without even thinking of making any payment for these things to them who after spending their time, money and labour, can hardly procure them for their own use. In short all the privileges of village life, as they were twenty years ago, are nowhere to be found

[12] DO no. 10x, 6 February 1917, from DFO, North Garhwal, to conservator of forests (CF), Kumaun circle, GAD file 398/1913, UPSA.

[13] *Report of the Kumaun Forest Grievances Committee* (thereafter KFGC), in Progs A, June 1922, nos. 19–24, file no. 522/1922, dept of rev. & agrl. (forests), p. 2, NAI.

now, still the officials hanker after the system of yore when there were everything in abundance and within the reach of villagers.[14]

As one can discern from this petition, the new laws and regulations were already beginning to threaten the considerable autonomy enjoyed by the Khasa community. Here, as in other colonial societies, unusual extractions and other forms of state encroachment upon the privileges of individuals or communities were regarded as transgressing the traditional relationship between ruler and ruled. By clashing with his notions of economic and social justice, increased state intervention breached the 'moral economy' of the peasant.[15] Anticipating that the hillman would react by 'throwing his forest loads down the khud and some day an unfortunate Forest Officer may go after them', Wyndham, commissioner of Kumaun, believed that the only way to prolong the life of the utar system would be for forest officials to use pack ponies. Government could hardly defend the use of utar by a money-making department which, if it continued to avail of begar, would hasten the end of the system.[16] Echoing the commissioner's sentiments, the Garhwal lawyer and legislative council member Taradutt Gairola pleaded for a 'vigorous policy of reform' failing which 'trouble [would] arise' at the revision of the revenue settlement.[17]

These warnings were to prove prophetic, but in the meantime the state hoped to rely on a series of ameliorative measures. The lieutenant-governor had in 1916 rejected the possibility of the utar system itself being scrapped; while it had caused 'hardship' in certain areas, the government, he emphasized,

[14] Petition to Sir James Meston, L-G, UP, by Pandit Madan Narayan Bist (village Ulaingad, patti Wallawigad, Almora), clerk on duty at the office of the director-general of archaeology at Ootacumund, 17 May 1913, GAD file 398/1913. Grammar and punctuation as in original.

[15] J. C. Scott, *The Moral Economy of the Peasant* (New Haven, 1976).

[16] 'Note on transport of Forest officials by Utar and pack ponies' by comm., KD, 17 August 1919, in file no. 21 of 1918–19, dept xv, Regional Archives, Nainital (RAN).

[17] 'Report of the Kumaun Sub Committee of the Board of Communications of coolie utar and bardaish in Kumaun', sd P. Wyndham, chairman, 9 October 1919; note on above report by T. D. Gairola, 17 October 1919, GAD file 739/1920, UPSA.

was concerned merely 'with checking any abuse of the system'.[18] In a move initiated by Gairola, coolie agencies were started in parts of Garhwal: by paying money into a common fund from which transport and supplies were arranged, villagers were not required to perform these tasks themselves.[19] In other parts registers were introduced to ensure that the utar burden did not fall disproportionately on any individual or village. Officers were advised to camp only at fixed places and procure grain from merchants subsidized by the government. Rules were framed prescribing what kinds of supplies could be indented for, and loads restricted to twelve pounds per coolie.[20] In a bid to 'raise the status of the soldier', retired and serving members of the Garhwal regiments were granted personal exemption from utar in 1900, although they were required to provide a substitute.[21] This was extended during World War I into an unconditional exemption for all combatant members of the 39th Garhwalis, and for the direct heirs of soldiers killed in battle.[22] The introduction of these 'palliatives which afford a considerable measure of relief', it was hoped, would ensure the continuance of the system itself.[23]

EARLY RESISTANCE TO FOREST MANAGEMENT

It is important to reiterate the dislocations in agrarian practices consequent on the imposition of forest management. The working of a forest for commercial purposes necessitates its division into blocks or coupés, which are completely closed after the trees are felled to allow regeneration to take place. Closure to men and cattle is regarded as integral to successful reproduc-

[18] Speech by Sir James Meston at durbar held in Nainital on 30 September 1916, GAD file 108/1918, UPSA.

[19] See, for example, 'Annual Report of the Coolie Agencies in Garhwal District for 1911–12', in GAD file 398/1913.

[20] No. 6544/xv/50, 10 October 1916, from comm., KD, to chief secretary, UP; 'Rules for touring officials in the hill pattis of the Kumaun Division', sd comm., 18 October 1916, both in ibid.

[21] No. 6056/xvi–19, 19 June 1900, from comm., KD, to chief secretary, NWP & O; no. 2503/1–303B, 4 August 1900, from chief secretary, NWP & O, to deputy adjutant general, Bengal, both in file no. 19 of 1899–1900, dept xvi, RAN.

[22] No. 1156/iii/398, 5 June 1916, from chief secretary, UP, to officers commanding 1st and 2nd 39th Garhwal Rifles, GAD file 398/1913.

[23] See note by under secretary to chief secretary, UP, 17 August 1913, in ibid.

tion, and grazing and lopping, if allowed, are regulated in the interests of the reproduction of favoured species of trees. Further, protection from fire is necessary to ensure the regeneration and growth to maturity of young saplings. Thus, the practice of firing the forests had to be regulated or stopped in the interests of sustained production of chir pine. While the exercise of rights, where allowed, was specified in elaborate detail, rightholders had the onerous responsibility, under section 78 of the act, of furnishing knowledge of forest offences to the nearest authority and of extinguishing fires, however caused, in the state forests. In general, as endorsed by the stringent provisions of the forest act, considerations of control were paramount (see chapter 3 for details).

We find evidence of protest at the contravention of traditionally held and exercised rights well before the introduction of forest management. Charcoal required for smelting iron in the mines of Kumaun was brought from neighbouring forests. Where these forests lay within village boundaries, villagers prevented wood being cut without the payment of malikhana.[24] And in the years following the constitution of the DPF in 1893, the deputy commissioner (DC) of Garhwal reported that 'forest administration consists for most part in a running fight with the villagers.'[25]

Even where discontent did not manifest itself in overt protest, the loss of control over forests was acutely felt. The forest settlement officer of British Garhwal commented thus at the time of the constitution of the reserved forests:

The notion obstinately persists in the minds of all, from highest to the lowest, that Government is taking away their forests from them and is robbing them of their own property. The notion seems to have grown up from the complete lack of restriction or control over the use by the people of waste land and forest during the first 80 years after the British occupation. The oldest inhabitant therefore and he

[24] J. O. B. Beckett, 'Iron and Copper Mines in the Kumaun Division', report of 31 January 1850, in *Selections*, vol. II, pp. 31–8. 'There is *not a single* malgoozar of any of the villages in the neighbourhood of the iron mines who has not at one time or other endeavoured to levy a tax on *all* the charcoal burners . . .' Ibid., 36, emphasis added.

[25] 'Note on forest administration for my successor', by McNair, DC, Garhwal, Feb. 1907, in FD file 11/1908, UPSA.

naturally is regarded as the greatest authority, is the most assured of the antiquity of the people's right to uncontrolled use of the forest; and to a rural community there appears no difference between uncontrolled use and proprietary right. Subsequent regulations—and these regulations are all very recent—only appear to them as a gradual encroachment on their rights, culminating now in a final act of confiscation . . . [My] best efforts however have, I fear, failed to get the people generally to grasp the change in conditions or to believe in the historical fact of government ownership.[26]

This brings out quite clearly that the root of the conflict between the state and hill villagers over forest rights lay in differing conceptions of property and ownership. There did not exist a developed notion of private property among these peasant communities, a notion particularly inapplicable to communally owned and managed woods and pasture land. In contrast, the state's assertion of monopoly over forests was undertaken at the expense of what British officials insisted were *individually* claimed rights of user. With the 'waste and forest lands never having attracted the attention of former governments',[27] there existed strong historical justification for the popular belief that all forests within village boundaries were 'the property of *the villagers*'.[28]

Discontent with the new forest regulations manifested itself in various other ways. The option of flight was considered by a group of villagers belonging to Tindarpur patti in Garhwal, who approached an English planter for land 'as the new forest regulations and restrictions were pressing on them so severely that they wished to migrate into another district and climate rather than put up with them any longer.'[29] Another time-honoured form of protest—non-compliance with imposed regulations—was evident when villagers gave misleading information at the time of fixation of rights.[30] As villagers were 'not

[26] J. C. Nelson, *Forest Settlement Report of the Garhwal District* (Lucknow, 1916), pp. 10–11.

[27] E. K. Pauw, *Report on the Tenth Settlement of the Garhwal District* (Allahabad, 1894), p. 52.

[28] T. D. Gairola, *Selected Revenue Decisions of Kumaun* (Allahabad, 1936), p. 211.

[29] District and sessions judge, Moradabad, to pvt. secretary to L-G, UP, 2 March 1916, in FD file 163/1916 (Forest Settlement Grievances in the KD), UPSA.

[30] According to the settlement officer, 'much was omitted and much exag-

in a frame of mind to give much voluntary assistance', one divisional forest officer (DFO) accurately predicted 'active resentment' at the fire protection of large areas and their closure to grazing and other rights.[31]

The year 1916 witnessed a number of 'malicious' fires in the newly constituted reserved forests. In May the forests in the Gaula range of Nainital division were set ablaze. The damage reported was exclusively in chir forests; 28,000 trees which were burnt had to be prematurely felled. For the circle as a whole it was estimated that at least 64 per cent of the 441 fires which burnt 388 square miles (as against 188 fires that had burnt 35 square miles in the preceding year) were 'intentional'.[32]

The 'deliberate and organized incendiarism' of the summer of 1916 brought home to the state the unpopularity of the forest settlement and the virtual impossibility of tracing those who were responsible for the fires. Numerous fires broke out simultaneously over large areas, and often the occurrence of one fire was the signal for general firing in the whole neighbourhood: 44 fires occurred in North Garhwal division, almost all in order to obtain a fresh crop of grass. In Nainital and in the old reserves of Airadeo and Binsar of Almora district—areas which had been fire-protected for many years—an established crop of seedlings was wiped out. The area chosen for attack had been under both felling and resin-tapping operations.[33] In Airadeo the fire continued for three days and two nights, with 'new fires being started time after time directly a counterfiring line was successfully completed'.[34] As a result of such 'in-

gerated, much extenuated and much set down in malice', while quarrels over rights 'were unfortunately always very bitter.' Nelson, 'Forest Settlement Report', pp. 2–4, 13, 25.

[31] A. E. Osmaston, *WP for the North Garhwal Forest Division, 1921–22 to 1930–31* (Allahabad, 1921), p. 67.

[32] *Report on the Administration of the United Provinces of Agra and Oudh, 1915–16* (Allahabad: Government Press, 1916), p. viii.

[33] *Annual Progress Report of the Forest Administration of the United Provinces* (hereafter APFD), 1915–16, p. 7.

[34] H. G. Champion, 'Observations on Some Effects of Fires in the *Chir* (*Pinus longifolia*) Forests of the West Almora Division', *Indian Forester*, vol. 45 (1919), pp. 353–63.

cendiarism' several thousand acres of forest were closed to all rights for a period of ten years.[35]

The protests against the forest settlement were viewed with apprehension in Lucknow, where the lieutenant-governor, anticipating the conclusion of World War I, observed that 'it would be a pity for the 39th Garhwalis to come home and find their villages seething with discontent.' Reporting on the situation the DC of Garhwal concluded, somewhat self-evidently, that government could not but affect village life in every patti by taking over the forests. The people's 'dislike of the forest department and the horde of new underlings let loose on the district' was shared by the soldiers, one of whom stated that if the war had ended before they left Europe they could have petitioned the king to rescind the settlement. The soldiers' discontent was evidently disturbing, for, as the district officer put it, 'if we can get them on our side it will be a great thing . . . They are already a power in the land and will be still more a power after the war.'[36] The forest department continued to be complacent about the possibilities of such discontent blowing over when the villagers had 'greater familiarity with the true aim of the department'.[37] Alternatively, they pointed to the strategic and financial results obtained in a few years of commercial working.[38] Percy Wyndham, as the commissioner of Kumaun the senior official entrusted with law and order, was considerably less sanguine. He preferred that the hills continue to provide 'excellent men for sepoys, police and all such jobs'—a situation jeopardized by the forest department which had demarcated the 39th Garhwali villages as if 'the world were made for growing trees and men were vermin to be shut in'. In a situation where 'the Revenue Department holds the whole country by bluff', without the help of regular police, Wyndham was clearly not prepared to enforce new rules on a 'dissatisfied

[35] H. G. Champion, *WP for the Central Almora For. Div.* (Lucknow, 1922), pp. 13–14.

[36] J. C. Meston (lieutenant-governor) to comm., KD, 5 March 1916; DC, Garhwal to L-G, 27 March 1916; 'Note on the Forest Settlement and the Garhwali Officers of the Regiment', by DC, Garhwal, 20 March 1916, all in FD file 163/1916.

[37] GO no. 197/xiv/163, 14 February 1918, appended to APFD, 1916–17.

[38] See GO no. 114/xivA/172 of 1918, 4 February 1919, appended to APFD, 1917–18.

people', preferring to do away with forest rules and staff altogether.[39]

Contravention of the new regulations concerning lopping, grazing and the duties of rightholders was, as Table 5.1 indicates, perhaps the most tangible evidence of the continuing friction. Figures from other forest circles are given by way of comparison. While the number of yearly convictions in the Kumaun circle far exceeded those obtained elsewhere, a comparison with 'criminal justice' in Kumaun itself is no less revealing. Over a ten-year period (1898–1908) an average of only

TABLE 5.1

Breaches of Forest Law in UP, 1911–22

Circle	Western circle		Eastern circle		Kumaun circle*	
Year	A**	B**	A	B	A	B
1911–12	786	1798	1167	2306	958	2159
1912–13	881	2182	1230	2424	1203	3374
1913–14	1006	2091	1365	2905	1309	3864
1914–15	1248	2681	1646	3293	1671	5857
1915–16	1401	2662	1514	3029	1610	5796
1916–17	1368	2517	1636	2944	2023	10264
1917–18	1242	2364	1530	2777	2197	11046
1918–19	1153	2058	1723	3167	2167	11024
1919–20	1162	2120	1378	2773	2136	13457
1920–21	926	1618	901	2154	1723	10328
1921–22	1248	2437	1622	839	2070	3799***

* The total area of reserved forest in UP equalled 4.32 million acres, of which 1.91 million acres lay in the Kumaun circle.

** A = cases; B = convictions (persons).

*** Cases dropped due to the recommendation of the Kumaun Grievances Committee.

SOURCE: APFD, relevant years.

[39] Wyndham to Meston, 26 June 1916; *idem*, 3 July 1916; 'Subjects for discussion at the conference of selected officers to be held at Government House, Nainital at 10.30 a.m. on the 28th August 1916', sd P. Wyndham, 14 August 1916, all in FD file 163/1916.

416 persons was convicted annually in Almora district, on account of cognizable crime of all kinds, ranging from non-payment of excise to murder.[40] Indeed, with the absence of an adequate patrolling staff, many breaches of the forest law went undetected.[41] Underlying the stiff resistance to the regulations of the forest department was a tradition of hundreds of years of unrestricted use.[42]

The continuing opposition to forest administration bore a strong similarity to traditional methods of social protest in Kumaun and Garhwal. The forms of protest—flight, strikes, occasional attacks on officials, marches—as well as its moral idiom, which reflected the state's failure to meet traditional obligations, were integral to the indigenous form of collective resistance known as the dhandak (see chapter 4). As the distinctive form of social protest specific to this area, the dhandak continued to be used, albeit with variations, in both the colonial territory of British Kumaun and the princely state of Tehri Garhwal.

THE UTAR AND FOREST MOVEMENTS OF 1921

Meanwhile, village opposition to the begar system was matched organizationally by the establishment of the Kumaun Parishad in 1916. This association of local journalists, lawyers and intellectuals, chaired in its initial years by Rai Bahadurs professing loyalty to the King Emperor, underwent a rapid transformation with the setting up of the forest department and the increased requirement of customary services. The impact of village-level protest and, indirectly, of upsurges elsewhere in India, contributed to a growing radicalization of the Parishad, best exemplified in the person of Badridutt Pande of Almora. As Shekhar Pathak has compellingly shown, Pande, far more than other Kumaun nationalists (such as Govind Ballabh Pant), was acutely aware of the growing discontent amongst the peas-

[40] Figures calculated from H. G. Walton, *Almora: A Gazetteer* (Allahabad, 1911), appendix.

[41] See, for example, GO no. 123-XIV-209, 2 November 1922, appended to APFD, 1921–2.

[42] See APFD, 1919–20, p. 8; Osmaston, 'North Garhwal WP', p. 89.

antry.[43] Convinced of the futility of memoranda presented to government by a few individuals based in Almora, Pande and his associates sought to establish branches of the Parishad in the villages of Kumaun. Simultaneously, his weekly, *Shakti*, published from Almora, became an important forum in which the begar system and forest rules were made the butt of strident criticism.[44]

In 1920 *Shakti* reported a strike against utar by villages in patti Kairaro, with villagers refusing to pay the fine levied on them. At the annual session of the Kumaun Parishad, held at Kashipur in December 1920, a major conflict arose between those who still hoped to negotiate with the state and village representatives who pressed for direct action. After the reformists had walked out the latter urged Badridutt Pande and other Parishad leaders to come to the Uttaraini fair.[45] Held in mid January at Bageshwar, the temple town at the confluence of the Saryu and Gomati rivers, this fair annually attracted fifteen to twenty thousand pilgrims from all over the hills.

Here, matters came to a head. In early January the conservator of forests was refused coolies at Dwarahat and Ganai, and, anticipating a strike, the DC of Almora, W. C. Dible, urgently asked government for a declaration of its future policy —a request summarily dismissed.[46] At Bageshwar a crowd of over ten thousand heard Badridutt pass on a message from Mahatma Gandhi that 'he would come and save them from oppression as he did in Champaran.' When almost everyone responded to a call to raise their hands to show that they would refuse utar, Pande continued: 'After abolishing coolie utar they would agitate for the forests. He would ask them not to extract

[43] However, most Parishad leaders were small landholders, like the majority of their kinsmen, and perhaps less alienated from the villages than urban nationalists in many other parts of India. See G. B. Pant's evidence to the *Royal Commission on Agriculture in India* (London, 1927), vol. III, p. 360.

[44] Shekhar Pathak, *Badridutt Pande aur Unka Yug* (Lucknow, 1982), pp. 12–24. Hereafter Pathak (3).

[45] Pathak (2), pp. 22–4. Prominent among the village activists was Mohan Singh Mehta of Katyur.

[46] HC no. C.3, Bageshwar, 17 January 1921, from DC, Almora, to comm., KD; extract from confidential fortnightly report of comm., KD, 10 January 1921, both in police department (PD) file 1151/1921, UPSA.

resin, or saw sleepers, or take forest contracts. They should give up service as forest guards which involves insulting their sisters and snatching their sickles.' Slogans in praise of Mahatma Gandhi and 'Swatantra Bharat' and cries that the government was 'anniyayi' (unjust) filled the air.[47] In a dramatic gesture, village headmen flung their coolie registers into the Saryu.[48]

In the weeks following the fair, several officials were stranded when the villages neighbouring Bageshwar declined to supply coolies. Elsewhere, only *khushkharid* (on payment) coolies were available, at extraordinarily high rates. With schoolmasters and other government functionaries extending their support to the movement, Dible hastily summoned the regular police.[49] Pathak has uncovered evidence of at least 146 anti-begar meetings in different villages of Garhwal and Kumaun, held between 1 January and 30 April 1921.[50] When the DFO of Almora complained of the continuing difficulties faced by touring officials, he was tersely told that the district administration was not in a position to 'give you or your department one utar coolie'.[51] Requests for utar were not made in tracts when they were likely to be refused.[52] In a matter of weeks the state's determination not to dispense with the system itself had broken down, and its abolition followed. In the following year over 1.6 lakh rupees were spent by the exchequer on the transport and stores of touring officials in the hills.[53]

The resistance to utar mirrored similar opposition in parts of Java, Africa and New Guinea, where attempts by colonial regimes to extract corvée labour were often met with sullen resentment. As in Kumaun, peasants sometimes expressed the

[47] Summary of Badridutt Pande's speech at Bageshwar, by S. Ijaz Ali, deputy collector, Almora, in ibid.

[48] Pathak (2), p. 28.

[49] DC, Almora, to comm., KD, no. C.3, 17 January 1921; *idem*, no. C.4, 20 January 1921; no. 43, C1.21, 29 January 1921, from comm., KD, to chief secretary, UP, all in PD file 1151/1921.

[50] Pathak (1), appendix III.

[51] No. 42, C.1.21, 28 January 1921, from comm., KD, to DFO, Almora, in PD file 1151/1921.

[52] Comm., KD, to secretary to government, UP, 4 March 1921, in GAD file 739/1920.

[53] Resolution passed by UP legislative council on 5 March 1921; table on transport of officers in camp, 1921–2, enclosed with DO no. 215, 17 June 1922, from comm., KD, to deputy secretary, GAD, UP, both in ibid.

wish that whites should carry their own loads, and in extreme cases, by striking, made this inescapable. The sentiments of Sindano, a Watchtower-movement preacher in Zambia during World War I, could serve equally well as an expression of the anti-utar campaign conducted around the same time in Kumaun and Garhwal: 'There they are, they who overburden us with loads, and beat us like slaves, but a day will come when they will be the slaves.'[54] However, in the Himalayan case resistance to corvée labour was greatly intensified by its association with the major indignity peasants had to suffer at the hands of colonial rulers: the loss of control over forests. And, as the press communiqué issued by the UP government emphasized, the growth of the forest department, with all that this implied for the social and economic life of the hill peasant, was at the root of the anti-begar movement.[55]

Peasant opposition to utar was conducted at a different level and for quite different reasons from that symbolized by the periodic memoranda—appealing to the instincts of a benign and civilized government—that liberal nationalists continued to submit to the state.[56] An English planter based in Kausani reported that while Hargovind Pant, an Almora lawyer, was asking that coolies be not supplied for utar, village leaders were prepared to go even further. Thus, local activists insisted that no coolies should be supplied at all, i.e. they were against khushkharid coolies as well.[57] After Bageshwar, the DC of Almora was tersely informed by a group of padhans that they had refused to supply coolies in order to compel attention to their grievances, chief among which was the taking away of their forests. Dible reported that proposals for closure to grazing had much to do with this intense feeling. A fund had

[54] Karen Fields, *Revival and Rebellion in Colonial Central Africa* (Princeton, 1985), p. 135; see also S. Moertono, *State and Statecraft in Old Java* (Ithaca, 1968), p. 75; Peter Worsley, *The Trumpet Shall Sound* (London, 1957), pp. 104–6.

[55] 'In recent years, mainly owing to the rapid expansion of the Forest Department, the demands for utar have greatly increased and the obligations of furnishing utar has caused growing resentment.' Press communiqué, 1 February 1921, sd H. S. Crosthwaite, secretary to government, UP, in GAD file 739/1920.

[56] See memorandum on coolie utar submitted by Kumaun Association (Ranikhet branch) to L-G, UP, 16 October 1920, in ibid.

[57] Letter from R. G. Bellaire, colonization officer of Soldier Settlement Estates, Kausani, to DC, Almora, 1 February 1921, in PD file 1151/1921.

been created by the villagers—anticipating punitive action—for defending anyone against whom the state had initiated proceedings, and for paying fines where they were inflicted.[58] While this unity and sense of purpose necessarily made their actions political, the politics of the peasantry was clearly not derivative of the politics of urban nationalism. Apart from a hazy perception of Gandhi as a saint whose qualities of heroic sacrifice were invoked against the inimical powers of government,[59] the utar movement had little in the nature of an identification with the Congress as such.

The Forest Movement of 1921

Following Uttaraini, Pande and his colleagues toured the different pattis of Almora, establishing local *sabhas* of the Parishad. Inspired by the success of the anti-utar campaign, Pande urged in his speeches the need for direct action in order to recover lost rights over forests. For, the 'government that sells the forest produce is not liable to be called a real government' —indeed, it was precisely these mercenary motives which had made God send Gandhi 'as an incarnation in the form of Bania to conquer Bania government'.[60] As the reference to Gandhi's caste indicates, the term 'bania' evoked images of power as well as deception; by selling forest produce the state was hastening the erosion of the legitimacy it had earlier enjoyed in the eyes of the peasantry. At Bageshwar Badridutt had depicted this transition in tellingly effective symbols. When forest resources and grass were plentiful and easily available, villagers had an abundance of food and drink. But now, he said, 'in place of tins of ghee the forest department gives them tins of resin.'[61]

[58] DC, Almora, to comm., KD, 17 January 1921; *idem*, no. C.15, 24 January 1921, both in ibid.; Wyndham was clear that 'the root of the whole evil and discontent is our d——d forest policy': no. 2, C.II.21, 1 February 1921, from comm., KD, to chief secretary, UP, in ibid.

[59] Cf. Govind Chatak, *Garhwali Lok Geet* (Dehradun, 1956), pp. 261–2.

[60] 'Report of Pandit Badridutt Editor's Speeches to Villagers in Almora District', in PD file 1151/1921.

[61] See criminal case no. 7 of 1921, *King Emperor vs. Motiram, Budhanand and Badridutt* of Totashiling, at police station Palla Boraraw, in the court of W. C. Dible, district magistrate, Almora, 7 July 1921, in FD file 157/1921 ('Forest fires in Kumaun'), UPSA. The implication, if it needs to be spelled out, was that while the forests had earlier supplied products like ghee and thus contributed to the

Sensing the peasantry's mood after the utar strike, Dible had with uncanny prescience predicted the shape of the impending agitation: '[The] next move will be against the Forest Department. Agitators will make a dead set for resin coolies and contractors' coolies engaged in sleeper work, and try to drive them from this work. The people will be incited to commit Forest offences and we shall have serious trouble with fires.' In the coming months breaches of the forest law increased daily. These included not merely the firing of forests for grass but also 'wholesale cutting of trees'.[62] In British Garhwal, too, the popular feeling against the forest policy continued to be 'very bitter'.[63]

The summer of 1921 was one of the driest on record. The failure of the winter rains had contributed to a poor *rabi* crop and money was sanctioned as subsistence *taccavi* in the hill districts.[64] In Totashilling, where the campaign was to be at its most intense, the local branch of the Kumaun Parishad passed a resolution that the people were themselves to decide whether or not to set fire to forest land falling within 'san assi' boundaries.[65] From the last week of April a systematic campaign, especially in Almora district, had been launched for firing the forest. When called upon (under section 78 of the forest act) to assist in extinguishing these blazes, villagers instead directed their energies towards helping the fire to spread. As a consequence the attempted fire protection by the forest department of commercially worked areas was a major failure. Of 4 lakh acres of forest in which fire protection was attempted, 2.46 lakh acres were burnt over.[66] The machinery

---

local economy, now they were used to produce resin which was of no use to villagers. The use of such a metaphor, it may be added, reiterates the strong emphasis placed on village autonomy.

[62] DC, Almora, to comm., KD, no. C.15, 24 January 1921; *idem*, no. C.63, 2 March 1921, both in PD file 1151/1921.

[63] Extract from fortnightly DO from comm., KD, for second half of March 1921, FD file 157/1921.

[64] See file no. 56 of 1921, A. Progs, nos. 1–2, May 1921, dept of revenue and agriculture (famine), NAI.

[65] See resolution printed in the *Shakti* of 12 April 1921 (extract found in FD file 157/1921). All archival sources in the rest of this chapter, unless mentioned otherwise, are from this source.

[66] Fortnightly DO no. CY.21, 23 May 1921, from comm., KD, to chief

for control of forest offences 'more or less broke down', and an estimated total of 819 offences occurred, of which 395 were definitely known to be 'incendiary'.[67]

Several features of a form of social protest summarily labelled 'incendiarism' by the state merit comment. On the one hand incendiarism represented an assertion of traditionally exercised rights—the annual firing of the forest floor—circumscribed by the state in the interests of commercial forestry. On the other the areas burnt over were almost exclusively chir pine forests being worked for both timber and resin, this wholesale burning of the chir reserves representing, as Wyndham acknowledged, a 'direct challenge to government to relax their control over forests'.[68] The intensification of the campaign in Almora and Nainital was confined to those areas well served by a network of roads that had been under commercial working for some time. When fires swept through nearly all the areas being logged, young regeneration was wiped out. Covering nearly 320 square miles of forest, these fires destroyed 11.5 lakh resin channels and 65,000 maunds of resin.[69] At the same time, there is no evidence that the vast extent of broad-leaved forests, also under the control of the state, was at all affected. As in other societies in different historical epochs, this destruction by arson was not simply a nihilistic release, but carefully selective in the targets attacked. As Eric Hobsbawm has argued, such destruction is never indiscriminate, for 'what is useful for poor men'—in this instance broad-leaved species far more than chir—is spared.[70]

A striking analogy with the burning of resin depots comes from nineteenth-century France, when peasants' rights in the forest were curtailed in favour of producing wood for iron forges. Believing that the 'wood supplying the forges was in the domain of their traditional rights of usage', villagers burnt the

---

secretary, UP; DO no. 348, 28 May 1921, from chief conservator of forests (CCF), UP, to governor, UP; no. 53-CC/XIV-1, 2 June 1921, from offg CF, Kumaun circle, to CCF, UP.

[67] APFD, 1921–2, pp. 7–8.

[68] DO no. 31.C.VI.21, 9 June 1921, from comm., KD, to home member, UP.

[69] S. B. Bhatia, *WP for the East Almora Forest Division 1924–25 to 1933–34* (Allahabad, 1926), p. 41.

[70] See his *Primitive Rebels* (3rd edn, Manchester, 1974), pp. 25–6.

forges to the ground.[71] Iron forges in nineteenth-century France, and resin depots in Kumaun a century later, both represented commercial uses of the forest that were taking priority over earlier subsistence-oriented uses. In either case this change, fostered from above, was fiercely resisted by peasants denied traditional rights of access and use. Indeed, as the analysis of court cases by the collector of Almora indicates, the act of burning the chir forests represented a direct confrontation with the colonial authorities. The decision to burn the commercially worked areas was predicated not merely on their containing the locally almost useless (in comparison with oak) chir pine. As Badridutt Pande well understood, the export of forest produce by the state clashed strongly with the subsistence orientation of the hill peasant. In the collector's classification—typical in its detail of the concern of the colonial state to understand, with a view to suppressing, any sign of protest—the fire cases were broken down into the headings shown in Table 5.2.[72]

Further details which may reveal more about the nature of protest can be gleaned from summary accounts of court cases. Gangua, aged sixteen, was one of the several youths 'put up by non-co-operators' to destroy 'valuable regeneration areas' by fire. Nor was participation restricted to men: thus, one Durga was sentenced to a month in jail when she 'deliberately set fire to Thaklori forest'. In at least four different instances, witnesses set up by the prosecution were 'won over' by non-co-operators and the cases had to be dropped. Chanar Singh and four others of the Tagnia clan of Doba Talla, Katyur, were 'affected by lectures' by 'Non-cooperators and a Jogi' and set fire to regeneration areas. This tantalizingly brief reference to the yogi, who was later prosecuted, leads one to speculate that the peasantry sought, as in the Uttaraini mela, a moral/religious sanction for their acts. No such sanction was required by Padam Singh and Dharam Singh of Katyur, awarded the

[71] John Merriman, 'The Demoiselles of the Ariege, 1829–1831', in Merriman (ed.), *1830 in France* (New York, 1975), pp. 102–3.

[72] This extremely revealing classification and the following paragraph are taken from the two 'Statements on fire cases in Almora', W. C. Dible, 23 July 1921 and 3 November 1921, respectively. Unfortunately, similar details could not be traced for Nainital and Garhwal.

TABLE 5.2

Fire Cases in Almora, 1921

Head	No. of cases	No. of persons involved
I. INTENTIONAL		
(A) To paralyse forest department (FD) by destroying valuable areas	8	21
(B) To cause loss to FD by way of revenge due to hatred	26	45
(C) To have good grass for cattle	11	17
(D) To cause loss to resin mates out of enmity	2	3
(E) To spite another out of enmity	3	5
(F) Whose agitation was direct cause of fire	NA	13
TOTAL	50	104
II. ACCIDENTAL (This includes smoking or carrying fire within the reserves, the spread of fire from cultivated fields or waste and not under government, etc).	23	45

SOURCE: Forest department (FD), file 157/1921, UPSA.

maximum sentence of seven years rigorous imprisonment, who expressed their opposition to state monopoly in no uncertain terms. In the words of the magistrate: 'The compartment fired was near the village and used by them. They resented the work of the Department in this compartment since it interfered with their use of the compartment. Therefore they set fire to it deliberately.'[73]

The firing of pine needles for grass occurred in Garhwal as well. With commercial forestry and the protection of regeneration areas from grazing and fire as yet restricted in their operations, the damage to the state-controlled forests was not as widespread as in Almora. Yet the DC had convicted 549 persons, 45 for 'direct or indirect incendiarism' and 504 for

[73] Cf. Eric Hobsbawm on the Luddites: 'In some cases, indeed, resistance to the machine was quite consciously resistance to the machine in the hands of the capitalist.' See his *Labouring Men* (London, 1964), p. 10.

refusing to extinguish fires, before the recommendations of the grievances committee led to all pending cases being dropped. Fires were reported to be most acute in the areas bordering Almora, and in the southern pattis of Lansdowne subdivision in the outer hills. With resin-tapping in its infancy, fires were most often started with a view to obtaining fresh grass.[74]

While all social groups participated, the involvement of soldiers in the forest movement of 1921—in the same way as the participation of village headmen in the utar campaign—bore witness to the failure of the attempt by the colonial state to create an indigenous collaborating élite. Like leaders of cargo cults in Melanesia, these soldiers were not always leaders in the old authority structure. However, they had a special experience of white rule, one that enabled them to exercise a moral claim on the rulers. When this claim was ignored and the forest regulations not withdrawn, expectation quickly turned to outrage; in consequence, soldiers were in the forefront of the opposition to commercial forest management. Like the demobilized soldiers who led their fellow peasants in the Mexican Revolution, these hill soldiers were 'proud veterans now and still full of fight, their revolutionary consciousness ironically enhanced by the official discharge papers they carried, [who] went back home as missionaries of the new unruliness'.[75] Thus, in Garhwal the fires were most often started by soldiers on leave, but as '99% of the population sympathized with them', their apprehension by the authorities became an impossible task.[76] After the Uttaraini mela, ex-soldiers were active among those who helped the Kumaun Parishad form sabhas in the villages of the Kosi valley. One soldier said in his speeches that 'Government was not a Raja, but a Bania and Rakshasi Raj and the King Emperor was Ravan.' Recounting his experiences in Europe, where he was wounded, the pensioner described the visit of the King Emperor to his hospital bedside. Asked to state his grievances, 'he complained against *Patwaris* and forest

[74] 'Fire cases in Garhwal district', sd P. Mason, DC, Garhwal, 9 September 1921; DC, Garhwal, to secretary, government of UP, 29 December 1921; DO no. 31.C.v.21, 9 June 1921, from comm., KD, to home member, UP.

[75] Worsley, *Trumpet*, p. 69; John Womack, *Zapata and the Mexican Revolution* (New York, 1969), p. 101.

[76] DC, Garhwal, to secretary to government, UP, 7 September 1921.

guards but all that has been given is the Rowlatt Act and Martial Law.'[77] No longer was the king perceived as being bestowed with the quasi-divine powers of intervening to restore justice and a harmonious relationship between the state and the peasant. As expressed through the symbolism of the epics, the government now embodied not merely the rapacious bania but the evil-intentioned demons of Hindu mythology. Ravan, the very personification of evil, was equated with the King Emperor, whose failure (or inability) to stem the expansive growth of the forest department and its minions had led to a rapid fall from grace.

SOCIAL PROTEST: 1921–42

The constitution of the Kumaun Forest Grievances Committee in the wake of the 1921 movement evoked mixed reactions in the hill districts. Meetings held at different villages expressed dissatisfaction at the composition of the committee. Soldiers who had voiced their resentment while fighting in Europe and figured prominently in the 1921 movement continued to be in the forefront of the opposition to forest policy. While the committee had only one non-official member, Jodh Singh, he too was regarded as being more on the side of the government than the people.[78] The chairman, Commissioner Wyndham, also came in for criticism for his attempts to drive a wedge between the two dominant communities in the hills, Rajputs and Brahmins. A famed shikari, Wyndham was held to be ignorant of 'true justice' (*asli-nyaya*). An example of his insensitivity to public opinion was provided by the 1918 report on qulibardaish, which he framed without asking the opinion of the inhabitants of Kumaun. As a consequence, the people had to take the initiative in stopping utar.[79]

As the committee did not contain any representative of the people, several villages resolved to boycott its sittings. A form was circulated, to be filled in by different villages in Garhwal and submitted to the KFGC. The form provided for the designation of different plots of forest near every village, over each of

[77] FD file 156/1921 ('Forest fires in Kumaun'), UPSA.
[78] *Garhwali* (hereafter GRH), 7 May and 21 May 1921.
[79] A. P. Bahuguna, 'Kumaun aur Janglat ki Committee', GRH, 21 May 1921.

which peasants would have exclusive rights of fuel, fodder, building timber and wood for agricultural implements, bamboos for basket-making and other crafts, and so on. It asked for villages to be given full rights over nearby forests, which would be managed by the panchayats. Further, it designated forests where afforestation could be carried out by the villagers themselves. Finally, the form asked the government to provide a forest patrol to each village to aid in protection.[80]

The committee itself toured the three hill districts in May–August 1921, examining 5040 witnesses in all. A particular source of bitterness related to the treatment of women and children who committed the bulk of the forest 'offences', but who did not appear in court as per custom. Attempts by forest officials to prevent them from lopping and cutting grass were greatly resented. Complaints were also made against the reservation of temple trees and oak groves which villagers had conserved for their own use. In some instances, forest boundary pillars were placed too close to cultivation, while 'in other cases the outcry against the forest pillars had been caused by a desire to get a freedom from the rules and restrictions which these pillars represent rather than by an existing need for more land.' The oft repeated act of the removal of these pillars symbolized the perceived threat to peasant autonomy and sovereignty that forest reservation represented.[81] In the circumstances, the committee concluded that 'any attempt to strictly enforce these [forest] rules would lead to riot and bloodshed.' It recommended the division of the existing reserved forests into two categories:

(1) Class I—containing forests of little or no commercial importance; (2) Class II—containing forests stocked with chir, sal, deodar, kail and other commercially exploitable species. In Class I reserves, management was to be almost nominal.[82] Of the existing forests, 1986 square miles were covered by Class II and 1090 square miles by Class I forests, respectively.

Table 5.3 gives details regarding breaches of forest rules during 1926–33, i.e. after the recommendations of the KFGC had taken effect. Several features merit comment. Forest

[80] 'Garhwal Janta ki Janglat Sambandi Mang', GRH, 18 June 1921.

[81] See Bhatia, 'East Almora WP', for details.

[82] KFGC, pp. 2–10.

TABLE 5.3

Breaches of Forest Law in UP, 1926–33

Year	Kumaun circle		Eastern circle		Western circle	
	Cases	Convictions	Cases	Convictions	Cases	Convictions
1926–27	1919	3661	1470	3078	1440	2646
1927–28	1992	3786	1435	3167	1568	2809
1928–29	2545	5482	1418	2740	1334	2323
1929–30	2675	6019	1457	3148	1531	2600
1930–31	2511	4500	1705	3821	1299	2226
1931–32	2534	5514	1621	3170	1524	2629
1932–33	2629	5968	1928	3085	1681	2871

SOURCE: APFD, relevant years.

offences in Kumaun circle still consistently exceeded those in the two other circles of UP. Although the area under which the old restrictions operated fell away sharply, better supervision was possible in the commercial Class II forests to which attention was now confined. A comparison with Table 5.1 is instructive, as summarized below:

Period	Cases per year	Convictions per year
1916–22	2053	9986
1926–33	2401	4990

While there is an increase to the order of 17 per cent in cases per year, there is a corresponding decrease in the latter period of 40 per cent in convictions obtained. A plausible inference one can make is that while better supervision enabled detection of individual cases of infringement, such as fuel and fodder collection, collective or group infringement was no longer so common. The latter would typically include collective grazing of village cattle, burning of the forest floor, and failure to inform the authorities when a forest fire occurred. With the large area of Class I under light supervision, these activities were no longer as liable to be deemed infringements of the law. Another contributory factor was the introduction of controlled departmental burning (cf. chapter 3). In 1928-9, for example, 81,000 acres were departmentally burnt in Kumaun circle, of which 35,000 acres were burnt with unpaid voluntary labour.[83]

An outbreak of what the state still preferred to call 'incendiarism' or 'malicious firing' did, however, take place in both 1930 and 1931. In the summer of 1930 a large number of fires occurred in regeneration areas of Almora district, notably within a few miles radius of Bageshwar, venue of the historic Uttaraini mela. Interestingly, the burning of the forest was contrary to the wishes of the Congress leaders. Of 63 fires that burnt 15,591 acres, 58 occurred in the two forest divisions of East and West Almora. As in 1921, peasants concentrated on the most vulnerable state-held areas—thus 21 per cent of the area under chir regeneration was burnt.[84] According to a later estimate the reserved forests were fired 157 times, with 37,000 acres of chir regeneration (or 50 per cent of the total) being destroyed.[85]

The campaign in 1931 was more widespread, with the abnormally hot weather favouring the spread of fires. It was observed that 'burning the hill forests in a dry year is so easy and the results obtained with the minimum of exertion so large that it is one of the first ways in which any general feeling of unrest manifests itself.' Not so localized, the campaign spread to the Kosi, Gaula and Ladhia valleys of Nainital, apart from Almora and some parts of Garhwal. Of 89 fires that burnt 38,512 acres, 34 occurred in Nainital, 49 in the two Almora divisions, and 6 in Garhwal.[86]

The year 1931 witnessed a burst of nationalist activity, coinciding with the Civil Disobedience movement. A procession bearing the national tricolour made its way from one end of the Nainital lake to the other. In Almora, on 25 May, an attempt to hoist the flag on the municipal board building was foiled by the police. The next day there was a lathi charge when a crowd tried again to mount the tricolour at the same venue.[87] In

[83] See APFD, 1928–9, pp. 5–9.

[84] APFD, 1929–30, pp. 8–9.

[85] See F. C. Ford Robertson, *Our Forests* (Allahabad, 1936).

[86] APFD, 1931–2, pp. 4–6, etc.

[87] D. S. Manral, *Swatantra Sangram mein Kumaun–Garhwal ka Yogdan* (Bareilly, 1978), pp. 70–4.

Garhwal shops were closed in several towns when Mahatma Gandhi was arrested upon the completion of the Dandi march.[88] The incarceration of the popular local leader Anusuya Prasad Bahuguna in August provoked a *hartal* or general strike in Badrinath town. A half mile long line of demonstrators hoisted the tricolour on the highest point of the Badrinath temple. Unnerved, the rawal or head priest sent telegrams to both the Tehri raja and the commissioner of Kumaun.[89]

Simultaneously, there was opposition by villagers to the new land settlement, which had enhanced revenue by as much as 30 per cent. In Salt patti of Almora district, labourers were asked not to work for forest contractors. Several hundred villagers went to the forest to enforce a collective decision to excommunicate anyone who did work. This culminated in a scuffle with the police and many arrests. In Garhwal telegraph wires were cut in Dontiyal and protests organized in Dugadda.[90]

The next major wave of protest occurred during the Quit India movement of 1942, when Almora was perhaps one of the most active districts in the state. Several strikes were organized in the towns. In Deghat police fired and killed two members of a crowd protesting the arrest of their leader. When the patwari of Salem, one of the most active pattis, fled, villagers burnt his records. A force sent to quell them was repulsed by the villagers, who confiscated their weapons. Another force comprising white soldiers was dispatched, but this force too was engaged by the villagers using sticks and stones. Two villagers were killed in the battle. In Salem's neighbouring patti of Salt, police fired on satyagrahis, prompting Gandhi to call the patti India's second Bardoli.[91]

A favourite target of the 1942 rebellion continued to be the forest department. Totashiling in Katyur, one of the most active localities in 1921, witnessed the burning of a resin depot. In Nainital district youths cut telephone wires and burnt the Mangoli forest rest house and the dak bungalow at Ramnagar.

[88] GRH, 17 May 1930.

[89] GRH, 9 August 1930.

[90] Manral, *Swatantra Sangram*, pp. 75–7; S. C. Dabral, *Uttarakhand ka Itihas*, vol. 8, pt 2 (Dugadda, n.d.,) pp. 251–3.

[91] Manral, *Swatantra Sangram*, pp. 85–93.

The office of the conservator of forests also went up in flames. In Garhwal the forest bungalow in Siyasen and the post office at Chamoli were burnt. Telegraph wires were also cut. An elaborate plan, never carried out, was framed to burn all the timber godowns from Hardwar in the west to Ramnagar in the east.[92]

The relative freedom enjoyed by the peasantry following the recommendations of the KFGC undoubtedly contributed to the diminution of social protest in the years following 1921. At the same time, Kumaun was more fully incorporated in the orbit of colonial capitalism, as males migrated outwards to be employed in the British Indian Army and in the lower echelons of the colonial administration. Yet the specific episodes mentioned above do exhibit a marked continuity with the rather more concentrated activity of 1916–21. Arson, neither haphazard nor indiscriminate, continued to be aimed at symbols of authority, such as forest offices or rest houses, or at points where the state was most vulnerable, e.g. chir areas under regeneration or, latterly, channels of communication. No less striking was the refusal of the peasantry to merge fully with the structured and highly restrictive stream of Congress nationalism. While the spread of Congress activities played a role in the 1930 and 1942 movements, the defiance of orders from 'above' during 'incendiary' campaigns and the violent episodes of 1942—which, it must be admitted, were in conformity with the countrywide character of Quit India[93]—testify to the imperfect control exercised by the Congress over peasant protest.

FROM CUSTOM TO CONFRONTATION

In their recent work, the Americans Michael Adas and James Scott have made a powerful case for the systematic study of forms of protest that minimize the element of confrontation between the peasantry and instituted authority. What Scott calls 'everyday forms of peasant resistance' and Adas 'avoidance protest' embrace a wide variety of protest forms, all of which

[92] Ibid; Dabral, *Uttarakhand*, pp. 288–90.

[93] See C. S. Mitra, 'Political Mobilization and the Nationalist Movement in Eastern Uttar Pradesh and Bihar 1937–42', unpublished D.Phil. thesis, Oxford University, 1983.

stop short of directly challenging the legitimacy of the rulers.[94] Clearly, as the extraordinarily rich material collected by Scott in rural Malaysia suggests, avoidance protest is more easily discerned through ethnographic research in contemporary societies. However, while the archival record may obscure, it can never completely eliminate evidence of everyday resistance. As elaborated in this chapter, many of the weapons of the weak described by Scott for Malaysia—including foot-dragging, false compliance, feigned ignorance, migration, breaches of the law, and social appeals to 'custom'—were effectively used by Himalayan villagers in thwarting the aims of colonial forestry. Yet my evidence also suggests that, over a period of time, peasants tended to discard these weapons in favour of more open and confrontational forms of protest: attacks on channels of communication, on state buildings, and most frequently on commercial forests and resin depots. This transformation in strategies of resistance was accompanied by a radical change in cultural perceptions of the overlord. Undoubtedly, the first century of British rule and the paternalist style of officials like Henry Ramsay may have seen a partial transference of an allegiance earlier owed to native kings. If early resistance drew on the dhandak tradition, by 1921 hill villagers were viewing the British authorities in distinctly unfavourable terms, equating the King Emperor with the very personification of evil, Ravan.

Nowhere was this transformation in rebel consciousness and forms of resistance more explicitly manifested than in the radicalization of an organization originally set up to mediate between the state and the peasantry. Established in the afterglow of the Coronation Durbar of 1911, the Kumaun Parishad initially swore undying loyalty to George Pancham (George V).[95] But the pressure from below, as it were, egged the Parishad leaders, and most noticeably among them Badridutt Pande, to adopt a more directly confrontationist position. By July 1921 their philosophy was being described as 'the anarchist doctrine

[94] Michael Adas, 'From Avoidance to Confrontation: Peasant Protest in Precolonial and Colonial South-east Asia', *Comparative Studies in Society and History* (*CSSH*), vol. 23, no. 2, 1981; J. C. Scott, *Weapons of the Weak: Everyday Forms of Peasant Resistance* (New Haven, 1986).

[95] The Coronation Durbar was a lavish spectacle held in Delhi to commemorate the accession of George V.

of direct action, which has been attempted in England by Labour Revolutionaries'.[96] Clearly, such a situation had been brought about by the 'inherent' elements of folk or popular ideology impinging upon, and transforming in the process, the 'derived' elements originating in the sphere of organized politics.[97] In this instance, at least, 'primitive' rebellion proved to be several steps ahead of 'modern nationalism', the rationale of its acts and the success which attended them being attested by the rapidity with which the state capitulated on both the begar and forest issues.

What are the sociological factors that explain the transition from custom to confrontation in the social history of protest in Kumaun? While early resistance may have utilized the idiom of the dhandak, Kumaun peasants later displayed, like their counterparts in Tokugawa Japan, 'the capacity, language and organisational ability to create a new world view when the old was inconsistent with reality'.[98] Evidence from other societies suggests that the fabric of customary rebellion normally contains within it the latitude for rebels to step outside the traditional relationship of dominance and subordination and challenge the very foundations of authority. Thus,

> to express rebellion against a lawful master the Javanese used the words *mbalik* (lit. to turn around and stand face to face), *mbeka* (to be recalcitrant), *mbalka* (to revolt), and the phrase *madeq kranan*, which can be translated as 'to set up one's own government', obviously with the purpose of establishing a new and independent territorial power or even a new government challenging an existing one.[99]

Closer to Kumaun, in the Hindu kingdom of Kathiawad in western India, peasants would resort to one of two kinds of protest against the government: (*i*) *risaaman*, indicating 'the

[96] Dible to Wyndham, DO no. C355, 24 July 1921, in FD file 157/1921, UPSA.

[97] These terms have been used by George Rudé, following Gramsci, in his *Ideology and Popular Protest* (London, 1980). Rudé, like some other historians, is rather more conscious of instances where 'derived' elements transform folk ideology.

[98] Irwin Scheiner, 'Benevolent Lords and Honorable Peasants: Rebellion and Peasant Consciousness in Tokugawa Japan', in Tetsuo Najita and Irwin Scheiner (eds), *Japanese Thought in the Tokugawa Period, 1600–1868* (Chicago, 1978).

[99] S. Moertono, *State and Statecraft in Old Java* (Ithaca, 1968), pp. 78–9, emphasis added.

temporary severing of relations between intimate friends or family members in order to emphasize one's grievances which, when applied to politics, led to peaceful protest and petition'; and (*ii*) *baharvatiya*, literally going outside the law—this implied the use of violence or other confrontational forms of protest.[100]

Its flexible 'repertoire of contention', to use Charles Tilly's phrase, throws further doubt on the interpretation of customary rebellion as a periodic release of discontent crucial to the integration and persistence of a society. What is more germane to our purposes, perhaps, is that the transition from 'avoidance' to 'confrontational' resistance in Kumaun followed a pattern quite similar to that observed in other colonial contexts. In Cochin China, for example, resistance to French colonialism in the early decades of this century 'passed from deferential petitioning in the tradition of Confucianism to an insurrection along anarchist lines'.[101] In Kumaun, as in Vietnam, Burma, Indonesia, and other parts of India, the imposition of colonial rule represented, in the Weberian sense, a transfer from traditional to legal/rational structures of authority. Traditional patterns of authority had, on the one hand, been flexible in their claims on peasant subsistence, and, on the other, bound by a cultural and personalized idiom of reciprocity. Under colonialism, however, a centralized and bureaucratic state apparatus increasingly impinged on village life; the rationalized and uniform tax structure, and the takeover of forests and other natural resources, rendered villagers far more vulnerable to economic fluctuations. As in Dutch-ruled Java, therefore, peasant risings in Kumaun 'can be regarded as protest movements against intruding Western economic and political control which were undermining the fabric of traditional society.'[102]

[100] Howard Spodek, 'On the Origins of Gandhi's Political Methodology: The Heritage of Kathiawad and Gujarat', *Journal of Asian Studies*, vol. 30, no. 2, February 1971.

[101] Scott, *Moral Economy*, p. 125.

[102] See Sartono Kartodirdjo, *The Peasant Revolt of Banten in 1888* (The Hague, 1966), pp. 3, 21–2, 28, 67, 94, 106, 321–2, etc. The framework of this fine work anticipates both the neo-Weberianism of Scott and Adas and the 'history from below' of the Subaltern Studies school; despite its unfortunate neglect by later scholars, it is a germinal contribution to the sociology of peasant resistance under colonialism.

The vantage point from which peasant rebels challenged the legitimacy of the colonial rulers in Kumaun provides an interesting twist to the following claim by Barrington Moore:

> Only when the obsolete character of a dominant group becomes blatantly obvious through *failure in competition with another society and culture* is it liable to lose its legitimate right to appropriate the surplus extracted from the underlying population. This is what happened to the Tsarist bureaucracy, the scholar gentry of China, and the armed knights of medieval Europe.[103]

In the examples advanced by Moore, the claim of the ruling class to rule was challenged from the perspective of the future, of a society in the making—state socialism in the case of Russia and China, capitalist democracy in the case of Europe. Colonialism, however, was challenged from the vantage point of the past, of the society which it had superseded. When the white rulers were deemed unfit to rule, their performance was compared not to the authority of a future millennium, nor to the ruling class in an adjoining state, but to the traditional rulers of the *same* society. Moreover, the persistence of customary forms of protest in the adjoining state of Tehri Garhwal must have acted as a reference point by which Kumaun peasants judged the responsiveness (or lack of it) of British officials to their demands.

While representing, as I have argued, a direct challenge to state authority, the actions of the Kumaun peasant do not conform to the picture of violence drawn by scholars reporting tribal and peasant revolts in peninsular India. The methods of resistance characteristically used by the hill peasant were strikes and the burning of the forest floor; physical violence was very rarely resorted to. In this connection one might refer again to the unusual political and economic structure of Kumaun, where the state dealt directly with the relatively egalitarian village communities without the help of an intermediary class enjoying a vested interest in land. The dreaded triad of 'Sarkar, Sahukar and Zamindar [which was] a political fact rooted in the very nature of British power in the subcontinent', was here conspicuous by its absence, as indeed was the 'total and integrated

[103] Barrington Moore, *Injustice: The Social Bases of Obedience and Revolt* (White Plains, NY, 1978), p. 43, emphasis added.

violence' of rebellion observed elsewhere.[104] Although 'impatient of control',[105] the hillman enjoyed an autonomy rarely found in other parts of India, as this description of the 'Garhwal village *paharee*' testifies:

> I suppose it would be difficult to find any peasantry in the world more free from the *res angustae domi* [i.e. straitened circumstances at home]: he is the owner of a well built stone house, has as much land as he wants at an easy rental, keeps his flocks and herds, and is in every sense of the word, an independent man.[106]

The absence of a culturally distinct buffer class between the body of cultivating proprietors and the state, and the relative autonomy these proprietors continued to enjoy, are germane to the particular forms assumed by the conflicts between the peasantry and the state, and the manner in which these conflicts were represented in popular consciousness. Thus, in Kumaun the absence of violent protest may be related to the structure of domination in hill society—this being one that did not quite correspond to the forms of domination in other parts of India—as well as to the distinctive tradition of peasant protest embodied in the dhandak. Moreover, while Adas is correct in suggesting that '*most forms* of the protest of retribution represent very limited responses that flaunt laws and threaten individuals . . . [but] have little lasting impact on existing systems of peasant elite exchange and social control',[107] this was certainly not the case in Kumaun in 1921. Given the strategic importance of the hill forests to colonial rule, and their vulnerability to fire, the forest movements left the state with no effective response but to abandon control over large areas of woodland. Likewise, labour strikes in an inaccessible and poorly connected region crippled the administration, forcing it to end

[104] Ranajit Guha, *Elementary Aspects of Peasant Insurgency in Colonial India* (Delhi, 1983), pp. 27, 157, etc.

[105] *Report of the Kumaun Forest Grievances Committee*, Progs A, June 1922, nos. 19–24, file no. 522/1922, dept of rev. agl. (forests), p. 2, NAI.

[106] Dr F. Pearson, 'Report on Mahamurree and Smallpox in Garhwal', in *Selections from the Records of the Government of the Northwestern Provinces*, vol. II (Allahabad, 1866), p. 300.

[107] Michael Adas, 'From Footdragging to Flight: The Evasive History of Peasant Avoidance Protest in South and South-east Asia', pp. 81–2.

the begar system. Clearly, the extent of violence will vary with different forms of domination. And in Kumaun the peculiar social structure, cultural history of resistance, and the relative efficacy of different methods of protest, all favoured the eschewing of physical violence on the part of agrarian rebels.[108]

NATIONALISM AND THE VANGUARD PARTY

The history of social protest in the Indian Himalaya also calls into question the received wisdom on the participation of the peasantry in anti-colonial movements in the Third World. The literature on Indian nationalism, in common with that on the Vietnamese and Chinese Revolutions, has focused on the role of the vanguard party—in this case, the Indian National Congress—in agrarian movements.[109] While this bias is in part a function of the historical record—namely the accessibility of source materials on organized nationalist campaigns—it is also informed by a scepticism of the power of the peasantry to act independently in defence of its interests. According to a prominent Indian historian, nationalism as represented by the Congress party 'helped to arouse the peasant and awaken him to his own needs, demands and above all the possibility of any active role in social and political development.'[110]

This perspective on the possibilities of peasant protest lies much in the tradition of social analysis that I called, in chapter 1, the S–O paradigm for the study of lower-class resistance. It posits a linear transition from unorganized to organized forms of resistance, with the former doomed to hopeless defeat, and the latter, by virtue of its association with an

[108] The violence/non-violence debate acquires a particular significance in the context of Indian nationalism, with Marxist writers often accusing Gandhi of adopting non-violence to wean the masses away from the revolutionary path. See, for the classic statement, R. Palme Dutt, *India Today* (Delhi, 1948). For a different reading of Gandhi's methods, which stresses their roots in Indian political tradition, see Dharampal, *Civil Disobedience and Indian Tradition* (Varanasi, 1971).

[109] Cf. Sumit Sarkar, *Modern India, 1885–1947* (Delhi, 1983); *idem, Popular Movements and Middle Class Leadership in Late Colonial India* (Calcutta, 1983).

[110] Bipan Chandra, *Nationalism and Colonialism in Modern India* (Delhi, 1979), p. 345. For another commentator, 'the patronage of politics from above helped agrarian discontent to get organized [and] it was in that sense a child [*sic*] of the politics of Indian nationalism.' Majid Siddiqi, *Agrarian Unrest in the United Provinces, 1918–22* (Delhi, 1978), pp. ix–x.

organized party, having a fair chance of success. A Korean scholar has this to say on the links between the peasantry and communists in his country:

If traditional peasant uprisings can be characterized as unorganized, amorphous and spontaneous, then modern peasant uprisings can be said to be more organized, systematic and contrived. The traditional uprising was a more or less natural [*sic*] phenomenon arising in the face of possible starvation; economic factors played a decisive role. The modern peasant uprising, in contrast, possesses a relatively clear goal as well as calculated strategies; political factors such as leadership and ideology play a decisive role.[111]

In this vision peasants stand closer to nature than to culture; it takes the intervention of urban intellectuals, whether nationalist or communist, to transform elemental peasant needs into a social movement worthy of the name. Curiously enough, scholars of diametrically opposed political persuasions are apt to overestimate the influence of the vanguard party. For their own very different reasons intellectuals of the Rand Corporation and party historians would tend to magnify the role (conspiratory in one version, emancipatory in the other) of the Communist Party in the Vietnamese nationalist movements. Similarly, apologists of the British imperium as well as official Indian histories have, by and large, uncritically accepted the Congress party's projection of itself as the initiator, director, and guarantor of Indian nationalism. As Richard Cobb not unfairly observes, these party-centred perspectives assume 'that a popular movement cannot be self-led and that the common people are too stupid to look after things for themselves. It is a thesis that, for obvious reasons, has always had an appeal to the right wing mind and to the intellectual, two studies in arrogance.'[112]

There are at least three ways in which historical research has begun to challenge theories of peasant nationalism centring on a 'hegemonic' party. First, a reinterpretation of historical source material is shedding more light on the everyday forms of

[111] Se Hee Yoo, 'The Communist Movements and the Peasants: The Case of Korea', in J. W. Lewis (ed.), *Peasant Rebellion and Communist Revolution in Asia* (Stanford, 1974), pp. 75–6.

[112] Cobb, *The Police and the People: French Popular Protest, 1789–1820* (Oxford, 1970), p. 78.

peasant resistance, the 'prosaic but constant struggle between the peasantry and those who seek to extract labour, food, taxes, rent and interest from them'. For, 'to understand those commonplace forms of resistance is to understand what much of the peasantry does "between revolts", to defend its interests as best as it can.'[113] Second, scholars have been recovering the numerous peasant revolts in the nineteenth and early-twentieth centuries (well before 'modern' nationalism penetrated the countryside), reconstructing the world view of the rebels and their own radical rejection of colonial rule.[114] Third, and perhaps most significant, recent work has stressed the relative autonomy of peasant participation in later movements formally led and directed by a nationalist party. While the rural masses joined the national movement for reasons of their own—which often did not coincide with the charter of demands laid down by the Congress Working Committee—on many occasions peasants on their own initiative adopted forms of struggle that broke the narrow confines of Congress-directed non-co-operation.[115] My own research strongly suggests that peasants joined nationalist movements only when such participation could redress local grievances. Finally, the linkages between the educated leaders and the rank and file were by no means as one-sided as some party histories suggest. In many parts of India, and clearly so in Kumaun, the leaders of the Congress, like the leaders of the Indochinese Communist Party in another context, were 'overwhelmed by their subordinates'.[116]

One could even argue that far from being stirred from their 'apathy' by larger political developments, peasants have historically seen these forces as an opportunity to settle old scores with their local oppressors. Within the restricted sphere of the conflict over forest rights, ample confirmation is provided by evidence from three continents of the links between political upheavals at the national level and the assertion of peasant claims at the local level: witness the massive invasions of forest

[113] Scott, *Weapons of the Weak*, p. 29.

[114] The major work for India is Ranajit Guha, *Elementary Aspects*. See also A. R. Desai (ed.), *Peasant Struggles in India* (Delhi, 1979).

[115] The pioneering regional studies are G. Pandey, *The Ascendancy of the Congress in Uttar Pradesh, 1926–34* (Delhi, 1978); D. Hardiman, *Peasant Nationalists of Gujarat: Kheda District, 1917–34* (Delhi, 1981).

[116] Morche Commission Report, quoted in Scott, *Moral Economy*, p. 149.

and grazing lands during the Russian Revolution of 1905–7, and the affirmation of peasant (as opposed to landlord or state) control over forests during the Mexican Revolution, the latter occurring almost simultaneously with the movements in Kumaun.[117] Indeed, as far back as 1688 the Glorious Revolution was a signal for English villagers to mount a 'general insurrection against the deer' protected in royal hunting preserves.[118] Perhaps the best documented of all such cases concerns the French Revolutions of 1830 and 1848, which the French peasantry welcomed as a golden opportunity to recover their lost rights in the forest.[119] This is precisely how the villagers of Kumaun seem to have viewed the nation-wide campaigns of 1919–22; in fact, peasants and tribals of other forest regions of India also rode the impetus of the Non-Co-operation movement and the promise of 'Gandhi raj' in pursuance of strikingly similar ends.[120] Larger historical forces—democracy in nineteenth-century France, mass nationalism in twentieth-century India—served to legitimize protests oriented towards forest rights, enabling peasants to claim these rights more insistently and with greater militancy.

As the comparative history of peasant resistance so abundantly illustrates, there is often a yawning gap between the concrete reasons for which peasants join larger revolts, and the more abstract goals of 'democracy' and 'nationalism' invoked

[117] Teodor Shanin, *Russia as a 'Developing' Society* (New Haven, 1986), vol. II, pp. 36, 84, 90–1, etc.,; Oscar Lewis, *Pedro Martinez: A Mexican Peasant and His Family* (New York, 1964).

[118] E. P. Thompson, *Whigs and Hunters* (Harmondsworth, 1975), p. 41.

[119] A mayor in Ariege during the 1830 Revolution wrote thus: 'The liberty which his majesty Philippe I [*sic*] has just given the French nation has been misinterpreted by our mountain peasants, who now believe themselves authorized to violate the laws, in delivering themselves, without any limit, to all the disorders that they can commit against the forest administration.' Thus, 'liberty in the Ariege did not mean the "essential political liberties", the *charte*, or an extended electoral franchise . . . it primarily meant the return of traditional rights of usage in the forest.' Merriman, *Demoiselles*, pp. 104–5. In 1848, at the first sign of the republic, peasants in the Var marched on a forest newly enclosed by a landlord, destroying his wall and uprooting newly planted fruit trees—'the idea was to regain the forest for the community . . . since "now we are a Republic".' Maurice Agulhon, *The Republic in the Village* (Cambridge, 1982), p. 172.

[120] See Ramachandra Guha and Madhav Gadgil, 'Forestry and Social Conflict in Colonial India', *Past and Present*, no.123, May 1989.

by the articulate leadership. Thus in rejecting the idea that the national assembly and the urban bourgeoise organized the rural jacquerie at the time of the French Revolution, Georges Lefebvre comments sharply: 'The peasants had their own reasons for joining the conflict, and these reasons were more than sufficient.' Likewise, when Madeiro initiated the Mexican Revolution in November 1910, rural leaders in the province of Morelos 'did not flock to his cause without weeks of hard reckoning and calculation. And when they did join him, it was for conscious, practical reasons—to recover village lands and establish security.' Half a century later, peasants gleefully recalled a conversation between Madeiro and their leader Zapata. When Madeiro says he is 'fighting for Effective Suffrage, No Reelection [for the strongman Porfirio Diaz]', Zapata replies that he, on behalf of the poor, is fighting for 'Water, Land and Justice'.[121]

These complex and often unexpected interconnections between organized nationalism and lower-class resistance are sufficiently illustrated in the trajectory of social protest in British Kumaun. For the Himalayan peasant the cohesion and collective spirit of the village community, and not the organized resources of urban nationalism, provided the mainspring of political action. Congress leaders in the towns of Almora and Nainital very likely believed themselves to be fighting for the nation-wide goal of Purna Swaraj (complete independence), yet peasants used the vehicle of nationalism to more effectively reclaim their lost rights in the forest. For forest administration had introduced a notion of property, one integral to colonial rule but previously foreign to Kumaun, which ran contrary to the experience of the Khasa village communities in which different jatis shared a 'remarkable amity', symbolized by their sharing of the common *hookah*.[122] Thus, the wide-ranging campaign of 1921, though differing from a modern social movement in its aims and methods, was far from being the spontaneous outburst of an illiterate peasantry, representing a blind reaction to the expropriation of a resource crucial to their subsistence. It expressed, albeit in a far more heightened

[121] Lefebvre, *Great Fear*, p. 99; Womack, *Zapata*, p. 220; Lewis, *Pedro Martinez*, p. 88.

[122] G. R. Kala, *Memoirs of the Raj: Kumaun* (Delhi, 1974), p. 20.

way, the motivations which underlay the sporadic and localized protests in the early years of forest administration. Expressed through the medium of popular protest were conflicting theories of social relationships that virtually amounted to two world views. One can meaningfully contrast state monopoly right with the free use of forest by members of the village community as sanctioned by custom, a pattern of use, moreover, regulated by the community as a whole. The exploitation of the pine forests on grounds of commercial profitability and strategic imperial needs was at variance, too, with the use of natural resources in an economy wholly oriented towards subsistence. The invocation of the symbols of Bania and Rakshas, with all that they stood for, was a natural consequence of this discrepancy. As the paternalist state transformed itself into an agency intruding more and more into the daily life of its subject population, so its claim to legitimacy floundered. Peasant opposition to this encroachment took the form of consciously determined actions that were incomprehensible to an observer unfamiliar with the social and cultural heritage of the Kumaun peasant. But set in their socio-historical context, these actions become intelligible and are seen to represent a frontal challenge to state authority. The seemingly docile peasantry had been thought incapable of this.

From the perspective of the sociology of domination, we can observe considerable differences between popular perceptions of an ancient dynasty and of a government alien in terms of both race and language. In Tehri Garhwal the king, sanctified as Bolanda Badrinath, enjoyed a status denied to representatives of the colonial state. The latter's workings were far more impersonal and lacked the sanctity of tradition. In Tehri it was the motif of the 'wicked official' that symbolized the impediment between raja and praja. As a consequence, peasant protest was directed exclusively at officials and the laws they implemented, not at the king as such. Rather, the monarch was required to restore justice by dismissing tyrannical officials or repealing unjust laws. Even the kisan andolan, which covered large parts of the state and led to the eventual fall of the monarchy, was not really anti-monarchical in its popular ideology. In Kumaun division, on the other hand, the social idiom of protest clearly revealed a growing separation of the state from the peasantry. Thus, the state was depicted as a Bania government, the caste appellation evoking images of power as well as deception. On another occasion it was called a Rakshas (demoniacal) government. As such, if the quasi-divine Tehri monarch exemplified the continuity—sometimes threatened but never fully breached—between the state and the people, in Kumaun division there had occurred by 1921 a near total rupture between the colonial state and its subject population.

CHAPTER 6

The March of Commercial Forestry

> **It is strictly forbidden for us to go into the [state] forests to cut lumber or firewood, but those who have money are free to exploit the biggest forests.**
>
> **—A Mexican peasant, *c.* 1960**

The rapid growth in forest industries, in consonance with the greatly expanded nature of industrialization since Independence, has necessitated an increased cut from the Himalayan forests. To facilitate increased extraction the building of roads into hitherto inaccessible forests became necessary. The relative isolation of many hill areas was ended as major highways and all-weather roads were built to transport timber and other forest produce to urban markets. Along with the communications network came the ubiquitous contractor whose job was to transport the produce to be processed by large-scale industries in the private sector.[1] In official circles the need was long felt for better communications, the lack of which was an impediment to greater exploitation of the hill forests. Though a rail line to the Alakananda valley, planned as early as 1920,[2] did not materialize, since 1947 road building in the hills has occurred at a rapid pace, especially after the creation of three new border districts in 1962. A Rs 56 million World Bank project was started in 1972 for the construction of 1330 kilometres of new roads and 16 new bridges, and the renovation of 620 kilometres of existing roads in the UP Himalaya. This project was initiated on the grounds that past road construction represented but a 'nominal fraction of the total requirements for the full

[1] Cf. Sunderlal Bahuguna, *Uttarakhand mein Ek Sau Bis Din* (Dehradun, 1974).

[2] Cf. R. N. Brahmawar, *WP for the Garhwal For. Div., 1930–31 to 1939–40* (Allahabad, 1938).

exploitation and proper development of these [hill] forests'.[3]

The building of roads into interior areas was viewed with satisfaction as a development which would enable the sale of hitherto untapped oak forest.[4] Now, the clear felling of oak and its replacement with planted conifers was being envisaged. However, road building, by opening up virgin forests for use as industrial raw material elsewhere, has failed to materially help the hill economy. The net benefits to the hill people have been 'starvation' wages as forest labour, while the fragile mountain ecosystem has deteriorated further through imperfect alignment and hasty construction of roads.[5] In addition, improved communications have made penetration by urban pleasure-seekers possible; and with the Himalaya 'being sold as a Mecca for climbers, adventurers and tourists', deforestation and allied ecological degradation to meet their needs for firewood has proceeded apace.[6]

Table 6.1 gives some details of the increased pressure on the forest department. The dramatic expansion of resin-tapping operations was a further burden, not reflected in the table. In the Alakananda and Bhageerathi valleys, this was greatly helped by road-building operations. Resin outturn after reaching a peak of 4.18 lakh quintals in 1974–5 (valued at Rs 74.8 million) averaged 1.30 quintals in 1978–9.[7]

These pressures of rising commercial and industrial demand called for a significant intensification of commercial forest operations. Important modifications introduced in forest working were the reduction in the diameter at which resin tapping was commenced, and the lowering of the age at which chir trees were cut. Incentives such as the awarding of bonus to resin mates who exceeded their targeted yield were also

[3] Uttar Pradesh Forest Department, 'Forest Development Project, Uttar Pradesh, India', mimeo, n.d. (1971 ?), pp. 117–21.

[4] Introduction by B. P. Srivastava in V. P. Singh, *WP for the West Almora For. Div., Kumaun Circle, 1966–67 to 1975–76* (Nainital, 1967).

[5] Madhav Gadgil, 'Towards an Indian Conservation Strategy', paper presented at the Workshop on a New Forest Policy, Indian Social Institute, New Delhi, 12–14 April 1982, p. 26.

[6] G. D. Berreman, *Himachal: Science, People and 'Progress'*, IWGIA document no. 36 (Copenhagen, 1979), p. 19 f.

[7] See *Uttar Pradesh Forest Statistics 1978–79* (Lucknow, n.d.), for details.

TABLE 6.1
Outturn of Selected Species in Uttarakhand
(cu. m. sawn wood)

Year	Deodar	Fir & spruce	Kail	Chir
1930–31	2,917	—	14,191	31,885
1934–35	4,333	—	—	30,299
1948–49	7,561	4,616	595	59,041
1950–51	9,542	10,987	5,135	87,415
1955–56	9,316	14,923	—	99,761
1960–61	9,571	39,502	5,380	1,07,435
1965–66	10,531	20,010	4,727	1,34,587
1970–71	11,612	39,766	5,166	2,00,030
1971–72	67,379	29,722	8,362	1,59,930
1972–73	48,623	60,106	5,162	2,06,645
1973–74	10,830	28,926	8,983	2,30,787
1974–75	15,464	37,463	9,742	1,86,114
1975–76	29,971	71,493	10,896	2,95,745
1976–77	14,712	37,980	5,632	2,67,458
1977–78	8,863	67,682	5,077	2,64,509
1978–79	7,965	84,954	6,023	3,19,081

SOURCE: *UP Forest Statistics, 1978–79* (Lucknow, n.d.).

suggested.[8] Meanwhile, the sale of chir wood was given a considerable fillip when laboratory trials of the Forest Research Institute (FRI) revealed that the utilization of chir waste (i.e. material left after the conversion of chir to sleepers) for paper making was a viable proposition.[9] With a view to selling the waste and utilizing the considerable areas of chir affected by twist (and hence unsuitable for sleepers) the forest department entered into a contract with Star Paper Mills of Saharanpur, owned by the Bajoria family. Under the terms of this contract, effective from 1 October 1961 to 30 September 1981, the mill

[8] See, for example, N. K. Agarwala, 'WP for the Kedarnath For. Div., Garhwal Circle, 1972–73 to 1981–82', mimeo (Nainital, 1973), pp. 168, 339–40.

[9] S. R. D. Guha, 'Chemical Pulps and Writing and Printing Papers from Chir (*Pinus longifolia Roxb*)', *Indian Forester*, vol. 84 (1958), pp. 235–40.

would be sold waste timber and twisted chir trees at ridiculously low prices.[10] Approximately 15 to 20 thousand tonnes of pulpwood were supplied annually to the mill.[11] When further research at the FRI established that ash and hornbeam could be used in the manufacture of sports goods, the Symonds Company of Allahabad were granted access to the high-level broad-leaved forests.[12]

The state's eagerness to further commercial working inevitably entailed further restrictions on village use. Cases were reported of the misuse of timber for their own use by high officials of the forest department. The high rates at which forest produce was sold to the surrounding population (as compared to the rates existing before 1947) and the takeover of disputed land by the department were also the subject of complaint. The department was widely believed to be in connivance with timber thieves.[13] In a bid to tighten control, the government had given the department extensive powers in the management of forest panchayats. Under the new rules, panchayats could only fell trees marked by the department. Local sale of slates and stones (used for housing) and export of resin were only allowed with the permission of specified senior forest officials who also directed the quantum of extraction and its destination. Finally, panchayats could retain only a fixed share (40 per cent) of any royalty on the sale of produce from their forests.[14]

More crucial, however, was the wilful neglect of the local population in the extraction and processing of forest produce. Initial hopes that road building would lead to industrialization and generation of local employment were belied by government policy which consistently favoured the export of raw materials to be processed by large industry in the plains. A sizeable proportion of the resin extracted—estimated at 85–90 per cent of the total output—was dispatched to the Indian Turpentine and Resin Co. (ITR) near Bareilly, in which government had the majority shareholding. Of the remainder, some was allotted to

[10] For details, see N. K. Agarwala.

[11] Estimated from figures given in different working plans; 1 tonne of paper requires 2 tonnes of pulpwood.

[12] Agarwala, 'Kedarnath WP', pp. 78–9.

[13] See *Yugvani* (YV), issues of 17 July 1960, 21 July and 18 December 1966, 4 October and 18 October 1970, and 18 April 1971.

[14] Agarwala, 'Kedarnath WP', pp. 28–30.

local co-operative societies and the rest sold by open auction. Initially, ITR and the co-operatives were sold resin at the same rates. This policy was changed in the 1970s, with ITR being supplied at the earlier (subsidized) rates, while local units had to buy resin at open auctions. In any case, these units were often allotted inaccessible forests where tapping was not economically feasible. As a result of such neglect, they rarely operated at more than 50 per cent capacity.[15] Requests to lower prices by Rs 15 per quintal to meet the costs of transporting processed resin to railheads were also not acceded to.[16]

Discrimination against small units by the government was matched by its refusal to end the contractor system of forest working. While policy documents recognized the need to do away with the intermediaries who, it was admitted, exploited both their labour and the forests, in practice the system continued to be patronized.[17] Under the initiative of Sarvodaya workers, forest labour co-operatives (FLCs) were started in different parts of Garhwal and Kumaun. Repeated pleas to the government to allot them blocks of forest at concessional rates went unheeded.[18] In fact, the chief conservator of forests had himself suggested at one stage that the department actively promote the working of FLCs in the hills. He was, however, tersely informed by the governor that 'since the forest department is a sort of commercial department, it cannot be expected to extend concession in the transaction of its business, even to co-operative societies.' The official was referred to the experience of Bombay state, where such a scheme had cost the government 'quite dearly and considerable amounts were lost to the exchequer'.[19] Apparently, the role played by contractors

[15] V. P. S. Verma, 'WP for the Tehri For. Div., Garhwal Circle, 1973–74 to 1982–83', mimeo (Nainital, 1973), pp. 44, 55; National Council of Applied Economic Research, *Growth Centres and Their Industrial Potential: Chamoli* (Delhi, 1975). Interview with C. P. Bhatt, May 1981.

[16] See YV, 17 February 1974.

[17] Cf. Ramachandra Guha, 'Forestry in British and Post-British India: A Historical Analysis', *Economic and Political Weekly* (in two parts), 29 October 1983 and 5 November 1983.

[18] YV, issues of 30 October 1960 and 14 June 1970.

[19] GO no. VOB 289/xiv–378–56, 23 July 1960, from assistant secretary, UP government, to chief conservator of forests, UP (office of the conservator of forests, Tehri circle, Dehradun).

(almost all of whom belonged to the plains) as political patrons stood in the way of the implementation of stated policy objectives.

Several features testify to the marked degree of continuity between colonial and post-colonial forest policies. While the pressure of industrial and commercial classes may have replaced strategic imperial needs as the cornerstone of state forestry practices, in both periods 'successful' implementation of policy has been at the expense of the hill peasantry and their life support systems. The use of silvicultural and other strategies of manipulation and control, designed to limit and carefully regulate the access of the surrounding population to the forest, has been remarkably invariant throughout this time span. Finally, the forest department, assigned the role of a revenue generating organ by both the colonial state and the Tehri durbar, has continued to be a veritable money-spinner for the government of Uttar Pradesh. Between 1967–8 and 1978–9 forest revenue from the hill region increased from Rs 962 to 2020 lakhs.[20]

ECOLOGICAL CHANGE AND THE MONEY-ORDER ECONOMY

In chapter 2 I had argued that in the period before commercial forestry, hill peasants were able quite comfortably to meet their subsistence requirements and have, occasionally, a surplus of grain for export. The egalitarian structure of the village community, the abundance of forests and other natural resources, and its insulation from the political instability of the Indo-Gangetic plain all contributed to the autonomy and relative prosperity of hill society. This depiction found verification from the numerous accounts of European travellers and officials, which repeatedly contrasted the fine, upstanding hill peasantry of the nineteenth century with poverty-stricken villagers in other parts of India and even in Europe.

The picture drawn in chapter 2 is, in fact, considerably at variance with the situation as it exists today. An element of continuity, no doubt, is provided by the continued dependence on agriculture. While population pressure has led to the

[20] See *UP Forest Statistics, 1978–79* (Lucknow, n.d.).

fragmentation of holdings, there exists little opportunity for the emergence of a class of capitalist farmers. Thus, in terms of the indices of 'modernization', for example the use of improved seeds, irrigation, commercial crops, etc., hill agriculture fares poorly.[21]

Table 6.2 presents data on the occupational structure of six exclusively hill districts in 1971, or just prior to the Chipko movement. The overwhelming importance of agriculture obscures one crucial fact: that while farming systems in the Himalaya continue to be subsistence-oriented, cumulative social and environmental changes have undermined the hill society's capacity to feed itself. Foodgrain output is no longer adequate for subsistence. Whereas for most families it was a point of pride not to purchase food from the market, declining yields and an increased population have forced a majority of peasant families to buy a significant portion of their grain requirements.[22] The substantial deficit between production and

TABLE 6.2

Percentage Distribution of Work-force, 1971

District	Cultivators	Agricultural labourers	Animal husbandry/ forestry	Agriculture as percentage of total population
Pithoragarh	78.01	1.30	1.62	80.93
Almora	80.51	1.99	1.02	83.52
Uttarkashi	85.90	1.00	1.55	88.45
Pauri	82.97	1.03	0.73	84.73
Tehri-Garhwal	90.96	0.55	0.68	92.19
Chamoli	86.52	0.49	0.19	87.15

SOURCE: Computed from 1971 census, in G. C. Tewari, *An Economic Profile of the Hill Region of Uttar Pradesh*, Occasional Paper No. 10, G. B. Pant Social Science Institute, Allahabad, 1982.

[21] Cf. Waheeduddin Khan and R. N. Tripathy, *Plan for Integrated Rural Development in Pauri Garhwal* (Hyderabad, 1976).

[22] Marcus Moench, 'Resource Utilization and Degradation: An Integrated Analysis of Biomass Utilization Patterns in a Garhwal Hill Village, Northern Uttar Pradesh, India', MS thesis, University of California, Berkeley, 1985, p. 22.

consumption—estimated at around 160 kgs of grain per person per annum—can only be met through purchase in the market.[23]

In order to keep pace with rising population, hill peasants have adopted two adaptive strategies. First, they have increased their holdings of livestock. The density of livestock has increased from an earlier estimate of 342 animals/km² to 474 animals/km² in 1980. This is because animal manure is the key input for arresting the decline in yields. Peasants have also colonized new lands. However, while the population has increased by 119 per cent in the last eighty years, cultivated area has increased only by 54 per cent, and cropping intensity has barely crept up by 14 per cent. At the same time, as Table 6.3 suggests, the yields of major agricultural crops have actually fallen.[24]

TABLE 6.3

Estimated Yields of Agricultural Crops in Uttarakhand (kg/ha)

Crop	1896	1979	Percentage of gross cropped area (1979)
Rice	1120	1133	17.6
Wheat	898	538	25.4
Barley	NA	362	5.7
Mandua	1120	924	24.6
Jhangora	1100	924	13.4

SOURCE: William Whittaker, 'Migration and Agrarian Change in Garhwal District, Uttar Pradesh', in T. P. Bayliss-Smith and Sudhir Wanmali (eds), *Understanding Green Revolutions: Agrarian Change and Development Planning in South Asia* (Cambridge, 1984).

Declining agricultural productivity can be directly attributed to the deterioration of the hill ecosystem, in particular

[23] S. C. Joshi, D. R. Joshi and D. D. Dani, *Kumaun Himalaya* (Nainital, 1983), p. 233.

[24] W. Whittaker, 'Migration and Agrarian Change in Garhwal District, Uttar Pradesh,' in T. P. Bayliss-Smith and Sudhir Wanmali (eds), *Understanding Green Revolutions: Agrarian Change and Development Planning in South Asia* (Cambridge, 1984), p. 125.

the degradation of the hill forests. Recent satellite data shows that of the 34,042 square kilometres of land declared as forests in Uttarakhand, good tree cover exists only on 6.6 per cent of the forest land, while another 22.5 and 13.8 per cent can be classified as medium and poor forests, respectively. According to satellite imagery, therefore, over half the land officially classified as forest has no tree cover at all: even allowing for the areas above the tree line and snowy peaks, this is an alarming figure.[25] There is a direct and reciprocal relationship between the loss and degradation of forests and the decline of hill agriculture. On a healthy vegetative slope a dynamic balance exists between the rate of erosion and soil formation. As the expansion of cultivable land in the hills can only take place at the expense of forests or on excessively steep slopes, this in itself increases the rate of soil erosion. Meanwhile, the increasing transfer of leaf manure to farms to maintain soil fertility for human consumption impairs the forests' regenerative capacity. Simultaneously, commercial forestry is radically altering the ecology of natural forests. The removal of large volumes of timber without the replenishments of nutrients—normally accomplished through the decay of wood and litter—also increases soil loss, especially in the monsoon season. These cumulative pressures lead to the impoverishment of the ecosystem, and hill agriculture enters a downward spiral from which there is seemingly no escape.[26]

Neither intensification nor expansion of agriculture, therefore, offers a viable solution to the growth of human population and the loss of control over forest resources. Faced with multiple environmental hazards, Uttarakhand society is in a 'state of continuing economic deterioration'.[27] A second and more widespread adaptive strategy is to look for alternative sources of employment. As these do not exist within the Himalaya, Uttarakhand peasants have no option but to emulate their counterparts from Nepal and 'follow their soils down the slopes'.[28] While this process was set in motion during

[25] N. C. Saxena, 'Social Forestry in the U.P. Himalayas', mimeo, ICIMOD (Kathmandu, 1987), p. 7.

[26] Whittaker, 'Migration and Agrarian Change', pp. 114–17.

[27] P. H. Gross, *Birth, Death and Migration in the Himalayas* (Delhi, 1982), p. 184.

[28] Cf. Eric Eckholm, *Losing Ground* (New York, 1976).

the colonial period, male migration out of the hills has greatly increased since 1947. These migrants work mostly in the armed forces, the police, and as clerical workers and menial servants in the towns and cities of northern India. Village studies have reported that over half of the adult male population does not reside in the village for most of the year, being forced to seek employment elsewhere. On my visits to hill villages I observed a preponderance of children, women and old men, testifying to the absence of able-bodied males. In some parts more than 60 per cent of the family income is generated outside by male migrants who remit a major portion of their earnings (by 'money order') to the village.[29] Uttarakhand now has, therefore, a dual economy—based partially on remittances and partially on the eroding basis of subsistence agriculture.[30]

In the absence of alternative energy sources, deforestation and the money economy have placed an additional strain on the women, left in the village to pick up the pieces of farm life. The customary tasks of fuel and fodder collection now require far more time and effort than they did earlier. Increasingly charged, too, with agricultural tasks, the woman's lot is a miserable one, poignantly captured in the writings of local activists.[31] Yet the malaise of hill society is by no means restricted to one section of its population. The processes of environmental change that came in the wake of commercial forestry have had a devastating impact on the social fabric of Uttarakhand: fragmentation of the family, erosion of local authority structures and co-operating institutions, and a crisis of confidence resulting from the decline and fall of a once prosperous system of agrarian production. As the commercial sector of the plains begins to cast a covetous eye on other natural resources of the hills (e.g. water and minerals), we begin to see a strong parallel with the exploitation of mountain peoples in other parts of the globe. Kai Erikson's description of Appalachia serves in its

[29] See 'Report of the Task Force for the Study of Eco-Development in the Himalayan Region', mimeo, Planning Commission (New Delhi, March 1982).

[30] Cf. Whittaker, 'Migration and Agrarian Change', p. 129.

[31] See, *inter alia*, Bahuguna, 'Uttarakhand'; Sarala Devi, 'A Blueprint for Survival of the Hills', supplement to *Himalaya: Man and Nature*, vol. 4, no. 6, November 1980; and for a treatment in fiction, C. P. Bhatt, *Pratikar ke Ankur* (Gopeshwar, 1979).

essentials, if not in fine detail, in capturing the economic and ecological exploitation of the Himalayan villagers:

[The] men and women of Appalachia are among the most truly exploited people to be found anywhere. In the beginning, they had rights to good land. It was covered with timber; rich seams of coal ran under its crust. It had soil fertile enough for the modest uses to which it was put and its forests were alive with fish and game. In the course of a few decades, however, dating from the last years of the nineteenth century, almost all of these valuable resources were cut or scraped or gouged away [by outsiders]; and when the land lay bruised and exhausted from the punishment it had received, the people of the region had virtually nothing to show for it.[32]

FRAGMENTS OF A PRISTINE CONSCIOUSNESS: 'COMMUNITY' MANAGEMENT

At the time of the reservation of the hill forests, settlement officers, in the belief that the management of the forests not reserved would be made over to the villages, restricted rights in many cases.[33] In anticipation of protest, villagers were in fact told that while the reserved forests would be in the strict control of the forest department, 'they would be given complete freedom of operation in the remaining areas...'[34] Although proposals were mooted at various times, there was no concerted attempt to establish village forests on land not vested with government. In British Kumaun, after the forest movement of 1921, the Grievances Committee did consider the establishment of village forests on land taken away from the forest department. An official sent to Madras to examine the system of communal management there strongly recommended the creation of similar reserves, to be controlled by villagers, in Kumaun. In face of the active opposition of forest officials, who argued quite falsely that village management of forests reflected a lack of concern for the needs of future genera-

[32] Kai Erikson, *Everything in Its Path: Destruction of Community in the Buffalo Creek Flood* (New York, 1976), p. 68.

[33] No. 3681/xxvi–2, 4 May 1915 from comm., KD, to chief secy, UP, in FD file 83/1909, UPSA.

[34] See note by J. R. W. Bennett, 26 August 1919, in ibid.

tions,[35] these proposals were implemented only in piecemeal fashion.

Despite official apathy, foresters, in both the colonial and post-colonial periods, have admitted that the panchayat forests in Garhwal, though small in extent as a consequence of government policy, were often well maintained,[36] with many having done 'exemplary work in connection with forest protection and development'.[37] Where ownership was still vested in the community, forests continued to be well looked after—such as the twenty-mile stretch between Rudraprayag and Karanprayag in the Alakananda valley, where the government had explicitly made over the forests to the neighbouring villages.[38] In Tehri Garhwal, too, informal management practices continued to prevail over forests not taken over by the durbar. A recent survey concluded that while some panchayat forests there are in better condition than the reserved forests in the area, they are uniformly better maintained than forests under the jurisdiction of the civil administration.[39] During fieldwork in the valley of Badyar, a tributary of the Alakananda, I came across a panchayat forest containing both banj and chir, with profuse regeneration of the two species coming up side by side. A village schoolteacher explained how extraction was carefully regulated, with monetary fines being levied on offenders. Exceptions were made only in the case of religious festivals, or when the timber was required for community purposes such as the construction of the panchayat *ghar* or a school.

In Uttarakhand the age-old panchayat system had been accustomed to handling diverse issues of which forest matters, though undoubtedly very significant, were only one aspect.[40] The partial breakdown of traditional mechanisms of allocation and control has been a consequence of the commercial penetra-

[35] Cf. A. E. Osmaston, 'Panchayat Forests in Kumaun', IF, vol. 58 (1932), pp. 603–8.

[36] C. M. Johri, *WP for the Garhwal For. Div.* (Allahabad, 1947), p. 20; D. N. Lohani, *WP for the North and South Garhwal Divisions, UP, 1958–59 to 1972–73* (Allahabad, 1962), p. 35.

[37] *Report of Kumaun Forest Fact Finding Committee* (Lucknow, 1960), p. 37.

[38] Note by D. Joshi in FD file no. 83/1909, UPSA.

[39] Personal communication from Madhav Gadgil, 25 July 1981.

[40] Cf. *Garhwali*, 14 February 1920.

tion of hill economy and society that followed in the wake of state forestry. Yet cases continued to be reported of the *lath* panchayat of the village (an institution not recognized by law) managing small blocks of forest 'for the common welfare of the village community as a whole'.[41] More rarely, it was individuals rather than the community that took the lead, a notable example being Vishveshwar Dutt Saklani, brother of the peasant leader Nagendra Saklani (martyred in the 1948 movement), who has over a period of forty years planted and raised to maturity thousands of broad-leaved trees in the Saklana area of Tehri Garhwal. As forest officials were constrained to admit, when oak forests were entrusted to nearby villages who appointed their own *chaukidars*, lopping was done systematically and the trees well protected.[42] And in Kumaun numerous instances were reported of panchayat land being closed to grazing by common consent, the copious regeneration in these forests presenting a 'striking contrast' to the heavily browsed reserved forests.[43] A recent study of the Aglar valley in Tehri Garhwal reports the existence of a large community grassland used equitably and without friction by the inhabitants of as many as seventeen villages.[44] In Ranikhet subdivision of Almora district, a civilian reported in the 1960s that there were a 'large number of successful forest panchayats'; and in certain localities the only forests that existed belonged to them.[45]

Admittedly, there are variations. In Kumaun, where commercialization had penetrated earlier, the experience of forest panchayats is far more mixed. Yet, whether judged on its own terms or against the manifest failures of state forestry, the fine performance of *van* panchayats in parts of Garhwal and Kumaun is instructive. This situation has prevailed where cohesive and largely egalitarian village communities have retained some control over their forest habitat. It also testifies

[41] Census of India 1961, vol. xv, pt vi, Village Survey Monograph, no. 5, *Village Thapli, Tehsil Pauri, District Garhwal*, p. 2.

[42] Uttarkashi Working Plan, quoted in Sunderlal Bahuguna, 'The Himalaya: Towards a Programme of Reconstruction', in K. M. Gupta and Desh Bandhu (eds), *Man and Forest* (Delhi, 1979).

[43] V. P. Singh, *WP for the West Almora For. Div., Kumaun Circle, 1966–67 to 1975–76* (Nainital, 1967), pp. 109–10.

[44] Cf. Moench, 'Resource Utilization', pp. 106–7.

[45] Prakash Kishan, *The Broad Spectrum* (Delhi, 1973), p. 58.

to a reservoir of local ecological knowledge that has managed to persist amidst a century of alienation and protest. It was left to the Chipko movement to awaken and crystallize this fund of local knowledge in the hill peasantry's latest and most sustained challenge to the march of commercial forestry.

CHAPTER 7

Chipko: Social History of an 'Environmental' Movement

As a popular movement that has focused worldwide attention on the environmental crisis in the Himalaya, the Chipko andolan provided the point of entry for the present work. In this chapter I explore the major dimensions of Chipko as a social movement. Essentially, a sociological study of the Chipko andolan must grapple with three sets of issues.

First, there is the understanding of the movement in its historical dimension. On the one hand, we need to interpret the social idiom of Chipko in the context of earlier movements (described in chapters 4 and 5) centring around the question of peasant access to forests. On the other hand, we need to examine the interconnections between Chipko and different aspects of state intervention, both scientific forestry in particular and, more generally, the administrative policies followed by different governments. In keeping with the overall emphasis of this work, both social participation in Chipko and its reflection in popular consciousness are sought to be depicted in terms of the changing relationship between the state and the peasantry.

Second, the links between specific forms taken by Chipko and its relationship to the social structure of Uttarakhand need to be spelt out. Here, one must emphasize the social changes that have created a 'money-order' economy and a lopsided demographic profile in the villages of Uttarakhand. Thus, Chipko can be read as a response to the fragmentation of the village community in recent decades. Again, women have always played an important role in economic life (chapter 2), and this structural constant may explain the widespread participation of women—marking an important departure from the pre-Independence period—in contemporary social movements.[1] At the same time, the participation of women in Chipko and its associated movements has been influenced by the impact of recent economic changes in intensifying their traditional dependence on the natural environment.

Finally, while Chipko lies in a direct path of continuity with an earlier history of social protest, as an organized and sustained social movement, at the same time, it represents an expansion in the scale of popular mobilization and the development of popular consciousness. This extension has two distinct aspects. First, the enduring nature of Chipko and its assumption of an organizational form has raised major questions: the nature of leadership, the ideological clashes between different subcultures of the movement, and the redefinition of the relations between the sexes. These were absent from many of the earlier, largely 'unorganized', movements of social protest in Uttarakhand. Second, notwithstanding its internal schisms, as an extension of popular consciousness Chipko attempts to combat the growing social and ecological disintegration of hill society. This attempt consists, on the one hand, of an expansion of the movement to embrace other social issues, and, on the other, of the presentation to the state and the general public with alternative strategies of resource use and social development.

CHIPKO: ITS ORIGINS AND DEVELOPMENT

The background

Not surprisingly, the continuation by the government of independent India of forestry practices inimical to local needs generated a certain amount of discontent. In 1958 a committee was formed to 'investigate . . . the grievances of the people' of Uttarakhand concerning forest management. It deplored the situation in the hill tracts where, even after the

[1] The narrative of social movements in chapters 4 and 5 mentions women only in passing. This fact should be taken only as indicative of the biases of the sources used. It is very likely that women played a key supporting role in the peasant movements in both Tehri Garhwal and Kumaun divisions, by keeping the household and farm economy going in periods of social conflict with the state, and perhaps even by aiding rebel movements. The sources are obviously biased towards reporting the activities of men, who, unlike women. came into repeated contact with the state and its officials.

attainment of independence, 'not only great discontent against the Forest Department prevails at several places, but it is also looked upon with extreme suspicion and distrust.' While recognizing the need to locally develop the resources of the hills, the committee considered as inevitable the continuance of restrictions viewed by the people as a 'forfeiture of their hereditary natural rights'. Its typically non-specific recommendations gave priority to the 'preservation, development and extension of the forests' and to meeting the 'genuine needs of the local people'. It also asked for a declaration from the government that it would respect village rights over forests and that, along with forest preservation, 'it would provide every opportunity for the economic progress of the people'.[2] In the absence of concrete programmes, local legislators warned, there was every chance of a popular upsurge in the tradition of movements against the British and the Tehri durbar.[3] In fact, Communist Party of India activists in the Yamuna valley had organized several satyagrahas against the highhandedness of different state agencies.[4] Great resentment continued to be expressed against the practice of large timber coupés being sold to 'outside' contractors. Villagers also refused to help the forest staff extinguish fires, as they were bound to do under the forest act.[5]

The undercurrent of protest against forest management was combined with opposition to other facets of commercialization and the continuing underdevelopment of the hills. Led by Sarvodaya workers, thousands of villagers, mostly women, opposed the widespread distillation and sale of liquor. Processions and the picketing of liquor stills were organized in different districts of Garhwal. In Tehri the prominent Sarvodaya leader Sunderlal Bahuguna and several women were arrested for defying prohibitory orders.[6] A partial prohibition was imposed on the occasion of the centenary of Gandhi's birth;

[2] *The Report of the Kumaun ForestFacts Finding Committee* (Lucknow, 1960), esp. pp. 26 ff.

[3] Speech by Ramachandra Uniyal in Vidhan Sabha, reported in YV, 3 April 1960.

[4] See YV, 20 November 1966.

[5] See Gopal Singh, 'WP for the Nainital For. Div., Kumaun Circle, 1968–69 to 1977–79', mimeo (Nainital, 1969).

[6] YV, issues of 2 April and 9 July 1967, 22 May 1970, etc.

when this was successfully challenged by liquor contractors in the high court, sale was recommenced. This led to a fresh wave of *dharnas*, with Bahuguna embarking on an indefinite hunger strike. Thirty-one volunteers were arrested in Tehri for picketing liquor shops.[7]

Meanwhile the demand for a separate hill state gathered momentum. Students went on strike demanding the establishment of universities in the hills. *Bandhs* were successfully organized in several towns. In a metaphor reminiscent of the forest movement of 1921 (chapter 5), the government was termed 'Bania', a government which yielded only under coercion. Consciously seeking to establish a continuity with earlier protest movements, the Uttarakhand Rajya Sammelan had organized a meeting at Bageshwar on the sacred occasion of the Uttaraini mela. Here, speakers stressed the looting of natural resources from the hills, the growing unemployment, and the cultural similarities between Garhwal and Kumaun. The government responded by setting up universities and autonomous development corporations in both Garhwal and Kumaun divisions.[8]

The 1970 flood

The unusually heavy monsoon of 1970 precipitated the most devastating flood in living memory. In the Alakananda valley, water inundated 100 square kilometres of land, washed away 6 metal bridges and 10 kilometres of motor roads, 24 buses and several dozen other vehicles; 366 houses collapsed and 500 acres of standing paddy crops were destroyed. The loss of human and bovine life was considerable. The Gauna lake, formed by the Alakananda flood of 1894, was filled with debris. Apart from the tributaries of the Alakananda, the Kali and Bhageerathi rivers also spilled their banks. Houses in Rishikesh, where the Ganga enters the plains, were also destroyed. Due to the blockage of the Ganga canal, 95 lakh acres of land in eastern UP went unirrigated.[9]

[7] YV, issues of 14 November, 21 November and 28 November 1971.

[8] See YV, issues of 13 June, 15 July, 29 July, 5 September, 12 September, 19 September, 26 September and 3 October 1971, 24 December and 31 December 1972, and 28 January 1973.

[9] C. P. Bhatt, *Eco-system of the Central Himalayas and Chipko Movement* (Gopeshwar, 1980), pp. 11–13.

The 1970 flood marks a turning-point in the ecological history of the region. Villagers, who bore the brunt of the damage, were beginning to perceive the hitherto tenuous links between deforestation, landslides and floods. It was observed that some of the villages most affected by landslides lay directly below forests where felling operations had taken place.[10] Preceding official initiative, 'folk sense was the only body that surveyed the grim scene and drew conclusions. The causal relationship between increasing erosivity and floods on the one hand, and mass scale felling of trees on the other, was recognized by [it].'[11]

The villagers' cause was taken up by the Dashauli Gram Swarajya Sangh (DGSS), a co-operative organization based in Chamoli district. Organized by several local youths in the mid 1960s, the DGSS had as its major objective the generation of local employment. Despite serious obstacles it operated a small resin and turpentine unit, manufactured agricultural implements, and organized the collection and sale of medicinal herbs.

On 22 October 1971 the DGSS organized a major demonstration in Gopeshwar, the district town of Chamoli. The demonstrators called for an end to liquor sale and to untouchability, and for giving priority to the local use of forests. Arguing that they had nurtured the forest growth themselves, villagers demanded that local units be given preference in the allotment of raw material. Led by Sarvodaya workers, such as Gandhi's English disciple Sarla Devi (who had set up an ashram in Almora district in the 1940s) and the leading local activist Chandi Prasad Bhatt, the procession was of a size never before seen in Chamoli district.[12] In the following year major public meetings were held at Gopeshwar and Uttarkashi, which demanded the replacement of the contractor system with forest

[10] S. Bahuguna, 'Uttarakhand mein Mrityu aur Tabahi ki Janam key Liye Jangalon ka Janaja Zimmedar', YV, 4 October 1970.

[11] C. P. Bhatt, 'Eco-development: People's Movement', in T. V. Singh and J. Kaur (eds), *Studies in Ecodevelopment: Himalaya: Mountains and Men* (Lucknow, 1983), p. 475.

[12] YV, 31 October 1971; *Uttarakhand Observer* (in Hindi), 25 October 1971, in Chipko file, Centre for Science and Environment, New Delhi (hereafter CSE file). The DGSS is now known as DGSM (M for Mandal). However, I shall continue to refer to it as DGSS.

labour co-operatives (FLC's) and the setting up of small-scale industries.[13]

Mandal[14]

In early 1973 the DGSS had asked for an allotment of ash trees in order to make agricultural implements. The forest department refused to accommodate this request. Instead, they asked the DGSS to use chir trees, totally unsuitable for the purpose. However, the Symonds Co. was allotted ash trees in the forest of Mandal, barely several miles from Gopeshwar. This blatant injustice inspired the DGSS to organize several meetings in Mandal and Gopeshwar to discuss possible action. Two alternatives presented themselves: (*i*) to lie down in front of the timber trucks; (*ii*) to burn resin and timber depots as was done in the Quit India movement. When Sarvodaya workers found both methods unsatisfactory, Chandi Prasad Bhatt suddenly thought of embracing the trees. Thus 'Chipko' (to hug) was born. Led by their headman, Alam Singh Bist, the villagers of Mandal resolved to hug the trees even if axes split open their stomachs. Young men cemented the oath with signatures of blood.

The birth of Chipko preceded the actual advent of Symonds Co. in Mandal. Hearing of the villagers' plan, the district magistrate wired the UP government, who responded by calling Bhatt for negotiations to Lucknow. A compromise was suggested, whereby the government would allot the DGSS ash trees on condition that the sporting goods firm could take away its quota. Despite raising its offer from one ash tree to five, the authorities could not break down the stiff resistance. The labour and agents of Symonds Co. were forced to turn away from Mandal without felling a single tree.

In June Symonds was allotted trees near the village of Phata in the Mandakini valley, en route to the shrine of Kedarnath.[15]

[13] See YV, 24 June 1973.

[14] This account is based on A. Mishra and S. Tripathi, *Chipko Movement* (Delhi, 1978), pp. 7–12, supplemented by S. Bahuguna, 'Uttarakhand ka Chipko Andolan', YV, 24 June 1973; news report in YV, 6 May 1973; interview with Alam Singh Bist (ex-pradhan, Mandal village), Gopeshwar, May 1982.

[15] The villagers rendered the firm's name as 'Simon Co.' Interestingly, the firm has been referred to as 'Simon Co.' in all subsequent literature on the Chipko andolan.

When the news reached the DGSS, they were able to contact (the late) Kedar Singh Rawat, a prominent social worker of the area. Despite heavy rainfall a huge demonstration was organized on 24 June. Dismayed, the company's agents returned to Gopeshwar, where they complained at the forest office that even after depositing the guarantee money they were unable to fell the trees marked for them.

Reni[16]

Despite these early protests, the government went ahead with the yearly auction of forests in November. One of the plots scheduled to be assigned was the Reni forest, situated near Joshimath, in the Alakananda valley—a locality affected by landslides in the recent past. Reni itself was a village inhabited by members of the Bhotiya community who had abandoned nomadic pastoralism in favour of settled agriculture.

Hearing of the auction, DGSS workers contacted the block *pramukh* of Joshimath, Govind Singh Rawat of the Communist Party of India. While trekking through the area they noticed that over 2000 trees had already been marked for felling. Ironically enough, the labour for marking had been provided by the villagers themselves. Meetings were organized at which the tragic 1970 flood was remembered, and the possible consequences of felling the marked trees highlighted. Bhatt suggested to the villagers that they adopt the Chipko technique. The village women huddled some distance from the meeting were clearly amused at the thought of 'Chipko'.

The fellings were scheduled for the last week of March 1974. On the 25th a massive demonstration was organized in Joshimath where college students from Gopeshwar threatened to embark on a Chipko andolan unless the fellings were called off. Fearing opposition to the felling operations, the forest department resorted to subterfuge. The conservator of forests, who was based at Pauri, hoping that Chandi Prasad Bhatt could be persuaded to stay on in Gopeshwar, arranged to visit the DGSS

[16] Based on Mishra and Tripathi, 'Chipko', pp. 16–18, 21–30; J. C. Das and R. S. Negi, 'The Chipko Movement', in K. S. Singh (ed.), *Tribal Movements in India*, volume II (Delhi, 1983), pp. 383–92; poster issued by Zila Chamoli Sangharsh Samiti, Joshimath, in CSE file; interviews with C. P. Bhatt, Gopeshwar, May 1982, and Pithoragarh, October 1983.

premises on the 26th. Bhatt stayed on to receive him. The same day the men of Reni and neighbouring villages were called to Chamoli to receive the compensation long overdue for lands appropriated by the Indian army after the Chinese invasion of 1962.

With both DGSS workers and local men out of the way, the lumbermen proceeded to the forest on the 26th. The same evening Govind Singh Rawat phoned Bhatt with news of the department's deceit. Now it was believed to be too late. A plan to *gherao* the conservator was foiled when the official fled from Gopeshwar.

At Reni events had taken a dramatic turn. The contractors' men who were travelling to Reni from Joshimath stopped the bus shortly before Reni. Skirting the village, they made for the forest. A small girl who spied the workers with their implements rushed to Gaura Devi, the head of the village Mahila Mandal (Women's Club). Gaura Devi quickly mobilized the other housewives and went to the forest. Pleading with the labourers not to start felling operations, the women initially met with abuse and threats. When the women refused to budge, the men were eventually forced to retire.

The government steps in

Reni's importance in the saga of the Chipko andolan is twofold. It was the first occasion on which women participated in any major way, this participation, moreover, coming in the absence of their own menfolk and DGSS activists. As Gaura Devi recounted,

> it was not a question of planned organization of the women for the movement, rather it happened spontaneously. Our men were out of the village so we had to come forward and protect the trees. We have no quarrel with anybody but only we wanted to make the people understand that our existence is tied with the forests.[17]

Secondly, no longer could the government treat Chipko merely as the reaction of motivated local industry deprived of raw material. For, until then, Reni was an archetypal hill village isolated from the market and dependent on the forests only as an input for subsistence agriculture. From now on Chipko was

[17] Das and Negi, 'Chipko', p. 390.

to come into its own as a peasant movement in defence of traditional forest rights, continuing a century-long tradition of resistance to state encroachment. The chief minister of UP, H. N. Bahuguna, who himself hailed from Garhwal, had earlier told the Chipko leaders that he could not meet their demands as he was 'the chief minister of the entire state, not only of the hill districts'.[18] After the Reni incident he conferred with them and agreed to set up a committee to investigate the incident. Headed by a botanist, Virendra Kumar, the members of the committee included Bhatt and secretaries of several government departments. Later, its terms of reference were extended to include the entire upper catchment of the Alăka-nanda. The committee concluded that one important reason for the 1970 flood was the widespread deforestation in the Alakananda catchment. Accordingly, commercial fellings were banned for a period of ten years in the upper catchment of the river and its tributaries.[19]

A second government committee, headed by K. M. Tewari of the forest department, was formed to investigate the existing practices of resin tapping.[20] The Tewari Committee found that tapping rules were rarely followed. In the several forest divisions toured by it, irregularities concerning the width, depth and length of cuts were observed to be widespread. Such maltreatment had made the trees particularly vulnerable to lightning.[21]

The UP government also promised to review the lease granted to Star Paper Mills. Proposals to set up units in the hills were examined by another committee, headed by a paper technologist from the FRI, and included Bhatt. The latter proposed that a number of small units, spread over the entire hill region, should be set up. Although eight sites were identified for the purpose, the scheme was found economically unviable. However, the committee found two sites suitable for the siting of units of a capacity of 25 tonnes per day, and where infrastructural and raw material facilities were available.

[18] Interview with C. P. Bhatt, Gopeshwar, May 1981.

[19] YV, issues of 17 November 1974 and 7 August 1977; Bhatt, *Eco-system*, p. 18.

[20] V. P. S. Verma, 'WP for the Tehri For. Div., Garhwal Circle, 1973–74 to 1982–83', mimeo (Nainital, 1973), p. 377.

[21] B. Dogra, *Forest and People* (Delhi, 1983), pp. 38–40; S. Bahuguna, 'Let the Himalayan Forests Live', *Science Today*, March 1982, pp. 41–6.

Although detailed project reports were prepared, these recommendations were never implemented by the government.[22]

One proposal that did materialize in response to Chipko was the constitution of a forest corporation or Van Nigam, to take over all forms of forest exploitation. As originally envisaged, the auction system would be abolished and a large proportion of forest lots were to be allotted to FLC's by the corporation. Over time, however, the corporation reverted to the old system wherein outside agents were subcontracted the task of felling.[23]

Chipko spreads to Tehri

Following Reni, forest auctions were opposed in different parts of Garhwal. In Dehradun the auction of the Chakrata division forests had to be called off following protests led by local students. At Uttarkashi's Hanuman Mandir, Sunderlal Bahuguna underwent a two-week fast in October 1974, calling for a change in the existing forest policy.[24] That summer youths from both Kumaun and Garhwal had embarked on a 700 kilometre trek from Askot village—the eastern extremity of Kumaun—to Arakot on the borders of Himachal Pradesh. The marchers traversed the breadth of Uttarakhand in forty-four days. They were accompanied for part of the distance by Bahuguna.[25]

The lack of co-operation between the newly constituted Van Nigam and labour co-operatives, coupled with the damage done to chir trees, was central to the next major form the movement was to take. On the occasion of Van Diwas (30 May, the anniversary of the Tiladi firing), Chipko activists in Tehri district informed the forest department that the resin-scarred chir trees would be bandaged. When the department did not respond to the call to save the trees, a direct action programme was commenced on another historic day, the anniversary of Sridev Suman's death (25 July). Villagers of Khujni patti started pulling out the iron leaves inserted to extract resin. In Advani forest, close to the Hemval river, the Sarvodaya

[22] File no. 15 (25), cellulose and paper branch, FRI, Dehradun.

[23] See YV, 5 September 1976.

[24] YV, issues of 20 October and 10 November 1974.

[25] Dogra, *Forest and People*, pp. 46–7; Shekhar Pathak, 'Chipko Andolan ki Nayi Lahr', *Dharmayug*, August 1977.

worker Dhum Singh Negi went on a fast which was called off when villagers assured him that they would save the marked trees. Signifying their close relationship with trees, women tied 'raakhees' around the wounded spots. A reading of the Bhagavad Gita was also organized.[26]

The monsoon of 1978 saw another major flood, this time in the Bhageerathi valley. The immediate cause was a blockage in the Kanodia Gad, a tributary of the Bhageerathi. The financial loss due to the flood was estimated at Rs 25 crores.[27] Despite the flood, forest auctions were held at Nainital under heavy police protection. Opposition to forest felling also took place in the Chamyala forest, near Bahuguna's ashram at Silyara.[28] Elsewhere, people's committees were formed which successfully opposed felling at Loital and Amarsar. Now Chipko moved on to Badyargarh, where over 2300 trees had been marked for felling by the forest corporation.[29]

Chipko in Kumaun

In Kumaun the Chipko andolan had first been introduced during the Nainadevi fair at Nainital in 1974, following which forest auctions were opposed at several places.[30] However, it gathered momentum following the major landslides at Tawaghat, a village situated close to the India–Nepal border, in 1977. In the landslide 45 men and 75 heads of cattle perished. Young activists of the Uttarakhand Sangharsh Vahini (USV) opposed the auctions that were scheduled despite the Tawaghat disaster. In October 1977 large demonstrations were organized in Nainital. When several leaders of the USV were arrested, a crowd of a thousand people surrounded the Rink Hall, where the auctions were being held. The auctions were rescheduled for November. This time too section 144 had to be enforced. In the presence of the police and the provincial armed constabulary, protesters sang the songs of the legendary folk poet, Gaurda. Again, the leaders were arrested. Some rowdies,

[26] Dogra, pp. 52–3; YV, issues of 14 August and 18 December 1977.

[27] YV, issues of 13 August and 27 August 1978.

[28] YV, 8 October 1978.

[29] YV, 17 December 1978; Dogra, *Forest and People*, pp. 53–4.

[30] YV, 29 September 1974.

probably not connected with Chipko, then set fire to the Nainital Club.[31]

In the following months different Chipko agitations were organized by the USV. On 15 December Chipko activities were commenced in the Hat forest of Almora, where 5000 chir trees had been marked for felling. The USV demands included the revision of the forest settlement and a ban on the export of raw material from the hills.[32] In Chanchridhar forest, situated in the sensitive catchment area of the Gagas river, protesters marched into the block where the forest corporation planned to fell 6000 trees. They camped in the forest for over a week till the foresters had to admit defeat. Later, fellings scheduled by the corporation were successfully stalled at Janoti Palri and at Dhyari on the Almora–Pithoragarh road.[33]

Chipko returns to Chamoli

Chipko witnessed a resurgence in Chamoli, when, despite its early successes, commercial fellings continued to threaten the ecological stability of different habitations. In the Bhyunder valley, adjoining the famous Valley of Flowers, oak trees were marked to meet the fuelwood needs of Badrinath town. In Badrinath, an important pilgrim centre, the temple alone consumed over 1000 quintals of wood between May and November every year, during the pilgrim season. The total fuelwood consumption of the town was estimated at 2500 quintals. When trees were marked near Pulna village, the village panchayat wrote to the divisional forest officer and the district magistrate. Officials replied that 250 villagers could not get precedence over 1.5 lakh pilgrims. On the second day of felling operations (5 January 1978) the women of Pulna, despite 40 centimetres of snow, surrounded the labourers, took away their implements, and gave them a receipt for the tools. In this manner 621 trees were saved.[34]

[31] *Dinman*, issues of 23–29 October and 18–24 December 1977 (CSE file); interview with G. B. Pant of the USV, Nainital, May 1983.

[32] *Janpath*, 15 December 1977, CSE file.

[33] Dogra, *Forest and People*, p. 60–1.

[34] Rosalyan Wilson, 'Phulon ki Ghati mein Chipko Andolan', *Dainik Nayi Duniya*, 1 March 1978, CSE file.

One of the more significant agitations occurred in the Pindar valley, near the village of Dungri-Paintoli. Here the men of the village wanted to sell their oak forest to the horticulture department, which intended to establish a potato farm on the land. If the forest, the only good one for miles around, had been cut, the women would have had to walk a long distance every day to collect fuel and fodder. When the women voiced their opposition, it went unheeded. At this juncture Chipko activists intervened and, helped by the district administration, ensured that the forest area remaining (some forest had already been cleared) was saved.[35] Angered at the women's success, the village headman threatened Bhatt and his colleague Ramesh Pahari with dire consequences if they came back to the area.[36]

The significance of Dungri-Paintoli lies in the open conflict of interest between the men and women of the village. Lured by promises of better communications and other 'modern' facilities, the men hoped to make some quick money. The women, for their part, 'raised some fundamental questions challenging the system. In their opinion, agriculture and animal rearing was entirely dependent upon them, both closely related to the forest, and yet they were not consulted with regard to any [decisions] taken relating to forestry.'[37]

The next Chipko agitation took place at Parsari, near the army encampment of Joshimath. Here, kharsu and *moru* (high-level oak) trees were being felled to meet the fuel requirements of Joshimath town. The appointed forest provided fuel and fodder to four villages nearby which had appointed a watchman to guard it. In fact, the Kumar Committee had recommended that there be no felling in this area. A people's committee headed by Narendra Singh and Narayan Singh organized the village opposition, which refused to allow the fellings.[38]

[35] Gopa Joshi, 'Men Propose, Women Dispose', *Indian Express*, 14 January 1982.

[36] Interview with C. P. Bhatt, Gopeshwar, May 1982.

[37] C. P. Bhatt and S. S. Kunwar, 'Hill Women and Their Involvement in Forestry', in S. S. Kunwar (ed.), *Hugging the Himalayas: The Chipko Experience* (Gopeshwar, 1982), p. 84.

[38] C. P. Bhatt, 'Joshimath mein "Chipko" Andolan', CSE file.

THE BADYARGARH ANDOLAN

Thus far, I have presented a broad overview of the major Chipko agitations that have occurred since the movement's inception. Let us now look more closely at one particular Chipko mobilization in order to properly appreciate its social and cultural idiom. The Chipko agitation that occurred in the Badyargarh patti of Tehri Garhwal district in the winter of 1978–9 forms the focus of the section, and my analysis of it is based largely on fieldwork conducted in early 1983. I present here an internal analysis of the movement, i.e. its patterns of mobilization and type of organization, the participation of different social groups, its ideology and methods, and the relationship between the leadership and the rank and file. I also highlight the changing perceptions of the state which has replaced the Tehri durbar as the unit of legitimate authority. The fundamental characteristics of Chipko, as the movement is conceived by its participants, may thereby become clearer.

The patti of Badyargarh is situated between the Bhageerathi and Alakananda rivers, about 130 kilometres north-east of Rishikesh. The social structure, in conformity with the rest of Uttarakhand, is built around relatively homogeneous and cohesive village communities. For the past few decades, however, grain production has been inadequate to sustain the population. In this money-order economy, women labour hard to perform household and agricultural tasks.

Badyargarh is a relatively prosperous patti, containing a large number of retired and serving army personnel. The growing opportunities offered to individuals by commercialization, education, government employment, etc. have definitely contributed to the erosion of the community co-operative spirit. The possibility of individual social mobility that the outside world offers is reflected in the village by the return of successful individuals to build cement structures. Although the community spirit is still present, as shown by Chipko, there is, simultaneously, a slowly growing differentiation within the village due to the impact of commercialization. There is, too, a sense of disruption of the traditional social fabric that the opening out of Garhwal has brought, as well as anger at the comparative underdevelopment of the hills.

Commercial forestry in the region started only around 1965, with the building of a motor road into the area. In the following years the extraction of resin and turpentine was commenced, alongside the felling of chir trees. In 1979 the Van Nigam gave out a big contract for the felling of chir pine in the area. The felling, which went on for several months, was, according to villagers, very destructive, with young regeneration being removed in addition to the logged trees. Several dozen trucks came and went daily, taking away all the wood, including the branches of trees. As people later reminisced, the contractor replied to early signs of protest by remarking that he would not leave any part of the tree behind ('*Hum ped ka koi hissa nahin choddenge*').

The andolan

Following upon this activity and just prior to the proposed logging in the Malgaddi forest, Sarvodaya workers, trusted associates of the Chipko leader Sunderlal Bahuguna, came to Badyargarh to enquire into the people's grievances. These leaders, Dhum Singh Negi, Kunwar Prasun, Pratap Shikhar and Vijay Jardari, among others, went from village to village informing people of the proposed felling and its harmful ecological consequences. At the same time Bahuguna's wife, Vimla, and other ladies mobilized the village women on the issue.

The andolan started on 25 December 1978 but acquired momentum only after Bahuguna went on a hunger fast from 9 January 1979. Conducted in a disused shepherd's hut in the forest, and in the middle of winter, the fast was a rallying point for people of the surrounding villages. Thus, over three thousand men, women and children participated, 'one for every chir tree in the forest'. An attempt at cutting by night was foiled by villagers taking night duty by turns. Classic non-cooperation tactics were adopted, there being no question of any violence used ('*himsa ka koi saval nahin tha*'). Bahuguna was carried away by the police on the night of 22 January and interned in Tehri jail, where he continued his fast. Meanwhile, a reading of the Bhagavad Gita was started on the 26th. Meeting determined resistance from the villagers even after the removal of their leader from the scene, the contractor and forest officials had to admit defeat and abandon felling.

Participation: A feature of the andolan was the active participation of all social groups. This was explained by the evident fact that all were equally affected by deforestation. The Bajgis, a caste of musicians, were solicited to mobilize villagers through their *dholaks* (drums). Women played a prominent part, as did government servants and defence personnel, though their support could only be covert.

Children too joined in a movement which recreated the atmosphere of joyous celebration in a fight against injustice. When police camped in Dhadi Ghandiyal High School, children went on strike in protest at the invasion of a 'temple of knowledge' (Vidya Mandir). While the strike itself lasted four days, all through the andolan students skipped school with the connivance of the teachers. As the principal recounted, he was placed in an awkward position, with the police harassing him on the one hand and, on the other, villagers imploring him to let his wards come to the forest. The schoolteacher, highly respected in Garhwal, symbolized in his person the conflict between government and people. As a figure of authority the state expected him to control the people, while the people wanted sanction for their acts by that very same authority.

The moral content of Chipko: Two further incidents that occurred after the successful completion of the andolan serve to illustrate the strong moral content of Chipko. When the contractor abandoned his labour, the locals fed them from village ration shops and petitioned officials to alleviate their plight. Only with the arrival of the labour commissioner could the grievances be redressed and the labour sent home to Himachal.

The second incident relates to the wood felled prior to Chipko, which was not allowed to be carried away for conversion to sleepers. The Badyargarh Van Suraksha Samiti (BVSS) resolved to release the wood only after the local people had fulfilled their needs. This entailed that the first claim would be exercised by those individuals and villagers who had not been granted timber rights, following which the requirements of the other inhabitants of Badyargarh and its neighbouring pattis would be met on payment of nominal rates. It was proposed that the income so generated would be used to regenerate the deforested areas of Badyargarh. Despite stern official warnings the BVSS stuck to their stand.[39]

[39] *Chipko Samachar*, datelined Badyargarh, 4 February 1979, in file of the Badyargarh Van Suraksha Samiti (BVSS).

Chipko and popular consciousness

There are several important characteristics of Chipko as the movement relates to popular perceptions.

The link between forests and humans: During my fieldwork I found that almost everyone I interviewed was aware of the importance of forest cover in regulating soil and water regimes. Chipko has contributed to a heightened awareness—the interesting question (to which chapter 2 provides one answer) is the extent to which this ecological consciousness predates Chipko. Thus, in Badyar village no grass cutting has traditionally been allowed on the steep hill overlooking the settlement. The cliff has a thick crop of grass and shrubs, in the absence of which boulders would come tumbling down the hill during the monsoon—hence the ban. As I argued in chapter 3, the link between humans and forests that existed before the inception of commercial forestry has been eroded by the loss of community control. In this context Chipko aims at halting the growing alienation of humans from nature, an alienation with potentially damaging consequences.

Chipko and community solidarity: An ecological consciousness, however attenuated, and the manifold benefits of forest cover to the hill economy (and ecology) can explain Chipko's success in mobilizing all sections of hill society. In response to criticism that the andolan depended largely on Bahuguna's appeal, the BVSS pointed out that if the movement did not enjoy popular support it would have terminated with Sunderlal's arrest and removal. As villagers see it, efforts to put out forest fires, which they are obliged to do under the settlement, are made in the belief that their property was being destroyed. Thus, when the government started indiscriminate felling (*andhadhun katai*) it was keenly resented.

Attitude towards officials: The lack of fulfilment of the basic needs of education, health and employment found the accumulated grievances being crystallized in Chipko. One BVSS activist put it thus:

> *Humme thoda sa anaaz mila, jab usse bhi*
> *nahin paka sake, tho andolan karna pada.*[40]

[40] Freely translated: 'when we could not obtain the wood to cook even the little grain we get, we had to resort to a movement.'

The implacable hostility towards state officials, particularly those belonging to the forest department, can be read as a symbol of such disillusionment. Chipko participants expressed delight in recalling the impotence of high officials (*ucchadhikari*) in the face of the andolan. Senior officials of the civil and forest administration, as well as the police, arrived but were powerless to resume felling operations ('*Ucchadhikari pahunch gaye, lekin kuch nahi kar paye*').

Women and Chipko: It has been stressed that hill women have agricultural tasks. This situation is further aggravated, in Badyargarh and elsewhere, by the absence of adult males. Some analysts see a direct causal link here. According to Bahuguna himself,

> Due to washing away of fertile soil, the menfolk were compelled to leave their families and wander in search of employment, thus making the women bear all the responsibilities, collecting fodder, firewood and carrying water, which form the main chores besides farming.[41]

This interpretation can be disputed: for, as I show in chapter 2, the important economic role of women is culturally specific to the hill family and not merely a result of changed ecological or economic conditions. Can one then relate the subordinate position of women in Uttarakhand to the enthusiastic support given by them to the Chipko andolan?

An interesting conversation at a teashop in Badyar village brought out the conflicts inherent in such a situation. One retired army man was strongly of the opinion that women's participation in Chipko was a consequence of their inferior position in hill society. Observing the men gathered around the shop, he asked rhetorically, 'We men are sitting drinking tea, but can we see any woman here? Why not?' A look at the far hillside, where women were gathering firewood, provided the answer: 'They are not here for they have work to do.' This feminist stand brought forth jeers from fellow villagers, who later advised me not to take him seriously.[42] Nevertheless, the local women's leader, Sulochana Devi, was emphatic that the success of Chipko depended on women. The movement,

[41] S. Bahuguna, *Chipko* (Silyara, 1980), p. 5. Emphasis added.

[42] This is in keeping with the tendency, often reported by anthropologists, to minimize internal criticism in the presence of outsiders.

she argued, was only the first step; women needed to be educated and dowry banned in order that others did not fritter away women's wealth (*'ladkiyon ka dhan na khoya jaye'*).

Chipko in a history of protest

Badyargarh was the scene of a wide-ranging peasant movement in 1948 that culminated in the merger of Tehri state with the province of UP (see chapter 4). Protesting against extortion of money by the king's officials, villagers gathered at a religious fair at Dhadi Ghandiyal, marched towards the capital, Tehri, capturing outposts on the way and symbolically replacing corrupt patwaris by their own men.

The 1948 dhandak remains vividly in the collective memory of the peasants of Badyargarh and their heroism then was invoked by the Chipko leaders in 1979. Apart from the participation of many in both, the movement itself has strong similarities—such as the identification of officials as the main exploiters, the belief that justice was on their side, and the forms of protest itself. In both instances the act of protest was seen as having a moral–religious sanction. While in 1948 the peasantry was mobilized on the occasion of a religious fair held once in thirteen years, an important event in Chipko was the reading of the Gita. Camped in the forests, Chipko volunteers commenced the reading of the epic and the rendition of folk songs. The conservator of forests who opposed the ceremony was firmly told that all the Vedas were written in the forest. And when the patwari threatened one of the priests with arrest the priest replied: 'Arrest me under any section of law, but what are the rules for the Nigam people?'

Bahuguna and the idiom of protest: The idiom of Chipko, then, can be understood in terms of the 'moral economy' of the Garhwal peasant, who could readily comprehend the tactics of the charismatic leader of the Badyargarh andolan, Sunderlal Bahuguna. Bahuguna concentrates his fire on the officials of the forest department who, in league with contractors, 'do not leave a splinter of wood in the forests'.[43] The call to forest officers to change their ways and serve local communities evokes a positive reaction from a people exposed to extortion by officials during earlier regimes.

[43] S. Bahuguna, 'Her Story: Women's Non-violent Power in the Chipko Movement', *Manushi*, no. 6 (1980), p. 31.

Bahuguna's method of functioning is far removed from that of self-seeking politicians. A non-political person, he was able to strike a chord in the hearts of those disenchanted with the hypocrisy of politicians and the electoral process. Gandhian methods of non-violence and Bahuguna's personal asceticism were appreciatively responded to by the predominantly Hindu peasantry. The capacity for physical suffering (vide the hunger fast in the bitter cold) and spirit of sacrifice (*tyaga*) in an age of selfishness were constantly marvelled at by villagers who read into these acts the renunciation of worldly ambition as exhorted by Hindu scriptures.

Sunderlal's charisma is undoubted and his deeds are still an object of wonder in Badyargarh. His success is clearly related to the distinctive character of social protest in Tehri Garhwal. The attacks on forest officials can be understood in the context of dhandaks aimed at the raja's minions. Sunderlal's remarkable physical endurance and sage-like appearance make him a natural leader whose followers look to him to restore a pristine state of harmony and just government. In fact, Bahuguna records that his life was changed by a chance encounter with Sridev Suman when he was a schoolboy. He 'proudly refers to Sridev Suman as his guru in all respects'—a theme he stresses repeatedly in his speeches.[44] Here one finds a striking parallel with other agrarian movements, where too the invocation of the spirit and memory of peasant martyrs is a primary 'means by which a sense of the past is revived, codified, and used'. References to predecessors like Suman reinforce Bahuguna's own credentials, as a notable ascetic of his time, to be the undisputed leader of the peasantry of these districts. The Tehri Garhwal case provides yet another illustration of what is a much more pervasive phenomenon so far as lower-class movements are concerned, for, as Eugene Genovese has pointed out,

> from the peasant revolts of medieval Europe, to revolutionary Puritanism, to the early working class organizations, to the great revolutionary movements of our own time, asceticism has provided a decisive ingredient in the mobilization of popular risings.[45]

[44] Interview in *The Telegraph*, 6 August 1983; S. Bahuguna, *Van Shramik* (Silyara, 1977).

[45] See Anne Walthall, 'Japanese *Gimin*: Peasant Martyrs in Popular Memory', *American Historical Review*, vol. 91, no. 5, December 1986; Eugene Genovese, *Roll, Jordan, Roll: The World the Slaves Made* (New York, 1973), p. 276.

For its practitioners, asceticism is a potent vehicle of cultural communication. Even as Bahuguna's own lifestyle evokes a sympathetic response among peasants, his message is conveyed through a local cultural idiom, both by his own acts and those of his followers—for example the noted folk-singer Ghanshyam Sailani, who has played a central role in the Chipko movements of Tehri Garhwal.

What is distinctive about Sunderlal Bahuguna's asceticism is that it is accompanied by a call to higher authority to side with the suffering peasants. During the course of the Badyargarh andolan, Sunderlal assured the villagers that even if the forest department was opposed to the movement, the prime minister, Morarji Desai, and Lokanayak Jayaprakash Narayan were on their side. While breaking the fast he commenced in Badyargarh in Dehradun jail Bahuguna said he did so only due to a request from 'JP', whom he called his general (*senapathi*). He recalled Suman's historic eighty-four-day fast in Tehri jail and also mentioned the support of home minister H. M. Patel for his *dharmayuddha* (holy war) to save the Himalayan forests.[46] After the victory of the Congress party in the elections of 1980 he invoked the support of the prime minister, Indira Gandhi, citing her concern at the situation in the Himalaya.[47] In this invocation leading politicians assume a role not dissimilar to that of the Tehri maharaja in earlier days. While their functionaries are viewed as being in league with corrupt contractors, those in power are believed to sympathize with the oppressed. Chipko then becomes, in a strikingly similar fashion to the dhandak, the only possible means to obtain justice by bringing the wrongdoings of officials to the notice of heads of government.

CUSTOM AND CONFRONTATION IN CHIPKO

As an organized movement of both national and international significance, Chipko can be analysed from the perspective of the sociology of social movements. In this study, too, I have highlighted several classic themes in the literature: the pattern of leadership, the forms of mobilization, the emergence of a

[46] S. Bahuguna, 'Badyargarh mein Itihas Ban Raha Hai', YV, 7 January and 21 January 1979. Cf. also YV, 4 February 1979.

[47] Cf. S. Bahuguna, *Walking with the Chipko Message* (Silyara, 1983).

codified ideology, and the relationship between leader and led.[48] I would, however, stress that this analysis of the formal characteristics of Chipko as a social movement must be supplemented by a study of its less formal features. Moving away from the public arena of Chipko and its popular stereotypes, through a case study of the Badyargarh movement I have tried to understand the transformations of meaning it has brought in the lives of its participants. An exploration of the less structured aspects of the movement reveals the existence of certain tenaciously held values, adhered to by village participants. The ideology that can be inferred from peasant actions is not entirely consistent with the formal ideology of Chipko as presented to the outside world. Finally, one of Chipko's central features is its historicity—i.e. its relationship with past movements which raised similar questions concerning the relationship between the state and the peasantry.

Locating Chipko culturally and historically provides a long overdue corrective to the popular conception of Chipko, which is that of a romantic reunion of humans, especially women, with nature. The dramatic act—often threatened but rarely brought into play—of hugging the tree to save it from the contractor's axe is the chief characteristic with which the movement is identified. Some writers have seen Chipko as having its origins in an incident believed to have occurred in Rajasthan in 1763, when members of the Bishnoi sect laid down their lives to protect trees being felled under orders from the maharaja of Jodhpur.[49] Within the movement, Sunderlal Bahuguna's writings and lectures have done much to propagate this view of Chipko.[50] Other writers have stressed the role of women, as the sex crucially affected by deforestation. It has even been suggested that Chipko is a 'feminist' movement.[51]

It will be clear from our study that the above stereotypes are

[48] Cf. J. R. Gusfield, 'Social Movements and Social Change: Perspectives of Linearity and Fluidity', in Louis Kriesberg (ed.), *Research in Social Movements, Conflict and Change*, volume 4 (Greenwich, Conn., 1981); J. C. Jenkins, 'Resource Mobilization Theory and the Study of Social Movements', *Annual Review of Sociology*, no. 9, 1983.

[49] Richard St Barbe Baker, 'Chipko—Hug to the Tree People', in S. Bahuguna, *Chipko* (Silyara, 1981), pp. 1–4.

[50] See, for example, S. Bahuguna, *Paryavaran aur Chipko Yatra* (Silyara, 1983).

[51] Centre for Science and Environment, *The State of the Environment: A Citizen's Report* (Delhi, 1982), pp. 42–3.

seriously inadequate in interpreting the origins, idiom and trajectory of the movement. The analogy with the incident involving the Bishnoi community obscures Chipko's origins, which are specific to the conditions of Uttarakhand. Chipko is only one, though undoubtedly the most organized. in a series of protest movements against commercial forestry dating from the earliest days of state intervention. Different Chipko agitations have invoked the spirit and memory of past upsurges against the curtailment of customary rights. This continuity is also strikingly manifest in the moral idiom in which protest has been expressed. Similar notions of morality and justice have permeated movements against the durbar and the colonial state as well as Chipko. As this case study of the Badyargarh andolan reveals, the peasantry was protesting against the denial of subsistence rights which state policy has wrought. Essentially, the movement was in response to a perceived breach of the informal code between the ruler and the ruled known as the 'moral economy' of the peasant.

Clearly, this continuity is more marked in the case of Tehri Garhwal. Here, Bahuguna's personal acquaintance with later movements against the durbar as well as the distinctive flavour of the dhandak has informed a movement whose contemporary character cannot be adequately grasped without reference to its historical context. The identification of officials as oppressors, the belief that Indira Gandhi or other high-level politicians—the contemporary equivalent of sovereigns—could intervene and dispense justice, and Bahuguna's own asceticism, which is reminiscent of Suman, all testify to this continuity.

In so far as Chipko constitutes a part of an overall tradition of protest, this continuity is present, albeit in an attenuated form, in other parts of Uttarakhand as well. Thus, certain variations in the different subcultures of Chipko can be explained with reference to the different socio-political structures in which they operate. Bhatt's identification of macro forces, such as overall state policy, as the major cause can perhaps be related to the rather different political history of the Alakananda valley, where, much earlier, the rupture between the state and the people had occurred as a result of British colonialism. Similarly, the adherence of the USV to a more radical posture may in part be a consequence of the earlier, and deeper, penetration of 'modern' political ideologies into Kumaun.

In Uttarakhand the participation of women in popular movements dates from the anti-alcohol agitations led by Sarvodaya workers in the 1960s. However, despite the important role played by women, it would be simplistic to characterize Chipko as a feminist movement. In several instances, especially the early mobilizations at Mandal and at Phata, it was men who took the initiative in protecting forests. Women came to the fore in Reni, when in the contrived absence of menfolk they unexpectedly came forward to thwart forest felling. In other agitations, such as Badyargarh, men, women and children have all participated equally. Dungri-Paintoli is the only instance of an overt conflict between men and women over the management and control of forest resources. As such, even at the level of participation Chipko can hardly be said to constitute a women's movement. Undoubtedly, the hill women have traditionally borne an extraordinarily high share of family labour—and their participation in Chipko may be read as an outcome of the increasing difficulty with which these tasks have been accomplished in the deteriorating environment. Interestingly, Chandi Prasad Bhatt does believe that women are capable of playing a more dynamic role than the men who, in the face of growing commercialization, are apt to lose sight of the long-term interests of the village economy.[52] On the other hand, it has been suggested that while they are the beasts of burden as viewed through the prism of an outside observer, hill women are in fact aware that they are the repository of local tradition. In the orbit of the household women often take decisions which are rarely challenged by the men. In the act of embracing the trees, therefore, they are acting not merely as women but as bearers of continuity with the past in a community threatened with fragmentation.[53] The conflict between men and women has surfaced much more sharply in other social movements in the hills, most notably in the anti-alcohol movement organized by the USV in 1984.[54]

Another possible source of confusion lies in the important

[52] Speech at a village meeting at Bakarkhatia, district Pithoragarh, October 1983.

[53] This is the position (as expressed in personal communications) of two scholars with an intimate knowledge of Uttarakhand, Shekhar Pathak and Jean Claude Galey.

[54] See Shekhar Pathak, 'Intoxication as a Social Evil: The Anti-Alcohol Movement in Uttarakhand', *Economic and Political Weekly*, July 1985.

role played by leaders owing an allegiance to the Sarvodaya movement. Gandhian institutions have been quick to hail Chipko as a modern example of satyagraha, calling it 'direct action in the best Gandhian spirit'.[55] In so far as the personal commitment and personal lifestyle of activists like Bhatt and Bahuguna exemplify the highest traditions of Gandhian constructive work, the characterization is not altogether incorrect. However, both Bhatt and Bahuguna, like the Praja Mandal activists of an earlier era, are anything but alienated from the historical and contemporary specificities of village life in Garhwal. Their involvement in Chipko is crucially informed, albeit in quite different ways, by a sharp historical sense and the experience gleaned from years of social activism in the hills. At the level of popular participation the Gandhian label is even less appropriate. It seems clear from the description of different Chipko agitations that the role played by external ideologies is a severely limited one. Villagers see Chipko as a fight for basic subsistence denied to them by the institutions and policies of the state. Although Chipko, like many Gandhian movements, has an important ethical dimension, its underlying notions of morality and justice are intrinsic to a history of protest against state restrictions on peasant access to forest produce. Nor should superficial similarities in methods of protest lead one to designate Chipko as 'Gandhian', its 'non-violent' method being an inspired and highly original response to forest felling rather than ideologically motivated.

At the same time, the Gandhian association may actually have helped Chipko in its largely successful bid to stop the onslaught of commercial forestry in the Himalaya. It is noteworthy that while the last decade has seen the emergence of several forest-based movements in peninsular India, none of these movements has had a comparable success in attracting public support or influencing the direction of government policies.[56] Indeed, they have on occasion been crushed with a brutality

[55] Foreword by Radhakrishna of the Gandhi Peace Foundation, in A. Mishra and S. Tripathi, *Chipko Movement*.

[56] For an analysis of these movements see, *inter alia*, Peoples Union for Democratic Rights, *Undeclared Civil War* (Delhi, 1982); Nirmal Sengupta (ed.), *Jharkhand: Fourth World Dynamics* (Delhi, 1982); G. De Silva, *et al.*, 'Bhomi Sena: A Struggle for People's Power', *Development Dialogue*, no. 2, 1979.

that has been notably absent in the state's attempt to deal with Chipko. Several factors account for the relative lack of success which these movements have enjoyed. First, the regions in which they have arisen have undergone rapid economic differentiation; wracked by internal contradictions, these struggles are unable (unlike in single-class hill society) to present a united front in opposition to forest policies. These movements have also tended to be more violent. Second, the cultural composition of forest dwellers in peninsular India is overwhelmingly non-Hindu. Chipko, on the other hand, located as it is in an area of enormous religious significance for the majority Hindu community, has struck a sympathetic chord in the heart of the Indian public. Finally, there is the veneer of Gandhianism with which Chipko is cloaked, a matter of some embarrassment for a state claiming to be the rightful successor of the freedom struggle and upholding Gandhi as the Father of the Nation. In this manner Chipko has, knowingly or unknowingly, successfully exploited the ambiguities in the dominant ideology of the Indian state. While this ideology is avowedly non-religious in its actions, the state goes to considerable lengths not to offend the Hindu sentiments of the majority of its subjects; and while its development policies are a strong repudiation of Gandhian economics, by paying daily obeisance to the Mahatma in its official rituals the state tries to symbolically appropriate the enormous prestige associated with his name. Faced with a popular movement which originated in the watershed of the holy Ganga, used techniques of non-violence and was led by Gandhians, the state has been hoist with its own petard.[57]

CHIPKO AS AN ENVIRONMENTAL MOVEMENT

I have repeatedly emphasized the fact that Chipko lies in a path of continuity with earlier peasant struggles in Uttarakhand; at the same time, as an organized and sustained social

[57] A relevant analogy within Uttarakhand is with the massive anti-alcohol campaigns organized by the Uttarakhand Sangharsh Vahini (USV) in 1984. Divorced from the Gandhian movement, the USV leaders do not enjoy the kind of access both Bhatt and Bahuguna have to several high officials. This element, and the more militant nature of their struggle, clearly played a role in the state's punitive response and its reluctance to concede the long-term demands of the movement.

movement it promises to go beyond them. Here it is useful to distinguish between the 'private' face of Chipko, which is that of a quintessential peasant movement, and its 'public' profile as one of the most celebrated environmental movements in the world. Thus, while the last Chipko agitation in Uttarakhand occurred in 1980, the movement's activists have since been tirelessly propagating its message. Within the Himalaya, foot-marches and environmental camps are organized at regular intervals. There has also been a significant attempt to contribute to the environment debate in India and abroad.

The widening of Chipko

In April 1981 Sunderlal Bahuguna went on an indefinite fast, urging a total ban on green felling in the Himalaya above an altitude of 1000 metres. In response the government constituted an eight-member 'expert' committee to prepare a comprehensive report on Himalayan forest policy. Although the thrust of the committee's report was to exonerate the forest department and 'sustained-yield' forestry, the government agreed to allow a fifteen-year moratorium on commercial felling in the Uttarakhand Himalaya.[58] Well before the moratorium, however, there was little doubt that the Chipko movement had significantly slowed the march of commercial forestry. Thus the output of major forest produce from the eight hill districts had declined, in the decade 1971–81, from over 62,000 to 40,000 cubic metres per annum.[59]

By successfully bringing commercial forestry to a standstill, Chipko marks the end of an epoch for the people and landscape

[58] 'Report of the Experts Committee to Look into the Policy Regarding Fellings and Protection of Trees and to Bring Improvement in the Maintenance of Environmental Balance in the Himalayan Region of U.P.', mimeo, Uttar Pradesh Forest Department, Lucknow, March 1982. In Uttarakhand proper, Bahuguna's fast marks an end to the activist phase of Chipko and its shift towards both publicity and reconstruction work. While Chipko-style movements (for example, the Appiko movement in Karnataka) have emerged in other parts of India, one must not make the mistake of seeing these movements as merely derivative of Chipko. Appiko, like Chipko, must be studied in its local historical and cultural contexts; assimilating it to Chipko, as some writers have done, does it as much violence as assimilating Chipko itself to abstract ideas of feminism, environmentalism, Gandhianism, etc.

[59] N. C. Saxena, 'Social Forestry in the Hill Districts of Uttar Pradesh', mimeo, ICIMOD (Kathmandu, 1987), Table 22.

of the Indian Himalaya. However, state forestry is by no means the only threat to the ecological and social stability of the hills, for the past decades have witnessed a rapid expansion in the scale of commercial penetration in Uttarakhand. This is exemplified by the location of large dams, increasing mining operations and the spread of alcoholism. This intensification of resource exploitation has been matched almost step by step with a sustained opposition, in which Chipko has played a crucial role, in catalysing and broadening the social consciousness of the Himalayan peasantry. Thus, movements against big dams, unregulated mining and the sale of illicit liquor have been organized by all three wings of the Chipko movement. While a detailed description of these ongoing struggles is beyond the scope of this study, in such a widening of the movement's horizons changes in forest policy are conceived of as only one element in an alternative development strategy. Moreover, despite insinuations that Chipko has a localized frame of reference, the bid to rescue hill society from the ravages of capitalist penetration does not call for a narrow 'regionalism'. As the agriculture of the Indo-Gangetic plain depends heavily on an assured supply of water from the rivers that originate in the Himalaya, the stabilization of Uttarakhand ecology and society has far wider implications.

Three environmental philosophies

Drawing on the experience of years of social activism, the leaders of the different wings of the Chipko movement have put forward their own interpretations of local and national processes of environmental degradation. One of the most forceful statements has come from Sunderlal Bahuguna, perhaps the best-known Chipko leader. Bahuguna holds commercial forestry and the close links that exist between contractors and forest officials as responsible for the deteriorating Himalayan environment. However, shortsighted forest management is a symptom of a deeper malaise—the anthropocentric view of nature intrinsic to modern industrial civilization. Thus, 'the ecological crisis in Himalaya is not an isolated event. It has its roots in the [modern] materialistic civilization, which makes man the butcher of Earth.'[60]

[60] Cf. Sunderlal Bahuguna, *Chipko Message*, p. 18.

While Bahuguna's group is active in the Bhageerathi valley, the wing of Chipko active in the Alakananda valley is associated with the name of Chandi Prasad Bhatt. Unlike Bahuguna, Bhatt does not deny the villagers' role in deforestation, stressing, however, that 'this has been a result of separating the local population from the management of the forest wealth.'[61] Further, Bhatt argues, both forest officials and commercial forestry are merely agents of a development process biased in favour of the urban–industrial complex and against local needs. He is also sharply critical of the growing separation between the state and the people, as clearly manifest in the framing of development schemes by urban-centred technocrats that have little relevance to the realities of rural India.[62]

Interestingly, the two leaders also affirm alternative systems of environmental activism. Bahuguna works in what one might call a prophetic mode: attempting to convert the uninitiated with a constant flow of articles, lectures and marches. In an inspired move, he undertook a 4000 kilometre foot march across the Himalaya, which was completed in April 1983, attracting wide coverage on the extent of environmental degradation in hill tracts outside Uttarakhand. Chandi Prasad Bhatt and his group work in what I would call the mode of reconstruction. Apart from several afforestation camps conducted yearly, they are also working on the installation of bio-gas plants and on other low-cost energy-saving devices. A remarkable fact about the afforestation camps organized by the DGSS has been the rate of survival of saplings (65 to 80 per cent)—the survival rate achieved in government plantations (around 10 to 15 per cent) seems pathetic by comparison.[63] Interestingly, the rate of survival showed a rapid rise following the greater involvement of women.[64]

The major differences between the perspectives of the two major leaders are presented in the chart on pp. 182–3. Here, the major schism in Chipko is interpreted along two separate

[61] Cf. C.P. Bhatt, Eco-Development: People's Movement'.

[62] C.P. Bhatt, 'Himalaya Kshetra ka Niyojan', mimeo, in Hindi (Gopeshwar, 1984).

[63] Personal communication to me from S.N. Prasad of the Indian Institute of Science, who conducted the study.

[64] See Anil Agarwal and Sunita Narain (eds), *India: The State of the Environment 1984–85: A Citizen's Report* (New Delhi, 1985).

but interlinked axes: historically, with reference to the earlier division of Uttarakhand into a traditional monarchy and a colonial bureaucratic regime; and ideologically, with reference to two distinct philosophies of development.

A third group, the Uttarakhand Sangharsh Vahini (USV), which is active in Kumaun, adheres to an ideology strongly influenced by Marxism. While attempting to move away from the public identification of Chipko with the two major leaders, USV insists that the human–nature relationship must not be viewed in isolation from existing relationships between humans. For the USV, social and economic redistribution is seen as logically prior to ecological harmony. It follows that the USV refuses to associate itself with state-sponsored development programmes, and in its own work it has occasionally come into sharp confrontation with the administration.[65]

These streams within Chipko reflect, in microcosm, different strands in the modern environmental debate. In his rejection of industrial civilization Bahuguna comes strikingly close to the American historians Lynn White and Theodor Roszak who stressed the role of religious beliefs in determining human attitudes towards nature. Modern science and technology are largely informed, in this perspective, by Judaeo-Christian ideals of human transcendence and rightful mastery over nature. This ethos is contrasted with the value systems of so-called primitive societies which, unlike Western science, viewed the ecosystem in its totality, thereby ensuring a rational and sustainable use of resources.[66] While accurately pinpointing the inability of Western science to come to grips with the eco-crisis, the alternative proposed by this school implies a return to pre-industrial modes of living—a vision perhaps as elusive as Western science's claim to bring material prosperity for all.

While acknowledging the alienation of modern science from the true needs of the people, Bhatt places a far greater emphasis on alternative technologies that could be more environmentally

[65] This paragraph is based on interviews with USV activists in Nainital and Pithoragarh, in May and October 1983.

[66] Cf. Lynn White, 'The Historical Roots of Our Ecologic Crisis', and Theodor Roszak, 'The Sacramental Vision of Nature', both in Robin Clarke (ed.), *Notes for the Future* (London, 1975). Cf. also John Passmore, *Man's Responsibility for Nature* (2nd edition: London, 1980).

CHART

Bahuguna versus *Bhatt: Personality and Ideology*

THEME	BAHUGUNA	BHATT
Historical influences	Specific to Tehri Garhwal—uses the symbols and targets of dhandaks. Invokes past protests and heroes like Suman. Sees high-level politicians as supporting movement (analogue with sovereign?)	Less specific—but recognizes and stresses overall history of deprivation of forest rights and protest in Uttarakhand
Identification of agents of deforestation	Representatives of forest dept in league with timber contractors	Forest policy influenced by commercial interests—villagers alienated from forest growth they helped to nurture
Broader underlying causes	Modern industrialization in which man is the Butcher of Nature	Development policy biased towards city and big industry and against local economic and ecological self-reliance
Methods of working	A prophetic mode—articles, lectures, pada-yatras, fasts—of late mostly outside Garhwal	Localized reconstruction work and appropriate technology of various kinds—in small industry, mini hydel plants, and bio-gas plants. Also the occasional article or lecture
Personal style	Ascetic, charismatic and all-inclusive. Relation with others in the movement more in the guru-shishya or master-disciple mould	Relatively low-keyed. More democratic, works closely alongside others in the DGSS. Ascetic, but less consciously so

Relation to Gandhian movement	Idealism, invocation of scriptures reminiscent of Vinobha Bhave, to whom he was close both personally and ideologically	Synthesis of Gandhianism and Western socialism—ideologically closer to J. P. Narayan and R. M. Lohia
Solution: local	Total ban on green felling—forests to revert to villagers. Trees for fuel, fodder, fertilizer, fruit and fibre to be propagated	Ban felling in sensitive areas. Large-scale afforestation drives involving state and villagers. Judicious extraction for local use only—aimed at generating employment through ecologically sound technology
Solution: global	Not specified—but a return to pre-industrial economy implied	Alternative path of industrialization—with political and economic decentralization. Based on technologies that promote self-reliance, social control and ecological stability

conscious as well as socially just. In this respect his views are similar to the pioneer formulations of the technologist A.K.N. Reddy, who emphasizes the role of appropriate technology in an environmentally sound development policy. The criteria of technological choice advocated by Reddy are, briefly: technologies that are employment generating, ecologically sound, which promote self-reliance (both in terms of invoking mass participation and using local resources), which tend to reduce rather than reinforce inequalities, and which build upon rather than neglect traditional skills.[67]

While the USV does share with the DGSS this vision of an ecologically oriented socialism, the two groups differ in their relative emphasis on political activism. The USV clearly prefers organizing social movements that confront the state to grassroots reconstruction work such as afforestation, arguing that it is the responsibility of the state to reverse the processes of capitalist penetration and environmental degradation. It does not share, either, the doctrinal emphasis on non-violence espoused by both Bahuguna and Bhatt.

In their own very different ways the three wings of Chipko have questioned the normative consensus among Indian intellectuals and political elites on the feasibility of rapid industrialization and technological modernization. Of course the environment debate is, worldwide, as yet in its very early stages. The linkages between technology and ecology, and politics and culture, will undoubtedly undergo significant changes in the years ahead. In the Indian context the Chipko movement and its legacy have helped define these issues with particular clarity and sharpness. It is likely that the continuing evolution of Chipko and of its three contending subcultures will define the outcomes as well.

[67] See A. K. N. Reddy, 'An Alternative Pattern of Indian Industrialization', in K. K. Bagchi and N. Banerjee (eds), *Change and Choice in Indian Industry* (Calcutta, 1982).

CHAPTER 8

Peasants and 'History'

THE UNQUIET WOODS: FOREST CONFLICTS IN TWO CONTINENTS

Liberty and Forest Laws are Incompatible.

—An English country vicar, *c.* 1720

Prior to the reservation of forests, hill society could be described as a conglomeration of village communities, with control over the means of production and over the resources needed to reproduce itself. In the ecological setting of Uttarakhand, forest management struck at the very root of traditional social and economic organization. Moreover, it operated on radically different principles from the customary use of forests by surrounding villages. This underlying conflict manifested itself, in a variety of forms, in virtually all the forest movements in Uttarakhand, including Chipko. The clash of two sharply opposed perceptions of the forest was captured in an insightful remark made by the commissioner of Kumaun during the 1921 movement. As Percy Wyndham saw it, the recurrent conflicts were a consequence of 'the struggle for existence between the villagers and the Forest Department; the former to live, the latter to show a surplus and what the department looks on as efficient forest management.'[1]

In its most elementary form, then, social protest was aimed at the restrictions on customary patterns of use entailed by scientific forestry. The takeover of the hill forests and their subsequent management on commercial lines were at once a denial of the state's traditional obligations and a threat to the 'subsistence dilemma' of the peasantry.[2] In response, peasant resistance to the new regulations typically made two claims. First, it unequivocally asserted continuing rights of control and

[1] DO no. 67/11/21 dt. 21 February 1921, from Percy Wyndham, comm., KD, to H. S. Crosthwaite, secy to govt, UP, in FD file 109/1921, UPSA.

[2] Cf. J. C. Scott, *The Moral Economy of the Peasant* (New Haven, 1976).

use. As the frequent attacks on forest officials in Tehri Garhwal showed, peasants objected to 'any state interference with the forest over which they claimed full and exclusive rights'.[3] In Kumaun, the idiom of agrarian protest similarly reflected the contending claims of villagers and the state. Here arsonists chose as their target blocks of forest and resin depots especially valuable for the administration, and official buildings that were the most visible symbol of alien rule. Second, the opposition to state management also contrasted the subsistence orientation of village use with the commercial orientation of the new forest regime. By initiating the commercial exploitation and export of forest produce earlier under the exclusive control of village communities, the governments of Tehri Garhwal, Kumaun division and independent India were, albeit in very different ways, placing at peril the legitimacy of their rule.

In this manner, protest has brought to the fore, on the one hand, alternative conceptions of property and ownership, and, on the other, alternative conceptions of forest management and use. The social idiom of protest in Uttarakhand bears a striking resemblance to the conflicts over forest rights that were an important feature of the transition to industrial capitalism in Europe.[4] The slow but steady growth of state forestry in Western Europe and the enclosure of communal forests by large landowners also substituted a uniform and rationalized system of forest administration in place of a flexible and informal system of customary use. As in Uttarakhand, this transition was neither smooth nor harmonious, with the peasantry protesting bitterly at the deprivation of their traditional rights of access and use.[5] In the mountainous region of Ariege in France,

[3] For the often violent conflict between state/commercial forestry and village use of common lands in Mexico, see Oscar Lewis, *Pedro Martinez: A Mexican Peasant and His Family* (New York, 1964).

[4] There is one notable difference, though. In the feudal system of Europe, peasants were continually fighting a battle for control of common property resources—thus, 'claim and counter-claim had been the condition of forest life for centuries.' See E. P. Thompson, *Whigs and Hunters* (Harmondsworth, 1975), p. 35. In Europe the commercial working of the forest under state auspices, which accompanied the rise of capitalism, was the final but decisive blow to customary rights. In Uttarakhand, by contrast, there was no ambiguity about who controlled the forest in pre-colonial (and pre-capitalist) times. Here the takeover of the forests by more powerful economic forces came through a sudden usurpation, not a gradual process of encroachment.

[5] See chapters 4 and 5.

for example, the development of the metallurgical industry in the second half of the eighteenth century initiated radical changes in the management priorities of crown forests and private forests. Landlords and the state came down heavily on peasant user rights, introducing in 1827 a forest code of 225 articles that forbade grazing in many areas and sharply limited supplies of fuel and timber to small agriculturists. In response, some peasants 'desperately searched for old deeds granting them rights of usage, checking the basements of deserted churches and going as far to look as [the town of] Montauban.' There was a rapid rise in forest offences, while groups of armed men disguised as women ('Demoiselles') attacked forest guards and the police—strangers to the region who symbolized the new and oppressive forest regime.[6] Elsewhere in France breaches of the forest law were by far the most common form of rural 'crime' in the early part of the nineteenth century.[7] Public records, especially those pertaining to the forest code, were burnt by angry peasants. Their rage was directed both at the state and at landlords; indeed, 'wherever landlords enclosed meadows and woods, they faced the rage and subversion of poor people who now had no place to pasture their animals.'[8] The villagers, Balzac observed in a thinly fictionalized account of this process, 'behaved as if they had an established right to cut wood in the forests.' As one woman defiantly says in *Le Paysans*, 'my man has sworn, I know, by all that's sacred, that we shall get our firewood and that all the gendarmerie on earth shall not hinder us, and that he will do it himself, and so much the worse for them.'[9]

In other parts of Europe as well, the battle for the forest was a central feature of the larger confrontation between an advancing capitalism and the peasant community. As in France, the development of the metallurgical industry in Germany and the growth of an urban market for fuelwood

[6] John Merriman, 'The *Demoiselles* of the Ariege, 1829–1831', in Merriman (ed.), *1830 in France* (New York, 1975), pp. 87–118.

[7] Maurice Agulhon, *The Republic in the Village: The People of the Var from the French Revolution to the Second Republic* (Cambridge, 1982), pp. 21–37.

[8] Charles Tilly, *The Contentious French* (Cambridge, Mass., 1986), pp. 15–16, 198–9, 214.

[9] Honore de Balzac, *The Peasantry*, volume xx of *The Works of Honore de Balzac* (New York, 1900), p. 170.

provoked landlords to enclose forests which were earlier open to the poor for grazing and fuel collection. Again, convictions for stealing wood and other forest offences showed an extraordinary rise in the first half of the nineteenth century. As Marx, commenting on the rash of forest 'crime', put it, a 'customary right of the poor' was, through force and fraud, transformed 'into a monopoly of the rich'.[10] Elsewhere, forests which provided fodder were taken over by the state for commercial timber production, forcing peasants to change grazing practices and rely on the cultivated meadow rather than the forest. Moreover, the relative valuation of different species was strikingly similar to Uttarakhand, with the state preferring species not especially favoured by villagers. Thus, in the state-owned forests, deciduous trees used for fuel and fodder were gradually replaced by conifers valued for commercial purposes. Inevitably, such changes met with opposition.[11]

As in the Himalayan villages covered by this study, in Europe too peasant protest was informed by alternative conceptions of property and use. What is common to the resistance to scientific forestry in nineteenth-century Europe and twentieth-century Uttarakhand is that in both cases it represented a defence of a traditional economic and social system, which afforded the peasantry some measure of stability, against the forces of a rising and expansionist capitalism. The spread of capitalism has everywhere radically redefined property relations and forms

[10] Peter Linebaugh, 'Karl Marx, the Theft of Wood, and Working-Class Composition: A Contribution to the Current Debate', *Crime and Social Justice*, Fall–Winter 1976, pp. 5–16; Karl Marx, 'Debates on the Laws on Thefts of Woods', *Rheinishche Zeitung*, 1842, reprinted in Karl Marx and Frederick Engels, *Collected Works*, volume 1 (Moscow, 1975), p. 235. As early as 1525 free access to the forests was a major demand of rebels in the German War. See F. Engels, *The Peasant War in Germany* (1850; English translation Moscow, 1956), pp. 51, 80, 88, 110. The conflicts over peasants' rights in royal hunting preserves, described both in E. P. Thompson, *Whigs and Hunters*, and several of the essays in *Albion's Fatal Tree* (Harmondsworth, 1975), are not strictly comparable. Although here too peasants were denied traditional use-rights, in so far as the forests were enclosed for pleasure (exclusive hunting by nobles) and not for profit (commercial forestry) one might say that these conflicts were more characteristic of feudalism than of the transition to capitalism.

[11] M. M. Postan (ed.), *The Cambridge Economic History of Europe: Volume I—The Agrarian Life of the Middle Ages* (2nd edition: Cambridge, 1966), esp. pp. 172–4; Franz Heske, *German Forestry* (New Haven, 1937).

of productive enterprise; just as inevitably, it has met its alter ego in the form of a '*rebellious* traditional culture'. A fine description of this culture is provided by E. P. Thompson in his study of eighteenth-century English society:

> The conservative culture of the plebs as often as not resists, in the name of 'custom', those economic innovations and rationalizations (as enclosure, work-discipline, free market relations in grain) which the rulers or employers seek to impose. Innovation is more evident at the top of society than below, but since this innovation is not some normless and neuter technological/sociological process ('modernization', 'rationalizing') but is the innovation of capitalist process, it is most often experienced by the plebs in the form of exploitation, or the expropriation of customary use-rights, or the violent disruption of valued patterns of work and leisure. Hence the plebeian culture is rebellious, but rebellious in defence of custom.[12]

In analysing the elements of a rebellious traditional culture, whether in Uttarakhand, France, Germany or England—and whether the genesis of rebellion is due to land tax, food prices, or forest rights—we must recognize that lower-class resistance typically has both instrumental and expressive dimensions. Faithfully reflecting disciplinary and ideological boundaries, anthropologists as well as Weberians are prone to emphasize the latter, while political economists and Marxists stress the former. However, lower-class rebels, whether in their actions or in their ideology, are not themselves inclined to strictly separate economic and cultural realms. The characteristic interpretation of utilitarian and symbolic elements in peasant revolt is clearly evident in the widespread opposition to scientific forest management in Uttarakhand; for the clash between scientific forestry and village management has not been merely an economic one. The conflicting perspectives rest on fundamentally different conceptions of the forest, on radically different systems of meanings. As chapter 2 documents, through a mix of religion, folklore and tradition the peasants of Uttarakhand had drawn a protective ring around the forest. As with other forest-dwelling communities, the continuity of their world rested on continuity in their relationship with the forest.[13]

[12] E. P. Thompson, 'Eighteenth Century English Society—Class Struggle without Class?', *Social History*, vol. 3, no. 2, May 1978, p. 154.

[13] For fine anthropological studies in the cosmology of forest-dwelling communi-

Scientific forestry threatened to disrupt this continuity, most obviously by denying villagers physical access, but perhaps more significantly by imposing an alien system of management on the forest. Thus the social idiom of agrarian protest has strongly reflected the threat to traditional cultural and communal values represented by scientific forestry. Most strikingly, there has been a close association of protest with folk religion: an association that was at once formal and informal, organizational and symbolic. The religious milieu of everyday peasant existence has influenced peasant resistance in two distinct ways. Protesters have, for one, sought a moral-religious sanction for their acts. This was accomplished either by involving priests and *sadhus* (ascetics), who enjoyed enormous prestige and influence locally, or in a more institutional form by using religious networks as means of communication. Thus, both temples and fairs have frequently served as locations where support was canvassed, or from which activities were co-ordinated.[14] Second, the ideology of peasant protest is heavily overlaid with religious symbolism. In the Kumaun movement of 1921, for instance, peasants invoked symbols from the Hindu epics while characterizing the colonial government as evil and demonic.

While the participation of priests testified to the involvement of figures of spiritual authority in social movements, holders of temporal authority were also prominent in the communal resistance to forest management. Both the colonial state and the Tehri Garhwal durbar tried without success to woo village leaders, especially headmen and retired soldiers. Almost without exception, the latter rejected these overtures and played a leading role in the mobilization and organization of the peasantry. In the Chipko movement too, retired schoolteachers, ex-soldiers and government officials—all prominent in the village authority structure—have played key leadership roles.

---

ties in peninsular India, see Verrier Elwin, *The Baiga* (London, 1939); Savyasachi, 'Fields and Farms: Shifting Cultivation in Bastar', mimeo (World Institute of Development Economic Research, Helsinki, July 1987).

[14] For examples of religious events turning into protest gatherings in early modern Europe, see Emmanuel Le Roy Ladurie, *Carnival in Romans* (New York, 1980); Georges Lefebvre, *The Great Fear* (rpt. Princeton, 1982); Paul Slack (ed.), *Rebellion, Popular Protest and the Social Order in Early Modern Europe* (Cambridge, 1984).

By choosing to cast their lot with their kinsmen, religious and community leaders have upheld their symbolic status as representatives of social continuity. The use of a religious idiom and of primordial networks of community solidarity suggests that the culture of resistance in Uttarakhand is simultaneously instrumental and symbolic. For if, as I have argued, scientific forestry represented a threat to the economic as well as cultural survival of the village communities, opposition to its workings has necessarily to invoke an alternative system of use *and* of meanings.[15]

AGAINST EUROCENTRICISM

> The blood of the villages is the cement by which the edifice of the cities is built.
>
> —Mahatma Gandhi

Reflecting on the century of social protest culminating in the Chipko andolan, what is especially striking from the perspective of the sociology of peasant protest is the persistence of conflicts over forest rights in India. The forest conflicts in Europe just described were representative of a particular historical epoch, when the rise of capitalism undermined the basis of subsistence agriculture. Bitter as these struggles were, they greatly diminished in scope and intensity with the maturing of the Industrial Revolution and the absorption of surplus workers in the cities or through emigration to the colonies. Simultaneously, the intensification of agriculture at home and the widening of the food production base through colonization greatly reduced the dependence of farming and stock-rearing on the forest. Subjected to commercial exploitation under sustained-yield silviculture, the forest has itself been transformed into an industrial enterprise run on capitalist lines. Of

[15] Although most accounts are silent on this score, the culture of peasant resistance to commercial forestry in Europe is likely to have invoked religious and cultural symbols in defence of the earlier system of forest use. A hint is provided by Linebaugh, who comments, apropos of German folklore, that 'the legends and stories of the forest testified to the fact that poor woodspeople and the peasants of the purlieus could find friends in the densest regions of the forest against the oppressions not only of princes and seigneurs, but also of their more recent enemies—the tax collector, the forest police, and the apostles of scientific forest management.' Linebaugh, 'Karl Marx', p. 13.

course, the forest continues to be an arena of conflict in Europe, as the labour force engaged in timber harvesting seeks to improve its wages and working conditions. The battle *for* the forest, however, between commercial forestry and the rural community, has, with the victory of industrial capitalism, been transformed into a battle *in* the forest. Although commercial forestry in India has created its own tensions between contractors and labourers, these conflicts pale into insignificance when compared with the continuing struggle between peasants and the state over control and use of the forest. The battle for the forest remains a very visible part of the social and ecological landscape. Thus the nature of social conflict in the transition to industrial capitalism in Europe differs greatly from the endemic conflict over forest rights in ex-colonial countries like India. B. H. Baden-Powell, one of the architects of Indian forest policy, had pointed to this distinction when he observed that in Europe, 'in a more advanced state of social life and occupation it has become more and more easy to alter an occupation that could not be continued if a forest right was taken away.'[16] The contrast with Europe holds good for peasant movements in general. Struggles over land and its produce continue to be very widespread in India, long after they have ceased to be significant in Europe.[17]

The continuing importance of peasant movements in the Third World challenges some of the basic assumptions of left-wing scholarship. In European historical writing, peasant movements are often treated as antiquarian, as pre-modern phenomena fated to disappear with the rise of modernity. As captured in the title of Eric Hobsbawm's classic work on the subject, these rebellions are 'primitive' and 'archaic', in effect against history.[18] This perspective on the historical significance of peasant movements makes a sharp distinction between spontaneous and 'organized' movements, viewing the latter as a *sine qua non* of the incorporation of the peasantry into the

[16] B. H. Baden-Powell, *Memorandum on Forest Settlements in India* (Calcutta, 1892), p. 5.

[17] See A. R. Desai (ed.), *Agrarian Struggles in India after Independence* (Delhi, 1986). For outstanding reportage on agrarian conflicts in India, see *Economic and Political Weekly* (EPW), Bombay, and *Frontier*, Calcutta.

[18] Eric Hobsbawm, *Primitive Rebels: Studies in Archaic Forms of Social Movements in the Nineteenth and Twentieth Centuries* (3rd edition, Manchester, 1974).

modern state and the march towards industrialization. A typical statement comes from the pen of a leading German scholar of the peasant war of 1525:

[A] peculiarity of traditional peasant movements in Europe is their general freedom from ideology. They were for the most part spontaneous movements with few informing ideas, characterized instead by concrete goals. Some historians have tried to raise the cry for the 'old law' to the level of a social idea, but such an expression is in reality not much more than a simple conservatism. Modern associational movements, however, do need an ideology, precisely because the actors do not interact personally and they do act over time. Of course, traditional types of movements take place constantly in modernizing societies. In such cases the peasant remains acted upon; the dynamic element is external to him. A modern movement makes the peasant part of the process of change as he expresses his demand for participation in the polity. In this transformation, however, he probably determines his own disappearance *qua* peasant.[19]

The thrust of this work has been towards challenging such simple-minded contrasts between unorganized, non-ideological, 'spontaneous' peasant protests on the one hand, and organized, ideological, 'modern' movements on the other. It is time to challenge, too, the theory of history that underlies the structural–organizational paradigm for the study of lower-class resistance. As the latter part of Sabean's statement makes evident, this paradigm confidently predicts the disappearance of the peasant from the modern world. Basing itself on what is arguably a narrow reading of European history, it further attempts to extend the lessons of that experience to the non-European world. It is imbued with a view of history in which the victory of capitalism, by allegedly preparing the way for industrial socialism, marks a major step in the march of human progress. The disappearance of the peasant, as a class that looks backwards rather than forward, is then accepted as axiomatic; its loss is indeed a precondition for the making of the modern world.

There is, however, another tradition of left-wing scholarship, one that is notably sensitive to peasant culture and ideology. Unburdened with a pejorative view of the peasantry but shar-

[19] David Sabean, 'The Communal Basis of Pre-1800 Peasant Uprisings in Western Europe', *Comparative Politics*, vol. 8, no. 3, 1976, p. 364.

ing nonetheless a teleological view of history based on the European experience, Barrington Moore could write:

The chief social basis of radicalism [in the early modern world] has been the peasants and the smaller artisans in the towns. From these facts one may conclude that the wellsprings of human freedom lie not only where Marx saw them, in the aspirations of classes about to take power, but perhaps even more in the dying wail of a class over whom the wave of progress is about to roll.[20]

In much of the Third World the 'wave of progress' has not yet rolled over the peasantry. In the incompleteness of this transition some scholars see a glimmer of hope. Concluding his fine study of Adivasi movements in western India David Hardiman writes: 'As yet, full fledged capitalism represents in these regions only a possibility, not an achievement. The adivasis' values have deeper roots with a resilience which provides us with at least some source of hope.'[21] In much the same vein, James Scott comments on the resistance to mechanization in rural Malaysia: 'The delaying of the complete transition to capitalist relations of production is in itself an important and humane accomplishment. It is often the only accomplishment within reach of a beleaguered peasantry.'[22]

This defence of traditional peasant values is of course based on a radically different interpretation of capitalism as a world historical process. Unlike in the paradigm case of Europe, in the Third World capitalism has been imposed from without, accelerating, even if not originating out of, the consolidation of the European imperium. Conceived by Europeans as essentially an extractive process, colonial capitalism greatly altered agrarian structure through the imposition of new taxes,

[20] Barrington Moore, Jr, *Social Origins of Dictatorship and Democracy* (Harmondsworth, 1966), p. 505.

[21] David Hardiman, *The Coming of the Devi: Adivasi Assertion in Western India* (Delhi, 1987), p. 217. In his last days, Marx himself seems to have gone back on one of his most cherished beliefs—namely the inevitably 'progressive' nature of capitalism. Through his correspondence with Russian revolutionaries who invoked the *mir* as an example of rural solidarity, Marx concluded that non-industrial societies could use their traditions of collective organization as a vehicle for a direct transition to socialism, bypassing capitalism. See Teodor Shanin (ed.), *Late Marx and the Russian Road* (London, 1983).

[22] J. C. Scott, *Weapons of the Weak: Everyday Forms of Peasant Resistance* (New Haven, 1986), p. 235.

landholding patterns and cash farming. More recently, the policies of post-colonial regimes have followed one of two paths. Where they are weak they have continued to exploit the predatory nature of colonial capitalism, which has now assumed grotesque and brutal forms unheard of in its original European home. Where they are strong they have embarked upon an ambitious programme of planned economic development, attempting to achieve in decades what it took the West centuries to accomplish. In this strategy small and landless peasants, and women and tribal minorities, are expected to bear the brunt of the forced march to industrialization. In either case post-colonial policies have continued to undermine the social, economic and ecological basis of peasant agriculture, without replacing it with a more viable or prosperous system of production. The familiar ills of Third World societies—land hunger, food scarcity, disease, urban decay, rising crime rates, civil strife and warfare—all testify to the cumulative impact of this process. In the ex-colonial world the ship of capitalism has finally run aground.

Third World capitalism, then, is a gross caricature of European capitalism, reproducing and intensifying its worst features without holding out the promise of a better tomorrow. Not surprisingly, scholars have seen in peasant resistance to its expansion a cause for celebration. There is another reason, barely hinted at even by writers as sympathetic as Scott and Hardiman, to see in such resistance 'the wellsprings of human freedom'. For if the transition to both industrialism and capitalism must necessarily remain incomplete in most of the Third World, the primary reason for this is *ecological.* The European miracle of successful industrialization was born out of a unique set of circumstances. The naïveté of both socialist and capitalist regimes notwithstanding, it is impossible to replicate that experience through the rest of the globe. Prior to the advent of colonialism most Third World societies consisted of a mosaic of long settled and sophisticated agrarian cultures which had a finely tuned but delicately balanced relationship with their natural environment. Colonial and post-colonial capitalism has disrupted this relationship in many ways. While the social consequences of this disruption are widely documented, what is less often observed are the devastating ecological consequences. In the absence of a 'frontier' such as was available to European colonists, even state-planned industrialization has to contend with a limited resource base and rapid environmental degradation. In most countries, and certainly in India, progress as conceived of in the energy-intensive, capital-intensive, western industrial model has already begun to meet with diminishing returns. Urban and industrial development, while not even successful on its own terms, has wreaked tremendous havoc on the countryside, pauperizing millions of people in the agrarian sector and diminishing the stock of plant, water and soil resources at a terrifying rate.[23]

From an ecological perspective, therefore, peasant movements like Chipko are not merely a defence of the little community and its values, but also an affirmation of a way of life more harmoniously adjusted with natural processes. At one level they are defensive, seeking to escape the tentacles of the commercial economy and the centralizing state; at yet another level they are assertive, actively challenging the ruling-class vision of a homogenizing urban–industrial culture. It is this fusion of what I have termed the 'private' (peasant movement) and 'public' (ecological movement) profiles that has lent to Chipko a distinctive quality and strength.[24] Far from being the dying wail of a class about to drop down the trapdoor of history, the call of Chipko represents one of the most innovative responses to the ecological and cultural crisis of modern society. It is a message we may neglect only at our own peril.

[23] For a fine documentation and analysis of environmental degradation in India, see Agarwal and Narain, *India: The State of the Environment 1984–85*. Cf. also Ramachandra Guha, 'Ecological Roots of Development Crisis', EPW, 12 April 1986.

[24] Within Western (especially American) environmentalism, there is, by contrast, a marked disjunction between intellectual prophets of doom, who point unerringly to the earth's inability to sustain infinite economic expansion, and popular environmentalism, which views nature primarily in aesthetic terms as a good to be 'consumed'. For the former, see, for example, the famous Club of Rome study—Donnella Meadows, *et al.*, *The Limits to Growth* (New York, 1971); for the latter, Samuel Hays, *Beauty, Health and Permanence: Environmental Politics in the United States, 1955–85* (New York, 1987).

EPILOGUE

The Afterlives of Chipko

APPROPRIATIONS AND ASSIMILATIONS

Social movements have a prehistory, and also an afterlife. Many popular struggles are kept alive long after they become inactive, their memory and myth continuing to inspire later generations. As a movement of the Himalayan peasantry against commercial forestry, Chipko was active from 1973 to 1981. Thereafter, it has faded away in the hills, but its echoes and resonances can still be picked up in places far distant from its original home.

The Unquiet Woods was first published in 1989. The research had commenced in the summer of 1981, coinciding with the movement's formal demise. Taking Chipko as its point of departure, the book filled in the historical context, narrating the stories of prior protests that were largely forgotten within the hills and completely unknown outside them. It sought also to provide a reasonably complete account of the development of the Chipko Andolan itself. One hoped thus to rescue Chipko from the master narratives of feminism, Gandhism, and environmentalism, and to firmly place it within the social history of Uttarakhand.

But the Chipko movement was simply too evocative and too glamorous to be contained by fact or history. Especially outside Uttarakhand, it is a case of 'every man his own Chipko', and quite often every woman too. People in general, and environmentalists in particular, have put their own interpretations on the movement, regardless of whether these interpretations can bear up to historical truth or scholarly scrutiny. The Chipko Andolan remains possibly the best-known and certainly the most widely misrepresented ecological movement in the world.

This epilogue deals with aspects of Chipko's 'post-history'. Let me begin with an invocation from London, made by Survival International, an organization that campaigns for the rights of indigenous people. In a booklet issued to commemorate its silver jubilee, Survival International printed a 'Dateline' of the milestones in the past twenty-five years. One entry reads as follows:

> 1972: India: tribal women in the Himalayas revive the ancient custom of hugging trees to protect them from the axe. This movement, known as 'Chipko', inspires similar protests around the world.[1]

How many errors can one make in a single sentence? The year the movement began was 1973, not 1972; Chipko's pioneers were caste Hindu men, not tribal women; their method was innovated on the spot rather than being a harking back to an 'ancient custom' (nor, it must be said, did they actually hug the trees).

Move on now, from the campaigners for cultural survival to a philosopher in the academy. 'Ecofeminism', writes Karen Warren,

> builds on the multiple perspectives of those whose perspectives are typically omitted or undervalued in dominant discourses, for example Chipko women, in developing a global perspective on the role of male domination in the exploitation of women and nature.[2]

The problems here are interpretive rather than narrowly factual. What is glossed over in this wish to build a global theory of ecofeminism are the deeply local roots of Chipko, the role played by men in the movement, sometimes with women, sometimes without them.

Consider, finally, this use of Chipko by Western environmentalists seeking to save a Malaysian forest:

> On the morning of July 5, 1991, a group of eight individuals from the US, UK, Germany, and Australia–most of whom had never met each other until just a few days before–walked onto the grounds of a timber camp at the mouth of the Baram River in Sarawak, East Malaysia, climbed up the booms of several barges, and chained themselves there. They hung banners from their perches and ignored the entreaties of officials who asked them to come down. After some eight hours they were brought down by police and arrested. To the great frustration of authorities, they gave their names as *Chipko Mendes Penan*, *Stop the*

[1] See *Survival*, newsletter of Survival International, no. 33, 1994.

[2] Karen Warren, quoted in Carolyn Merchant, *Radical Ecology: The Search for a Livable World* (New York, 1992), p. 185.

Logging, *Save the Forests*, and so forth. When subsequently their identities were established, they were tried and most were sentenced to 60 days in prison. They were there to protest the destruction of Sarawak's forests by timber companies, and the effects of that destruction on a small group of hunter-gatherers, the Penan.[3]

Chipko is here clubbed with the struggle of Brazilian rubber-tappers (led by the late Chico Mendes), these two unrelated movements drawn in to service a campaign in a third place still, among the Penan of Sarawak. One sees here, more clearly even than in the claims of Survival International or Karen Warren, how for Western environmentalists the historical specifics of Chipko are largely irrelevant. Disenchanted with the mores and values of the society they live in, they take Chipko (and Chico, and the Penan) to be signs of a hopeful alternative. To locate this generalized and abstracted love for a social movement that took place thousands of miles away, one needs to go back to a famous essay by the California historian Lynn White, which argued that the roots of the ecological crisis lay in the Judeo-Christian ethos and its insistence that man must dominate nature. White further suggested that the roots of an ethic of respect for nature lay in Eastern religions.[4] In the Chipko Andolan the alienated Westerner has at last found the alternative. The message s/he takes from this movement is simple: Good Hindu women protect and revere nature, just as surely as bad Christian men destroy and devastate it. More generally, 'primal' and 'indigenous' people (Amazonians, Himalayans, the Penan) are praised as protectors of nature, while 'modern' and 'industrial' people (with whom the Chipko admirers are, unfortunately, compelled to live) are condemned for destroying the environment.[5]

[3] J. Peter Brosius, 'Arresting Images: Post-Colonial Encounters with Environmentalism in Sarawak, East Malaysia' (Manuscript, Department of Anthropology, University of Georgia, 1996). I am grateful to Professor Brosius for allowing me to quote from this paper.

[4] Lynn White Jr., 'The Historical Roots of Our Ecologic Crisis' (1967), reprinted in Robin Clarke (ed.), *Notes for the Future* (London, 1975).

[5] Although grossly vulgarized, this reading of Chipko can be traced, at one remove or more, to Sunderlal Bahuguna. Especially in the West, where he frequently travels and lectures, his is the name most readily identified with the movement. In any case his cultural-religious 'spin' on Chipko resonates more easily with foreign audiences than Chandi Prasad Bhatt's more materialist in-

Though disregard of the truth can be irritating, the attractions of a certain reading of Chipko in the West do not come as a surprise. Indian environmentalists also tend to be worshipful of Chipko, if slightly better informed of the facts. For them Chipko fulfills the function of a myth of origin. This is where their movement began. Before Chipko, political and popular discourse was dominated by the ideology of a resource-intensive, socially disruptive, and environmentally destructive pattern of development. After Chipko, opposition to this model crystallized. It became possible to talk of alternative ways of relating to the poor and to nature. The baton has now passed to the movement against the Narmada dam, which has been for some time the most influential environmental campaign in the country. But Chipko shall always occupy a distinctive place as the originator of environmental concern in contemporary India.[6]

A good—or bad, depending on one's worldview—place to look for representations (and misrepresentations) of Chipko is of course the world wide web. Type 'Chipko Andolan' into Google and you are directed very quickly to an entry in an 'environmental encyclopaedia' prepared by William P. Cunningham and Jeffrey Muhr. This begins by locating—or mislocating—this autonomous, materialist, peasant movement in traditions of Hindu and Gandhian pacifism and spiritualism.[7] (The writers are Western men—had they been Western women perhaps the feminist motif would have been more dominant.)

Also on the web, the Wikipedia entry (probably written by a combination of Western and Indian hands) is quite long and mostly accurate. (Full disclosure: *The Unquiet Woods* is cited as one of the sources consulted.) One bit of myth-making it indulges, though, is the claim that while 'the modern Chipko movement started in the early 1970s in the Garhwal Himalayas of Uttarakhand . . . the first recorded event of Chipko, however, took place in village Khejarli, Jodhpur district, in 1730 AD when 363 Bishnois, led by

terpretation. The bias is made more pronounced because Bhatt travels little outside Uttarakhand and, unlike Bahuguna, does not speak English.

[6] See, as one example among many, the homage to Chipko in the dedication and text of Anil Agarwal and Sunita Narain (eds), *India: The State of the Environment 1984–5: The Second Citizens' Report* (New Delhi, 1985).

[7] http://findarticles.com/p/articles/mi_km4449/is_200510/ai_n16261396/ (accessed 10 June 2009).

Amrita Devi sacrificed their lives while protecting Khejri trees, considered sacred by the community, by hugging them, and braved the axes of loggers sent by the local ruler . . . [This] is today seen as an inspiration and a precursor for the Chipko movement of Garhwal.'[8]

The precision of those dates and numbers notwithstanding, there are no independent sources to confirm that this tale is true. The story first began to feature in the environmental discourse only in the late 1980s, well after Chipko had begun, indeed somewhat after the activist phase of Chipko had run its course.

The origins of this postmodern myth are as follows. In 1980 the anthropologist Kailash Malhotra and the ecologist Madhav Gadgil were doing fieldwork in Rajasthan. They interviewed a group of Bishnois, who told them a legend about their forbears, which had them being killed by soldiers while seeking to protect Khejri trees. The legend, in this telling, had no dates, no numbers, and no invocation of tree-hugging. It was retold by Malhotra and Gadgil in a newspaper article, which happened to be read by Sunderlal Bahuguna. The story appealed immensely to Bahuguna, in part because of its romantic and spiritual underpinnings. At the time, there was a biter dispute in certain circles as to who was the 'real' leader of Chipko—whether it was Chandi Prasad Bhatt, who had organized the first Chipko protests in 1973 and 1974, or Bahuguna, who was the acknowledged father of the Gandhian movement in Uttarakhand. The Bishnoi legend was a way out of this controversy—it placed Chipko in a very distant past, centuries before either leader was born.[9]

One expects greens in New Delhi or San Francisco to go to town on Chipko. More startling is the praise for the movement expressed by its historic enemies. In 1995 I attended a national workshop on 'Joint Forest Management' in New Delhi. In his inaugural address the Inspector General of Forests—the most powerful forestry official in the country—spoke generously of the contribution of the Chipko movement towards the growing concern with the fate of India's forests. 'Women are the real conservators', he said, 'they are the embodiment of service and sacrifice.' To take forward the programmes of joint forest

[8] http://en.wikipedia.org/wiki/Chipko_movement (accessed 10 June 2009).

[9] This paragraph is based on conversations with Madhav Gadgil and Shekhar Pathak.

management, one needed to marry 'ancient wisdom and modern ecological knowledge'.[10]

In the last decade, forest policy in India has taken a decided turn away from the past. There is, on the one side, a greater appreciation of the value of species diversity–no longer are monocultures of commercially valued trees assiduously promoted. On the other side, the pressures of popular movements have forced the state to move, at least on paper, towards a more decentralized and participatory form of management. In this ecological and social reorientation of forest policy the heritage of Chipko has played more than a walk-on part. Its own criticisms of commercial forestry and authoritarian forest officials have become the conventional wisdom, accepted not just by activists elsewhere in India but also by bureaucrats and donor agencies.[11]

Possibly the most innovative recent initiative in the forest sector is the programme of Joint Forest Management, or JFM. In different parts of India, the Forest Department has signed agreements with individual village councils, making them the chief beneficiaries of forest working and consulting them in management decisions. There are now tens of thousands of village forest committees, helping take care of land previously guarded strictly by the state. This turnaround is a product not so much of rethinking within the forest bureaucracy as of continuing social conflict between communities and the state. That is to say, the concessions to local use and village right have not been granted from above but wrested from below.[12]

The demands now codified in the JFM policies were made implicitly by numerous Himalayan struggles, and explicitly in representations made to the Kumaun Forest Grievances Committee of

[10] Address by M.A. Ahmed, National JFM Workshop organized by the Society for Promotion of Wastelands Development, New Delhi, 29 November 1995.

[11] Cf. Madhav Gadgil and Ramachandra Guha, *Ecology and Equity: The Use and Abuse of Nature in Contemporary India* (London, 1995), Chapters III and VII.

[12] Cf. Mark Poffenberger and Betsy McGean (eds), *Village Voices, Forest Choices: Joint Forest Management in India* (New Delhi, 1996); Sarah Jewitt and Stuart Corbridge, 'From Forest Struggles to Forest Citizens? Joint Forest Management in the Unquiet Woods of India's Jharkhand', *Environment and Planning*, vol. 29, no. 12 (1997).

1921 (cf. pp. 120–1, above). These demands were, of course, made most forcefully and repeatedly by the Chipko Andolan itself. It is therefore a curious irony that the state of Uttar Pradesh lags far behind other parts of India in the spread of JFM. In states such as West Bengal the Forest Department has genuinely taken aboard the message of 'participatory management'. By contrast, UP forest officials have, with only the odd exception, continued to prefer the old-fashioned methods of policing and exclusion. The principal reason for this divergence lies perhaps in administrative history, in the continuation in northern India of older, more feudalistic styles of governance.

After those protests of 1921, the colonial state did mandate the formation of *van panchayats* (village forest councils) in parts of Kumaun and British Garhwal. Alhough small in extent, these village forests have been in operation now for seventy years. Citing studies from the 1960s (see pp. 148–50 above), I had suggested that these forests were in as good—or as bad—a shape as forests controlled by the Forest Department. This conclusion has been confirmed by a recent study based on satellite imagery of the forests of Uttarakhand. Using sophisticated statistical techniques, the study demonstrates that so far as crown cover is concerned, there is no noticeable difference between state forests and village forests—one is as dense, or as degraded, as the other. At the same time, state forests are seven times as expensive to manage as village forests—largely because of the burden of salaries to an overstaffed bureaucracy. The authors thus conclude that 'substantial savings could be realized by decentralizing [forest] management' in the Himalaya. Their findings further suggest that 'decentralization deserves wider attention in conservation strategies in developing countries with limited financial resources.'[13]

Ironically, the trend of forest policy in Uttarakhand has been exactly the reverse—namely, to strengthen the control of the state. No new areas have been allocated for decentralized management; at the same time, fresh curbs have been placed on the autonomous functioning of the van panchayats that already exist. Although technically under the control of the villagers, the Forest

[13] E. Somanathan, R. Prabhakar, and Bhupendra Singh Mehta, 'Decentralization for Cost-effective Conservation', *Proceedings of the National Academy of Sciences*, vol. 106, no. 11, 2009, pp. 4143–7.

Department can veto schemes for improvement, while of the revenue generated 40 per cent is swallowed by the state exchequer. And 40 per cent of the rest is by law granted to the village, but this money too first finds its way into a 'consolidated fund' controlled by the District Magistrate, to which individual panchayats have then to apply.[14] There are signs of an emerging movement to do away with these constricting rules. A chronicler of this discontent writes that 'those who know the history of forest struggles say that after Chipko the van panchayat andolan will be the biggest such movement in the hills.'[15] To Khas Patti (1906), Bageshwar (1921), Rawain (1930), Totashiling (1942), Mandal (1973), Reni (1974), and Badyargarh (1979) might yet be added other milestones in the history of forest movements in Uttarakhand.

HISTORY ENDS, HISTORY CONTINUES

There is a clever remark, attributed to John F. Kennedy, that 'success has many fathers but defeat is an orphan.' This is at best a half-truth. Success, especially runaway success, certainly attracts snipers and detractors.

A massive prick in the Chipko bubble came in the form of a cover story in the New Delhi fortnightly *Down to Earth.* The magazine's editor Anil Agarwal—one of the world's most highly regarded environmentalists—had often emphasized his own debt to Chipko.[16] On the movement's twentieth anniversary, in April 1993, he dispatched a reporter to Uttarakhand to find out what remained. The question that the magazine posed was: 'Chipko influenced the world, but have its local objectives been met?' The answer was an unequivocal 'no'. The reporter found former participants bitter about the consequences of Chipko. They had fought for their livelihood, but the portrayal and acceptance of the Andolan as pre-eminently an 'environmentalist' movement had seriously backfired. In Uttarakhand the 'state used the

[14] Cf. E. Somanathan, 'Deforestation, Incentives and Property Rights in Central Himalaya', *Economic and Political Weekly*, 26 January 1991.

[15] Jai Prakash Pawar, 'Chipko ki Parampara Mein ab Van Panchayatain Janta ko Andolit kar Rahi Hain', *Naini Tal Samachar*, 1 September 1994 (my translation).

[16] Cf. Anil Agarwal, 'An Indian Environmentalist's Credo' (1985), reprinted in Ramachandra Guha (ed.), *Social Ecology* (New Delhi, 1994).

environmental concern that was first enunciated in the country by Chipko to centralize forest management, instead of decentralizing.' Under the Forest Conservation Act of 1980, numerous development projects–schools, bridges, roads, hospitals–had been stalled. If these projects required even a tiny plot of land legally designated as 'forest', and even if this land actually had no trees within it, the central government had to be petitioned for clearance, leading to unconscionable delays. The state's new-found enthusiasm for 'conservation' had led also to the constituton of new 'national parks' where the traditional activities of grazing and fuel and herb collection were prohibited.

Down to Earth also criticized the later work of the two major Chipko leaders. Other observers had praised Chandi Prasad Bhatt and his Dashauli Gram Swarajya Mandal for their afforestation drives, with their creative release of the energies of women. In villages around Gopeshwar, the DGSM has successfully mobilized women in the protection and plantation of forests, encouraging them also to take control of the village panchayats.[17] But *Down to Earth* suggested that by taking grants for this work Bhatt had 'governmentalized' Chipko. Bahuguna, meanwhile, was chastized for having '"internationalized" Chipko by putting it at the service of the world conservation community.'[18]

Six months later, another funeral oration was printed in the pages of the Kathmandu periodical *Himal*, also a respected voice in subcontinental journalism. Chipko, it complained, might thrive elsewhere but it was dead and buried in Uttarakhand. The movement 'has migrated from the hills of its origins to seminars and conferences further south and overseas. It lives in university courses, academic tomes and in articles like this one, which keep the controversy, but not the issues alive.' Once again, the torchlight was made to shine fiercely on the icons of Chipko. 'Bhatt's DGSM', wrote *Himal*'s woman on the spot, 'is now a more passive NGO than a grassroots initiative taking organization.' If 'Bhatt's organization is but a ghost of Chipko', Bahuguna too 'seems today a holdover from a more involved past.' In a sharp reference

[17] See Mukul, 'Villages of Chipko Movement', *Economic and Political Weekly*, 10 April 1993.

[18] Amit Mitra, 'Chipko: An Unfinished Mission', *Down to Earth*, 30 April 1993.

to Bahuguna's solitary fasts against the Tehri hydroelectric project, the journalist wrote that 'one cannot help feeling that without the dam he would be a man without a cause, a following, and an audience.' The scepticism was reinforced by a photograph of Bahuguna posing for the Smithsonian's magazine, hugging a pipal tree. The verdict, overall, was harsh and unforgiving: 'Chipko as a definable movement got wound up too quickly, its energies sapped by excessive adulation. While study of the movement has become *de rigeur* in universities in India and abroad, within Uttarakhand itself Chipko is spoken of in the past tense.'[19]

In some circles in India and abroad, the story of Chipko is told principally as '*our* story', the narrative of the coming of age of a dissident tradition, namely, environmentalism. Within the movement, however, there has long been a tussle for control over the history of Chipko. Chandi Prasad Bhatt and his supporters claim that he should be seen as the principal figure for having founded the Andolan. Sunderlal Bahuguna's camp claim, to the contrary, that only he made Chipko a properly 'environmentalist' movement.[20] The attempt in each case is to construct the story as '*My* Story', or more accurately perhaps as '*Not*-His story'. A further complication is provided by the ecofeminists, who seek to diminish the role of both Bhatt and Bahuguna, and of Chipko men in general. Here, if a story is to be told, it is emphatically of the Chipko Andolan as 'Her Story'.

Our Story, My Story, Her Story. It was left to *Down to Earth* and *Himal* to impartially but comprehensively rubbish these competing narratives of Chipko. It seems the story was that were was *no* story. The movement was dead, finished. The participants of Chipko had themselves put a final full stop to it. It remained only for the scribes to write a epitaph to the End of History.

My own view is that both magazines were insufficiently appreciative of what it takes to start and build a social movement. Indeed, before they came to Chipko, both Bhatt and Bahuguna had spent years in the service of their people. From social workers they became, for a while, leaders of a popular struggle. After

[19] Manisha Aryal, 'Axing Chipko', *Himal*, January–February 1994.

[20] See, respectively, Anupam Mishra and Satyendra Tripathi, *Chipko Movement* (New Delhi, 1978); Bharat Dogra, *Forests and People* (Rishikesh, 1980); also the exchange cited in the preface to the first edition of this book.

some years of intense activity the movement exhausted itself–as movements do. When Chipko ended, Bhatt and Bahuguna had already entered late middle age. But they did not renounce the world, or take *sannyas* as a tired Hindu would. Bhatt has encouraged villagers to take care of their forests, and also written perceptively on the larger ecological problems of the region.[21] Bahuguna has risked his life in three long fasts against the Tehri dam project.[22]

Instead of respecting Bhatt and Bahuguna for what they have done, the journalists complain that they haven't done enough. 'Bahuguna's public relations ability and international appeal and Bhatt's organizing ability, put together', comments *Himal*, 'might have taken the people of Uttarakhand further than where they are today.' *Down to Earth* writes that 'a movement that could have given the world its most powerful green party with village self–governance at its heart, fell apart.'[23] The lack of sympathy is manifest and unfortunate. This is a classic case of the projection of the hopes of the middle-class intellectual onto the 'people'. The intellectual seeks total, systemic change, but the task of bringing this about is always left to others, in this case Bhatt, Bahuguna, and the like. Such agents do mobilize mass energies and, for a time, bring about significant social change. But the journalist-intellectual chooses only to remember what they have not done.

History has ended for some analysts of Chipko, but history continues for the people of Uttarakhand. The summer after the latter of these two stories was printed, the hills were set alight by a massive popular upsurge. In a region not unfamiliar with social movements, the struggle for a separate state of Uttarakhand was unprecedented in its scope, spread, and scale of participation. In July and August 1994 there was a series of strikes, lockouts, processions, and demonstrations. These were held in all eight districts of Uttarakhand, in all of its towns, and many of its villages too. The unity and sense of solidarity were noteworthy.

[21] Cf. Chandi Prasad Bhatt, 'Uttarakhand Mein Bade Jalashyon va Vidyut Pariyojanaon ka Bhavishya', *Pahad I* (Nainital, 1983), revised and translated as *The Future of Large Projects in the Himalaya* (Nainital, 1992).

[22] See Praveen Swami, 'Blundering Progress: The Tehri Project and Growing Fears', *Frontline*, 30 June 1995.

[23] Aryal, op. cit., p. 19; Mitra, op. cit., p. 36.

In both Nainital, towards the eastern end of the region, and Mussoorie, towards the western end, public meetings were held daily, where news of the struggle in other parts was collated and conveyed. As one local newspaper commented, this was 'an expression of popular sentiment such has never been seen or heard of before.'[24] Or, as a more dispassionate observer remarked, 'no movement in contemporary Indian politics has been able to muster so much popular support, and that too in such a short timespan, as the movement for a separate hill state of Uttarakhand in Uttar Pradesh.'[25] The authorities were worried enough to send seventy battalions of the Central Reserve Police to keep the 'peace'.[26]

The demand for a separate hill province was first clearly enunciated at a public meeting in Haldwani in 1946. The prime mover was our old friend Badridutt Pande, 'Kumaun Kesari', the leader of the *begar* and forest movements of 1921.[27] It was argued that the hills were distinct from the rest of Uttar Pradesh—distinct geographically, socially, culturally, economically, and linguistically. The argument continued to be made over the years, as the costs of being part of UP became more apparent. It seemed clear that Uttarakhand remained poor largely because its natural resources—forests, water, minerals, herbs—were diverted for use elsewhere. By some calculations, this expropriation of resources was ten times more than the budgetary allocation for the region made by the central and state governments.

Over the years, as the resentment built up, the Uttarakhand demand took organizational shape. Various forums and fronts were floated to take it forward: one such, the Uttarakhand Yuva Morcha, organized a padayatra from Badrinath to New Delhi in 1978. The Uttarakhand Kranti Dal (UKD) was formed in the following year. The UKD set up successful candidates in the legislative elections of 1980 and 1985. On 23 November 1987 it led a

[24] In the more expressive Hindi: '*Ek aisa jan ubhaar jaisa na kabhi dekha, na kabhi suna.*' 'Andolith Uttarakhand', *Nainital Samachar*, 1 September 1994.

[25] Pradeep Kumar, 'Uttarakhand Movement: Areas of Peripheral Support', *Mainstream*, 9 August 1997.

[26] A good account of the protests in July–August 1994 is provided by Jagdish Chandra Bhatt, in his reports printed in the Delhi edition of the *Times of India*.

[27] This and the subsequent paragraph are largely based on the information contained in Govind Pant (ed.), *Aaj ka Uttarakhand, Kal ka Uttarakhand Rajya?* (special number of *Nainital Samachar*, August 1989).

large procession in Delhi, culminating in a petition offered to the President of India. Critical support for such activities was provided by the *prabasi*, the migrant from the hills working in the cities and towns of the plains.

The upsurge of 1994 was, however, of a different order of magnitude. It was sparked by the decision of the Uttar Pradesh government to extend its new reservation policy to the hills. This mandated that 27 per cent of all government jobs and, in time, of all seats in state-funded colleges would be reserved for candidates belonging to the 'Other Backward Classes', or OBCs. Now the social structure of Uttarakhand (cf. Chapter 2) is polarized between Bith and Dom, between high-caste Brahmins and Rajputs on the one side and the so-called Scheduled (or 'untouchable') castes on the other. The OBCs constitute less than 2 per cent of the population of the hills. Thus the implementation of the new policy would lead inevitably to an inflow of outsiders from the plains, to take up jobs in a region already marked by scarce employment opportunities.

The Uttarakhand movement is an illustration of 'nonseccessionist regionalism'.[28] Like the Jharkhand movement, but unlike the Kashmir insurgency, it did not wish to secede from the Indian union. Its demand, rather, was for a separate province, to be hived off from the larger province of which it was presently part. Both leaders and supporters took inspiration from the ecologically comparable state of Himachal Pradesh. Himachal was given separate status in 1972: till then it had formed part of Punjab, a state otherwise dominated by *maidani* (plains) economy and maidani culture. Since its separation Himachal has steadily progressed, economically as well as socially. Literacy rates have dramatically increased; public medical facilities are better than in most other states; fruit cultivation has generated much income for peasant households; and tourism is on the rise. The participants in the Uttarakhand movement likewise believed that a state of their own would allow them to more constructively use their natural bounty and generate revenue through pilgrim and nature tourism. Rule by their own politicians and administrators would, they

[28] The term is used in Emma Mawdsley, 'Nonseccessionist Regionalism in India: The Uttarakhand Separate State Movement', *Environment and Planning A*, vol. 29, no. 12 (1997).

also hoped, be more conducive to the provision of desperately needed social services such as health and education.

The geographer Emma Mawdsley has pointed to several areas of overlap between the Chipko and Uttarakhand movements. Both identified the problem in terms of exploitation, by external agencies, of the patrimony of the hills. Both criticized an imported culture of administration that has, over the decades, facilitated this exploitation. Both saw the solution as, broadly, local control over natural and political resources. One important point of divergence was the attitude towards the state. Past movements, including Chipko, had defined themselves in opposition to the state. The Uttarakhand struggle, however, sought not to reject the state but to capture it.[29]

Which it eventually did. After the mass protests of 1994, the political elite of Uttar Pradesh decided it would be better off without the turbulent hill districts. The UP assembly thus passed a resolution mandating the creation of a new state of Uttarakhand. This resolution had then to be drafted into law, and approved by the union parliament, a process that took all of five years. At last, in November 2000, the hill state that Badridutt Pande and many others had fought for came into being. However, its birth was attended by two misfortunes. One was symbolic, namely, that the state had been named 'Uttaranchal' rather than Uttarakhand, apparently because the Bharatiya Janata Party, then in power in New Delhi, thought this a more traditional name. The other was substantive, the fact that the capital was located at Dehradun, a large town at one extreme of the state and in the lowlands, unsuited geographically and otherwise to represent a province meant for highlanders discriminated against and living in interior villages.

Those who had left and staffed the popular movement for a new state protested against both these developments. In 2007 the name of the state was officially changed to Uttarakhand. But the demand to relocate the capital to the inner hills, ideally to Gairsain, a village on the Kumaun–Garhwal border, has been rejected out of hand. The politicians and bureaucrats have become accustomed to Dehradun, which provides the comforts and seductions of city life and is only a few hours away by train from New Delhi.

[29] Emma Mawdsley, 'After Chipko: From Environment to Region in the Uttaranchal', *Journal of Peasant Studies*, vol. 24, no. 4 (1998), pp. 36–54.

Meanwhile, debates are also brewing about the form of economic and social development most appropriate to the state. The state government of Uttarakhand is keen to promote large hydel projects that would dam the rivers of the Himalaya and generate power and money (as well as substantial kickbacks for those who promote them). Critics point out, however, that large dams are unwise in this seismically active zone; besides, they would displace many villages and destroy rare natural habitats.[30] Chandi Prasad Bhatt, among others, has called for a form of resource use that is more sensitive to the ecological specificities of the Himalaya. He notes that the great Himalayan rivers are receding because of climate change. He urges that every village be asked to nurture its own forest, and that water management focus on promoting small, decentralized, run-of-the-river projects rather than massive dams. The 'fundamental thinking process for Himalayan development', says this Chipko pioneer, 'must be conservation of water, soil and plant resources and their sustainable development.' This reorientation of approach is vital for India as much as for Uttarakhand, since the Himalaya, as 'a source of water, soil and vegetation, is also a controller of [the] nation's weather. Its rivers provide [the] foundation of prosperity for the plains. Himalayan conservation must, therefore, be considered as central to [the] nation's planning process.' In this framework, the state and citizen must be equal partners, for, as Bhatt writes, 'our experience is that people should be involved in all natural resource conservation programmes.'[31]

The creation of a new province in the hills might be seen perhaps as the logical culmination of a century of popular struggle against forms of rule and types of rulers inimical to the autonomous social development of the hills. That conclusion may not be inaccurate, but it is certainly safe to say that the formation of Uttarakhand will not lead to the end of social protest. If the new state merely repeats the politics of capitalism and cronyism, or if it continues the rapacious and shortsighted exploitation of nature, then it will not be welcomed. For the administration of

[30] See Dunu Roy, 'Hydropower in Uttarakhand: Is "Development" the Real Objective', *Economic and Political Weekly*, 11 October 2008.

[31] Chandi Prasad Bhatt, 'Himalaya's Enviromental Conservation, Upgradation and Development', text of Millennium Lecture to the Indian Society of Geometrics, Bhopal, 18 February 2008 (translated from the Hindi by P.C. Maithani).

Uttarakhand to continue the practice of previous governments is to encourage the revival of protest and struggle, to see the birth of new movements against what its participants perceive to be unjust and insensitive governance. Indeed, the history of peasant protests in Tehri Garhwal suggests that the expectations placed on 'indigenous' rulers can be higher still.

I must admit here to a vested interest in the creation of the new state of Uttarakhand. I support it for political reasons, as a critic of the excessive centralization of the Indian polity. But there is also a personal stake, for the Uttarakhand movement inadvertently—but emphatically—'proved' a major thesis of the present work, as this last vignette explains.

A leading part in the upsurge of the summer of 1994 was played by the students of Garhwal University, based in the old town of Srinagar, on the Alakananda. Students of both genders participated with equal fervour. The boys organized themselves as a 'Chandra Singh Garhwali dal', naming their group for the hero of the Peshawar mutiny of 1930, who later became something of a father confessor for activists in the Tehri peasant movement of the 1940s. The girls, for their part, called their group the 'Gaura Devi dal', invoking the memory of the Bhotiya from Reni who first brought women into the Chipko Andolan. Far more effectively than an academic work, the students of Garhwal had rescued their struggle from the dominating discourses of the outside world. Chipko was returned to where it originally belonged, put back in the social history of Uttarakhand, back in the history of social movements in Uttarakhand.

The Unquiet Woods and Indian Environmental History

Amita Baviskar

Looking back at the fields of environmental history and sociology in India over the last two decades, the debt that we owe to *The Unquiet Woods* becomes immediately apparent. Ramachandra Guha's monograph not only inaugurated these fields of enquiry, it continues to define their contours even today. Through *The Unquiet Woods*, and his numerous essays and biography of Verrier Elwin, as well as his work in collaboration with Madhav Gadgil and Joan Martinez-Alier, Guha offers a master narrative for understanding the shifts in social relations around forests which has been enormously influential and provocative. Whether scholars following in his wake have extended and refined his arguments or refuted them,[1] Guha's analysis has commanded our

[1] Guha's key contention that colonial forest policy was chiefly driven by the imperial quest for natural resources was challenged by Richard Grove who argued that ecological concerns were equally important. Grove's *Green Imperialism: Colonial Expansion, Tropical Island Edens and the Origins of Environmentalism, 1600–1860* (Cambridge: Cambridge University Press, 1995) described the stirrings of environmental anxiety among colonial officials dealing with drought; the divergence between his work and Guha's can be attributed to their focus on different scales, regions, and time periods. The tension between extraction and conservation was also the subject of Mahesh Rangarajan's *Fencing the Forest: Conservation and Ecological Change in India's Central Provinces, 1860–1914* (Delhi: Oxford University Press, 1996). Following this debate, other scholars further refined our understanding of colonial state policies regarding forests and pastures. Vasant Saberwal's *Pastoral Politics: Shepherds, Bureaucrats and Conservation in the Western Himalaya* (Delhi: Oxford University Press, 1999) showed internal dissension within the state on the question of agrarian expansion versus forest protection, laying to rest the notion that a singular imperial logic prevailed across South Asia for a century and more.

attention by defining the terms of engagement and the themes around forestry and the environment at large. However, reading *The Unquiet Woods* in 2009, twenty years after it was first published, allows us to do much more than simply read a classic monograph or trace the contours of disciplinary trajectories. Reading *The Unquiet Woods* today also gives us an opportunity to reflect on its contemporary relevance in a political and economic context that has changed profoundly since the 1980s. So I will first discuss how the fields of environmental history and sociology in India have been shaped and enriched by *The Unquiet Woods*, and then focus on the book's significance in contemporary India's cultural politics of environment and development.

As its subtitle says succinctly, *The Unquiet Woods* is about 'ecological change and peasant resistance in the Himalaya'. By 1989, when the book appeared, peasant resistance was a well-established area of sociological and historical interest. Ranajit Guha's *Elementary Aspects of Peasant Insurgency in Colonial India* had been published in 1983 and the Subaltern School had produced an

---

K. Sivaramakrishnan's outstanding work, *Modern Forests: Statemaking and Environmental Change in Colonial Eastern India* (Stanford: Stanford University Press, 1999), placed forestry on a larger canvas of cultural history, where governance demanded new forms of knowledge, bureaucratic devices for standardizing and ordering the obstinate substance of forests and fields, and the agrarian communities who depended on the land. Questions of science and modernity in colonial forestry first raised by Guha also figure in Kavita Philip's *Civilizing Natures: Race, Resources and Modernity in Colonial South India* (New Brunswick, NJ: Rutgers University Press, 2004) and S. Ravi Rajan's *Modernizing Nature: Forestry and Imperial Eco-development, 1800–1950* (Oxford: Clarendon Press, 2006). Essays dealing with similar issues in the contemporary period can be found in Vasant Saberwal and Mahesh Rangarajan, eds, *Battles over Nature: Science and the Politics of Conservation* (New Delhi: Permanent Black, 2003). Guha's attention to local perceptions of the colonial state and its impact on people and resources resonates through Ajay Skaria's *Hybrid Histories: Forests, Frontiers and Wildness in Western India* (New Delhi: Oxford University Press, 2001), an innovative study that used archival and oral sources (much like Guha did) to describe tribal understandings of their gradual political marginalization and economic impoverishment. The monographs mentioned here are just a sample of the writings on forestry that directly followed *The Unquiet Woods*, making it a shared point of reference from which to start and depart towards varying analytical concerns, concepts, and conclusions. Guha's continuing influence on the wider field of environmental history in South Asia is far greater than can be glimpsed in this brief sketch.

impressive body of work delineating history from below, as produced by peasants in places like Avadh, Gorakhpur, and Kheda in Gujarat. Like other Subaltern historians, Ramachandra Guha (no relation of Ranajit Guha) wrote about peasant resistance; unlike them, his focus was not agricultural land but the centrality of forests in such conflicts. A more radical departure was his treatment of forests as a resource, for Guha emphasized that forests were not abstract or inert objects of value but had their own specificities–mixed deciduous stands of oak and rhododendron were decidedly different from pine monocultures. Ecological changes like deforestation and road-building were of enormous consequence in changing the political economy of the hills.[2] Appreciating ecological specificity and change was critical for understanding place as a cultural artefact that provides a meaningful basis for social being and resistance. Guha's choice of place is also noteworthy. By focusing on the Garhwal and Kumaun hills–not on the Indo-Gangetic heartland or the Cauvery delta, or for that matter Bengal (the region that continues to claim hegemonic status in the social sciences as representing all of India if not the entire postcolonial world)–*The Unquiet Woods* drew attention to the 'marginal' areas of the country which sustain millions of people. The hills matter, not only to those who live there, but also to those who inhabit the plains watered by Himalayan rivers, and to those for whom the subcontinent's sacred geography would be unimaginable without the towering presence of Himalayan places.

Like other Subaltern histories, *The Unquiet Woods* too is eclectic in the provenance of its conceptual and empirical sources even as it works within a broadly Marxist analytical frame. It combines history with sociology and political science, empirical exactitudes with generalized abstractions. Yet–and here again it forged new ground–the book is not only concerned with providing a culturally- and ecologically-informed account of peasant resistance that illuminates insurgent consciousness in the past. It uses its historical canvas to frame a contemporary social movement–Chipko–and to delineate collective struggles around the environment in

[2] Elizabeth Whitcombe's study of the economic impact of ecological change in the Indo-Gangetic plains, *Agrarian Conditions in Northern India* (Berkeley: University of California Press, 1972) is perhaps the only previous historical work on India to have been as attentive to environment–society relations.

postcolonial India.[3] By bringing history to bear on present-day political questions, Guha far exceeds the mandate that the Subaltern School set for itself. By 1989 the story of Chipko and women hugging trees had captured imaginations across the world, thanks in part to its peripatetic spokesman Sundarlal Bahuguna. In 1982 the Centre for Science and Environment had published *The State of India's Environment: A Citizen's Report*, educating a generation of upper-class urban Indians into an environmental sensibility that went beyond a class-blind 'love for nature' by showing how 'red' and 'green' issues were inseparable. Into this emerging understanding of environmental politics Guha introduced the notion of moral economy, a historically grounded appreciation of the ties that create community in relation to the state and form the basis for collective action.

The move to moral economy not only allowed Guha to situate Chipko in line with a longer history of peasant struggles in the hills, it enabled him to highlight aspects that heralded the presence of an alternative politics which resisted dominant definitions of development and democracy. The Chipko movement offered a critique of knowledge and truth—of knowledge that claimed the authority of scientific expertise and truth that posed as common sense—forcing us to re-examine the seemingly self-evident verities of developmentalism. In its idioms of protest and ideology Chipko drew explicitly on a Gandhian social vision and political vocabulary, bringing a distinctively Indian tenor to its critique of development. In espousing an environmental ethic that challenged the ideology of industrial development and the class and regional inequalities that sustain it, Chipko embodied an engagement with European modernity without being defined or encompassed within its terms. By adopting the discipline of satyagraha and struggling for swaraj for ordinary Indians, Chipko (and later the Narmada anti-dam movement) revived the possibility of imagining alternative utopias based on agrarian self-sufficiency, ecological sustainability, and political self-governance. It is this notion for which Guha's account of the Chipko movement provides compelling

[3] A later work, also a superb monograph on forest politics in the past and present, and striking in its resemblance to *The Unquiet Woods* in terms of structure and method, is Nandini Sundar's *Subalterns and Sovereigns: An Anthropological History of Bastar, 1854–1996* (Delhi: Oxford University Press, 1997).

testimony: that, if one strives for it, another world is possible—a world more just, humane, and respectful of nature's limits. The power of this notion to inspire hope and the collective action to realize that hope cannot be overstated.

The distinctive attributes of Guha's work have left a lasting impression on studies in environmental history and sociology in India. Subsequent scholars have grappled with these elements, not always consistently or successfully. *The Unquiet Woods* emphasizes holism and interconnectedness, frequently trespassing across disciplinary boundaries, creating a productive hybridity that is an antidote to the compartmentalized approaches of the past. Second, it treats the environment not simply as a set of 'factors of production' but as a material *and* symbolic resource, sustaining livelihoods but also life in the larger sense, including a life of the imagination that strives to understand the mundane but also transcend it through individual and collective projects both secular and spiritual.

Third, it respects much more the notion of *ecological* as well as social limits to growth. For generations of Marxists brought up on technological optimism, social relations were the primary constraints on equality and prosperity, for the productive forces of industrialism created the potential of plenty for all. Later, for a post-materialist generation of scholars, especially those influenced by science studies and social constructivism, 'objective' ecological constraints were not relevant; what mattered was the discursive production of things. This focus on perceptions, on how authoritative versions of truth were produced, led to a form of pluralism that emphasized how nature was capable of being appropriated in an infinite variety of ways. Both the Marxist and post-materialist schemas failed to appreciate the biophysical properties of nature, all the elements one cannot get around—that the 'social construction of forests' cannot be independent of the specific properties of forests in particular locales. It is this respect for the biophysical, for ecological as much as social limits, that is the defining tenet of environmental history and sociology, even though we have not always done justice to it.

Fourth, Guha's approach encompasses the social relations that produce hegemonic forms of knowledge and the set of cultural practices through which inequality is reproduced. It offers a focused view of the operations of power, addressing squarely the question that Lenin asked so precisely: What is to be done? This is the question that recent studies have shied away from, preferring a more hands-off delineation of power as diffuse and immanent, a characterization that, perhaps inadvertently, lends itself to political quietism.

Quietism is a cop-out in these unquiet times and Guha's book needs to be read again to reflect on how contemporary political and economic shifts may be addressed by scholars of environmental history and sociology. It is a major paradox for our times that while peasant resistance is alive and growing, the peasantry as a subject of study is now entirely absent in the academy. 'The peasant question', or the issue of changing agrarian relations that preoccupied intellectual energies in the four decades after Independence, and to which entire journals and volumes were once dedicated, is now passé. The fact that scholarly pursuit has abandoned agrarian issues in favour of urban and service sector settings, identity politics, and cultural studies is clear from the themes addressed in recent publications and research proposals. Yet, on the ground, in Nandigram and Singur, Kalinganagar and Raigada, and in the mobilization around the Forest Rights Act 2006, more and more peasants are staking their lives to defend their rights to land against the great enclosure movement unfolding in rural India. From Manipur, Sikkim, Orissa, Maharashtra, Andhra Pradesh, Kerala, and West Bengal, to name only a few of the states where displacement by mining and dam projects and Special Economic Zones has encountered fierce resistance, come accounts of sustained collective action that testify to the continued centrality of land and related resources for a majority of Indians. But historians and sociologists of agrarian movements are missing from this scene.

Underlying contemporary peasant resistance is an even bigger story, one that demands scholarly attention on a comparable scale. Economic liberalization has induced an agrarian crisis that has destroyed agriculture as a viable mode of production for most farmers, perhaps forever. Thousands of suicides in places as disparate as Punjab, Kerala, and the Deccan point to the desperation of peasants unable to sustain themselves against the onslaught of changing terms of trade and the demands of resource-intensive agriculture. These transformations call for a social and economic analysis that is as alive to history as Guha's account of the

Chipko movement: one could, for instance, explain the agrarian crisis by tracing the career of one crop and commodity, namely cotton, from the introduction of long-staple varieties in the colonial period at the time of the American Civil War to the conflict around Bt cotton and the spate of suicides in the last decade.[4] There is enormous potential for research that moves between past and present to offer a cogent and compelling interpretation of agrarian conflicts in the manner exemplified by *The Unquiet Woods*.

While noting the continued importance of the analytical themes and approach that *The Unquiet Woods* epitomizes, I am struck by a profound change that peasant life has undergone in the last two decades. When Guha wrote his book, he assumed the integrity of peasant community and collective life. The ability of Chipko to challenge extractive state policies derived from its sense of itself as embodying an alternative utopia based on a vision of rurality that drew upon distinctive cultural values, modes of social organization, and relationships with nature. In the intervening twenty years that vision seems to have been extinguished. The 'moral' core of peasant economy–its normative sense of itself as the right or the good life–is now dead. As small peasants will tell you, there is no future in farming any more. By most accounts the teleology of modern development as industrialization and urbanization has triumphed. The unlamented death of the peasant is merely the future foretold.

Even if the material foundations of the agrarian crisis can be repaired and peasant economy reconstructed, what of the foundering of its ideological coherence, its moral core? How do we address this undermining of alternatives? *The Unquiet Woods* depicts ideologies in contention: subsistence versus profit-orientation, princely rule versus the colonial state; can we bring a similar Gramscian understanding to bear on the problem of cultural hegemony

[4] Sidney Mintz's study of sugarcane in the world economy, *Sweetness and Power: The Place of Sugar in Modern History* (New York: Penguin, 1985) is a masterpiece of this genre, though it does not discuss ecological changes at any length. For a highly readable combination of agrarian political economy and ecology focused on the United States, it is hard to beat Michael Pollan's *The Botany of Desire: A Plant's-Eye View of the World* (New York: Random House, 2001) and his *The Omnivore's Dilemma: A Natural History of Four Meals* (New York: Penguin, 2006).

in the present? This is the challenge confronting scholars of environmental history and sociology who have been influenced by Guha's work: how does one engage in the politics of hope in the face of the seemingly impossible odds against agrarian life?

The viability of agrarian life is also in question in the hills where *The Unquiet Woods* situates itself. Despite a ban on commercial forestry and the expansion of community-managed forests, especially in the Kumaun hills, and the creation of the separate state of Uttaranchal (now renamed Uttarakhand) in 2000, peasant economy hasn't really looked up. Statehood has, in theory, allowed regional and local concerns to be better articulated and addressed. More decentralized and democratic management has meant more effective mechanisms for resolving forest-related grievances. Yet the problems that Guha identified in the preface to his work: 'the eroding base of subsistence agriculture, large-scale outward migration, and the creation of a "money-order" economy in the villages of Uttarakhand'—seem as pervasive as ever, and are probably even more dire. This indicates that the connections between political control and local resource management on the one hand, and economic self-sufficiency on the other, are more complex than our accounts have led us to believe. As researchers, sometimes it is our proximity to social movements that draws us towards simplified explanations when we try to establish our political correctness by cleaving too closely to a social movement's analysis and manifesto. A movement's political statements and 'public face', to use Guha's term, have a different purpose from a scholarly analysis that must delve into aspects that are generally kept from public view: the complexities and contradictions of building alliances, addressing various audiences, representing issues and people as politically compelling: in sum, the work of making history under conditions not of one's choosing. While social movements have undoubtedly enriched our scholarship in manifold ways, if we curb our critical faculties when engaging with them we undermine ourselves as scholars and impoverish the larger world of political debate and action. And our analyses fail to stand up in the court of history .

The persistence of the predicaments of peasant life in Uttarakhand, despite changes in state–society relations, suggests that we re-examine the connections between ecology and economy. One way of doing this may be to adopt Guha's comparative approach to the question. While *The Unquiet Woods* considered the princely state of Garhwal and colonial Kumaun side by side to highlight variations in relations of rule, forest-related conflicts, and differences in the cultural idioms of protest, one could today compare Uttarakhand with the hill state of Himachal Pradesh which has similar ecological and social attributes but diverges widely in terms of economic prosperity, social welfare, and cultural attitudes towards out-migration and the integrity of village life. Comparative sociological and historical studies are rare in the Indian academy and re-reading *The Unquiet Woods* reminds us of the analytical purchase that we stand to gain from them.

For my generation of environmental sociologists and historians, *The Unquiet Woods* offered a map for traversing and situating ourselves in the ecological landscape of India, respectful of local particularities and in solidarity with people's struggles. This was a radically different way of conceiving the scholarly enterprise: it was not about demonstrating one's techno-scientific prowess in environmental policy discourse, nor about precious ethnological description of 'forest people' hermetically shut off from the operations of power. For bringing to life the connections between past and present, nature and culture, we in the academy owe an enormous debt to *The Unquiet Woods*.

The Unquiet Woods as Comparative History

JOAN MARTINEZ-ALIER

The success of *The Unquiet Woods* (1989) over the last twenty years is evident from its two editions and repeated reprints in India and the United States. The reasons for the book's success are various, the first being its literary quality. Its author Ramachandra Guha is by academic origin a sociologist who became a social historian as well as an accomplished cultural and political journalist who writes with concision, precision, and verve, reducing technical expression to a minimum and avoiding the pretentiousness of some sociologists; he has been referred to as 'perhaps the best non-fiction Indian writer in English.' The second reason is the fascinating and intricate story that Guha's book tells. Not being a specialist on India and the Himalaya, I was, the first time I read this book, perplexed by several issues within it: the historical differences between the kingdom in Garhwal still under colonial rule and the neighbouring district of Kumaun; the role of the king as a Badrinath deity or perhaps a super-priest; and the very different ways of being Gandhian made manifest by the two leaders of the Chipko movement, Sunderlal Bahuguna and Chandi Prasad Bhatt. So, this is a book with many nuances that make one aware of the very long history of India, and the complexities of its social, cultural, and political systems. I am not surprised that *The Unquiet Woods* has become a classic of peasant studies and socio-environmental history, read by graduate students all over the world.

It is not, however, an easy introduction to the forest struggles of India. It is primarily a scholarly monograph on the subject: Guha frequently makes his points using documentary evidence from national and regional archives (including that of the Forest

Research Institute of Dehradun, where his father had worked), and at other times through expressions in local languages from the many actors he interviewed—as anthropologists do. It is, all the same, a book that can be read many times, allowing the discovery of new connections each time.

I have visited several regions of India since my first visit to Karnataka in 1988, and although I have not yet joined any pilgrimage to Badrinath I have been a tourist in Kausani, Karanprayag, Rudraprayag, and Deoprayag (the divine confluence of the Bhagirathi and Alakananda rivers). I have also lectured at the G.B. Pant Institute near Almora. This is part of the territory covered in *The Unquiet Woods*. A difficult geography, a beautiful landscape, many uniformed children on the roads going or coming back from school, and down below the narrow green valleys where rice is grown. I am speaking of the year 2006, more than thirty years after the Chipko movement took place. While there, I remembered Guha often mentioning the impact of population growth and the migration of men to the plains. I saw many chir trees, many lopped *banj* trees, many women carrying home headloads of twigs. I had no reason to disbelieve what I read in his book about the relative lightness of the caste system in the region—although as a passing tourist I was not asked to take part in intercommunal smokings of the hookah.

The book, I now understand, goes over the history of a region that has a deep significance for India's culture across many centuries preceding the Chipko movement. All this is explained in detail, so that the persevering reader is able to acquire a clear image of the reasons why, in Garhwal, peasant resistance in defense of access to the forest took the form of ritual petitions to the king backed by demonstrations (the *dhandak*); while in Kumaun, on the other hand, there were less structured rebellions and massive arson in the *chir* forests around 1920–1. This varied history and its protagonists were remembered in the 1970s, when the Chipko movement started.

COMPARATIVE HISTORY

A third factor that explains the success of this book is the comparative international perspective discernible within it. Although it is not a long work—just about two hundred pages—it provides enough ideas for at least three separate books. The first of these would be on the history of peasant resistance and its varying forms in Garhwal and Kumaun. The second would be on the rise of the Chipko movement in the 1970s. It would ask: was this a new environmental movement or only another form of peasant resistance—this time with an explicit ecological content—a form that had also existed earlier but remained hidden to analysts? Finally, there is a third book inside the book in the shape of its running commentary comparing peasant resistance in these two regions of Uttarakhand (when they were still part of Uttar Pradesh) to instances of peasant resistance or peasant acquiescence in other countries: the enclosure of forests in western Germany as described by the early Marx; descriptions of peasant or rural labourers' movements by the great British social historians E. P. Thompson and Eric Hobsbawm; work by James Scott in South East Asia on the moral economy of peasants and their everyday forms of resistance; rural novels by Balzac; and analyses of the peasantry by historians of the *Annales* school in different parts of France as well as in Andorra in the Pyrenees—a place Guha was to visit much later.

Guha did not share Hobsbawm's dislike for, or at most doubtful praise of, peasants as "primitive rebels" (as compared to a proletariat organized on union and party lines). He preferred E. P. Thompson's enthusiasm for anti-feudal or anti-capitalist sabotteurs of all kinds. In 1989 the journal *Past and Present* published Guha and Gadgil's article titled 'State Forestry and Social Conflict in British and Post-British India: A Study in the Ecological Bases of Agrarian Protest'—possibly the first time that the word 'ecological' appeared in the title of an article within that celebrated journal of British Marxist social history. *The Unquiet Woods* also includes interesting comments on the Mexican revolution of 1910 (based on work by Womack and Oscar Lewis), which was about land and water rights; and on the history of peasant revolts in Java under colonial rule (citing work by Sartono Kartodirdjo). Within the limits of his knowledge of non-Indian languages when he was not yet 30 years old, Guha, it was apparent, had made a strong effort not to be Eurocentric. He had looked also towards Latin America, Africa, and other regions of Asia, anticipating his later work on the global history of environmentalism with its emphasis on the 'environmentalism of the poor'. Complementing this international perspective was what one might see as a nationalist one: Guha acknowledged and often praised other scholarly work on the Himalaya—whether in English or Hindi—such as that of Shekhar Pathak. He also traced comparisons between his area of research and those on other regions of India, adding his Himalayan case study, with its new environmental awareness, to the famous contributions by the 'Subaltern School' historians on peasant rebellions and resistance in colonial India. (This was before the 'Subaltern School' set Gramscian-Marxist influences aside and became addicted to the deconstruction of discourses.) In sum, though following the detailed local narrative of *The Unquiet Woods* requires careful attention, there are many refreshing paragraphs and footnotes for the international reader: indeed whole pages, in almost every chapter, of well informed comparative analyses where one re-encounters the classical authors of social history and historical sociology alongside more recent debates on property rights and institutions for natural resource management.

Some names are missing, however, and their absence is the basis of a minor criticism. Guha assumes that there must be similarities across the different mountain areas of the world in relation to fights over forests. He mentions the Andes. But in the central Andes (Bolivia, Peru, Ecuador) the historical struggle, as analysed by Florencia Mallon (1983) and others, was between the agricultural and pastoral haciendas of colonial origin and the indigenous communities. In the Andes no one explicitly studied the *ecological* content of such struggles—the fights specifically linked with access to natural resources (pastures, water, dung) which can be called 'socio-ecological distribution conflicts'. Ecological anthropologists did pursue the idea of complementarities in production at different ecological levels—this applies to mountain areas in general—and therefore looked for the institutions (of tribute, barter or markets) that linked this 'vertical economy'. And there have also been studies as well as famous novels on social conflicts between local populations and mining companies. But there was in fact little socio-environmental history in the Andes, and indeed in Latin America, until twenty years ago. My own favourite monograph on Latin American environmental history is by Elinor Melville (1994), not on a plague of chir but, in this case, on a 'plague of sheep'. It explains how, in the sixteenth and seventeenth centuries, a valley near Mexico City turned into a semi-desert while the Otomi indigenous to it nearly disappeared. So there are significant differences between the colonial experiences of Latin America and India, not least in the demographic consequences of the conquest in America (Crosby, 1986). Moreover, the rural struggles of peasants and labourers against haciendas and plantations in Latin America have a strong ethnic component, making them different from caste conflicts in India, and different too from adivasi resistance. But to say this is not to obscure the main point, which is that *The Unquiet Woods*, born as the doctoral thesis of a young Indian scholar, displayed so much knowledge of the history of rural social movements in many countries of the world.

While in India Ramachandra Guha is the father of environmental history, outside India he has had many followers. An early one was Nancy Peluso who, in her work on natural resources and peasant resistance in Java (Peluso, 1992), showed how German forestry in the mid-nineteenth century put in place a system that pushed whole villages outside the law. In Spain, recent socio-environmental history by González de Molina and Ortega Santos on Granada province in Andalusia has followed Guha in counting and classifying several kinds of forest crime as a sign of discontent with the disentailment of forests (and shrub areas) in the nineteenth century. While in India forests became state property under colonial rule, in Europe there was bourgeois privatization—another form of the 'tragedy of enclosures' (Ortega Santos, 2002). The explicit common ground between Ortega Santos and Guha is enclosures leading to the overexploitation of natural resources, and the 'discovery' of the ecological content within historical struggles over such resources. In this manner, social and environmental history come together.

There is, however, a problem within environmental history that I do not know how to solve. When did environmental movements—in the sense of social movements with an ecological content—start? For instance, around 1900 Tanaka Shozo in Ashio, Japan, and peasants and miners' families in Rio Tinto, in Huelva, Spain, opposed the pollution of water and air that came with copper mining and foundries (Martinez-Alier, 2002: 55–61). These movements did not of course use the word 'ecological'. So were these proto-environmental movements? Certainly they were: as were the many complaints against the exploitation of forest resources by external forces in the Himalaya much before Chipko.

The movements precede the analysis, naturally; but there is the danger of anachronism.

FOREST ECONOMICS

Forests became state property in India under colonial rule. The main technical advisers were German experts trained in forest economics, or, rather, tree plantation economics. Their policy was to grow uniform stands of trees as long as it was financially viable to do so, which meant comparing the rate of growth of trees (multiplied by expected price, net of cutting costs) to the rate of interest in the bank. In 1849 Faustmann introduced another factor: the rent obtainable from the land for some years (as pasture, for instance) once the trees were cut and while waiting for the next 'crop' of trees. This additional factor would be reason for a shorter rotation. This severely economistic and utilitarian training was the kind of management expertise that German foresters had when they arrived in India, with its rich tropical and diverse forests, its local populations that depended so much on the forests for their subsistence livelihood.

The logic of multiple use could not be totally ignored by the administrators. It was obvious that forests in India were used by the local populations for 'non-timber' products; they held much biodiversity; and they provided flood control and other 'environmental services' (to use today's jargon). In fact, in India the debate on the multi-functionality of forests goes back 150 years. The new institutions of Joint Forest Management since the late 1980s (partly the result of the Chipko movement) and the older institution of the Van Panchayat in Kumaun, especially after the revolt of 1920–1 (Agrawal, 2006), have a long intellectual and social history. While in *The Unquiet Woods* Guha tends to blame German forestry science for too single-mindedly imposing the logic of chir plantations over the various uses to which the Himalayan peasantry deployed oak forests, in a more recent book he quotes Dietrich Brandis, the Inspector General of Forests between 1864 and 1883, to the effect that village forests should be preserved. The German argued that forests ought to provide free-of-charge firewood for home consumption or for sale by poor people with headloads; he also saw them as desirable for wood in the making of agricultural implements and carts; for bamboo, wood, and grass in thatching, flooring, and fencing; for leaves and branches in the preparation of manure; and for grazing, except in areas that had been closed for forest regeneration (Guha, 2006: 206–7). These humane considerations notwithstanding, in Garhwal and Kumaun the main trend—towards the commercial exploitation of uniform tree plantations under state ownership—was clear. Demand from the railways was the main factor. But later, in the 1950s and 1960s, to this would be added the demand from other industries such as paper, plywood, and sportsgoods.

DISCOURSE ANALYSIS

I spent the year 1999–2000 at the programme of Agrarian Studies at Yale University near the place where, by a coincidence, Ramachandra Guha had given the final touches to *The Unquiet Woods* some twelve years earlier. My connection with James Scott, who directs this programme, goes back thirty years. My first book, *Labourers and Landowners in Southern Spain* (1971), was one minor source of ideas for Scott's *The Moral Economy of the Peasant* (Scott, 1977). I was at the time writing *The Environmentalism of the Poor* (2002), the words in the title being those that Guha and I had been using since we met for the first time in August 1988 in Bangalore. We had noticed, then, how his work on Chipko fitted with the work I was starting to do on Latin American environmental movements. More importantly, the time we met, twenty years back, also coincided with the murder of Chico Mendes, who was killed in December 1988 defending the Amazon forest in Brazil. Mendes, as is now well recorded, was defending the material uses which the rubber-tappers made of the forest in Acre. He was a local union leader. The rubber-tappers, with some inspiration from the left-wing Catholic 'Theology of Liberation' (but largely unaware of Gandhi's forms of struggle), developed a technique for opposing the cattle ranchers who came to destroy the forest. They sat down or stood up peacefully, with women and children confronting the armed invaders in a series of *empates*—a Portuguese word to which they gave new meaning. This was a clear case of 'the environmentalism of the poor'.

At Yale—where I had gone because of the libraries, and the work on environmental issues at the old Forestry School founded by Gifford Pinchot who had been trained in German-style forestry—I was surprised by the fashion among graduate students and even post-docs to dismiss empirical history or careful fieldwork, and to indulge instead in discourse analysis. Foucault had written on the historical treatment of issues like insanity, crime, and sexuality, convincingly showing the political use of pseudoscientific theories. So far so good. Foucault was writing in the Rive Gauche, or somewhere else in Paris, a city with streets named after Gay-Lussac, Sadi Carnot, Jussieu, Boussingault, some of the great names of science. Foucault could not have meant that there was in general no difference between truth and fantasy. Anyway, there was a passing epidemic of discourse analysis in some seminars at Yale in 1999–2000. Because of this, in *The Environmentalism of the Poor* (2002: 256) I wrote: 'Thus, the Chipko movement briefly described in Chapter 6 disintegrates in some armchair seminars on political ecology-cum-cultural theory taught in the USA into an analysis of the discourses by different authors who write on the discourses produced by the putative actors of the Chipko movement (which perhaps never did exist at all), certainly an economy of research effort compared to old-fashioned concern with checking the facts.'

Some friends thought I was overdoing it. However, I had seen the future. In Paul Robbins' textbook, *Political Ecology* (2004), which I did not read until 2006, the factual narrative and interpretation of the Chipko movement by Guha is put on the same level as another discourse—the book *Staying Alive* by Vandana Shiva (1988), written with no scholarly apparatus or aspirations. A feminist-economist working on rural issues in India, Bina Agarwal, soon dismissed Shiva's 'essentialist eco-feminist' interpretation of the Chipko movement when she carefully analysed the material reasons why women are often so active in socio-environmental conflicts and movements (as for example Gaura Devi in the village of Reni during the Chipko movement, as explained by Guha in *The Unquiet Woods*: Agarwal, 1992).

Robbins, an associate professor of geography at Ohio State University, wanted to become the Foucault and the Derrida of Chipko. He is not the only one in that line. Curiously, most of his ilk are in the United States, not in Paris or India. Robbins first summarized Shiva's interpretation, then Guha's, whose 'parallel account . . . is written in an equally urgent voice . . . This similarly prominent book insists that Chipko is one in a long line of peasant movements . . .' Both Vandana Shiva and Ramachandra

Guha (who was in his mid twenties when he started publishing on peasant resistance in Garhwal and Kumaun) appear to Robbins as 'veteran scholar activists'. It is known in India that Guha is not an activist. I never saw him at the World Social Forum in Porto Alegre, not even at the one in Mumbai. Vandana Shiva is a world activist against the World Bank, the IMF, and some transnational companies, greatly admired by many people, including myself, in this capacity.

Once the equal validity or lack of validity of both interpretations is established, and once both authors are fitted into similar slots of veteran activism, the conclusion reached by Robbins is that 'the movement about which Guha and Shiva are arguing is a *myth*' (Robbins, 2004: 194–6). Further evidence of the calibre of his scholarship is shown by his failure either to mention Bina Agarwal's discussion of Guha and Shiva (Agarwal, 1992), or Jayanta Bandyopadhyay's work on Chipko (1986 [coauthored with Vandana Shiva], 1999). It was Bandyopadhyay who first advised Guha to work on the Himalaya; he coauthored early articles with Shiva on Chipko and other topics (like eucalyptus plantations, Shiva and Bandyopadhyay, 1985) where 'essentialist eco-feminism' was not in evidence; and he became very critical of Shiva's *Staying Alive*. Some deconstruction would have been welcome here, just to see where the weight of the evidence tends to lie in regard to the history of the Chipko movement.

So, Ramachandra Guha, so successful and so highly praised for his literary enterprises over the last twenty years, subject perhaps now and then to small doses of envy in his own country, has had his share of silly, unfair, and parochial criticism coming from abroad. A more substantial critique of his Chipko book could be as outlined below.

The world significance of peasant resistance was emphasized by Guha against economic liberals as well as against Marxists (except for those who followed the late Marx in his exchanges with the Russian *narodniki* of 1880). In other works, notably in his outstanding biography of Verrier Elwin, Guha analysed and praised the values not of mainstream peasants but, even more, of adivasi societies because of their relative freedom from caste and religious constraints and because of their sustainable economies. We could now ask Guha: 'Does the resistance to state or private capitalism shown by the environmental movements of the rural poor provide a social and economic alternative, as you believed in the late 1980s and in the 1990s? Has this not become more doubtful in the last decades of economic growth?' In India today the flows of fossil energies and materials are growing at least at the same rate as the economy, and therefore there is no lack of socio-environmental conflicts against mining and large dams. Modernization has also caused many suicides among farmers. The twentieth century has witnessed a fourfold multiplication of humans, and a duplication of peasants. In short, it is still too early to tell if the message of Chipko—the idea of a sustainable rural economy—will prove to be a relevant worldwide response to the great ecological crisis of our time.

Finally, I shall disclose a family secret. The secret is known in some circles in Bangalore. This is that Ramachandra Guha once had a nice dog named Foucault. I last saw and talked to Guha's Foucault a couple of years ago. Unfortunately, he died. I wonder if Guha's next dog will be called Derrida.

REFERENCES

Agarwal, B. 1992. 'The Gender and Environment Debate: Lessons from India'. *Feminist Studies*, 18 (1).

Agrawal, A. 2006. *Environmentality: Technologies of Government and Political Subjects*. Durham: Duke University Press, and Delhi: Oxford University Press.

Bandyopadhyay, J. 1999. 'Chipko Movement: Of Floated Myths and Flouted Realities'. *Economic and Political Weekly,* 10 April, pp. 880–2.

——, and V. Shiva. 1986. 'The Evolution, Structure and Impact of the Chipko Movement'. *Mountain Research and Development*, 6 (2), pp. 133–42.

Crosby, A.W. 1986. *Ecological Imperialism: The Biological Expansion of Europe, 900–1900.* Cambridge: Cambridge University Press.

Guha, R. 2006. *How Much Should a Person Consume? Thinking through the Environment.* Ranikhet: Permanent Black, and Berkeley: University of California Press.

Martinez-Alier, J. 1971. *Labourers and Landowners in Southern Spain.* London: Allen & Unwin (St Antony's Publications).

——, 2002. *The Environmentalism of the Poor: A Study of Ecological Conflicts and Valuation*. Cheltenham: Edward Elgar; with a new introduction, Delhi: Oxford University Press, 2005.

Mallon, F.E. 1983. *The Defense of Community in Peru's Central Highlands: Peasant Struggle and Capitalist Transition 1860–1940.* Princeton: Princeton University Press.

Melville, E. 1994. *A Plague of Sheep: Environmental Consequences of the Conquest of Mexico.* Cambridge: Cambridge University Press.

Ortega Santos, A. 2002. *La Tragedia de los Cerramientos: Desarticulación de la Comunidad en la Provincia de Granada.* Preface by M. González de Molina. Valencia: Fundación Instituto de Historia Social, Alzira.

Peluso, N. 1992. *Rich Forests, Poor People: Resource Control and Resistance in Java.* Berkeley: University of California Press.

Robbins, P. 2004. *Political Ecology.* Oxford: Blackwell.

Scott, J. 1977. *The Moral Economy of the Peasant: Rebellion and Subsistence in Southeast Asia.* New Haven: Yale University.

Shiva. V. 1988. *Staying Alive: Women, Ecology and Development.* London: Zed.

——, and Bandyopadhyay, J. 1985. 'Eucalyptus in Rainfed Farm Forestry: Prescription for Desertification'. *Economic and Political Weekly*, vol. 20, no. 40, pp. 1687–8.

When Environmental Traditions Collide: *The Unquiet Woods* and U.S. Environmental History

PAUL S. SUTTER

In January 1986, after finishing his dissertation at Calcutta, Ramachandra Guha left his native India for a year and a half in the United States, where he had a lecturership at Yale University's School of Forestry and Environmental Studies. While at Yale he penned an essay that, when it appeared in 1989, sent tremors through the U.S. environmental community. Titled 'Radical American Environmentalism and Wilderness Preservation: A Third-World Critique', the essay took on the powerful role that deep ecology had played in pushing U.S. wilderness advocacy in a radical direction.[1] It was a critique not only of deep ecology's ethical case for wilderness preservation, built as it often was upon biocentrism, purism, and the misappropriation of Eastern spiritual traditions, but of the dangers of exporting the wilderness ideal to developing nations. Less well recognized, but as importantly, it was a trenchant case for getting American environmentalists–and, by association, members of the adolescent field of environmental history–to consider consumption as a category of analysis, and to think critically about the implications of gaping global disparities in rates of consumption. As indictments go, though, it was uncommonly generous, for Guha, though he rejected the universal moral imperative of wilderness preservation, did suggest that there were good reasons why wilderness arose as a distinctively American preservationist ideal. His goal in exposing wilderness as a

[1] Ramachandra Guha, 'Radical American Environmentalism and Wilderness Preservation: A Third-World Critique', *Environmental Ethics* 11 (Spring 1989): 71–83.

potentially dangerous cultural construct, then, was not so much to dismantle it as to contain it.

I cannot recall exactly when I first read Guha's 'Third World Critique'; it was probably in the early 1990s, during my initial years of graduate study at the University of Kansas, where my advisor, Donald Worster, impressed upon all of his students the need to think beyond national borders. But I do know that I embodied its target audience, and that it shook me to the core. Like Guha, I too had been on the move in January 1986. In the midst of completing an undergraduate degree in American Studies at Hamilton College in snowy northern New York State, I departed for California, on what I facetiously came to call my 'junior year abroad' at the University of California at Santa Cruz. (We Americans can be parochial, but Santa Cruz did seem like another country to me.) It was there, on a campus laid out in the midst of a coastal redwood forest, that I first embraced both environmental activism and environmental history. I read (and re-read!) Roderick Nash's classic study, *Wilderness and the American Mind* (1967), under the tutelage of environmental studies professors who had been on the front lines of the American environmental movement of the 1960s and 1970s. I also fell in with a group of students smitten with the philosophy of deep ecology—Bill Devall and George Sessions' *Deep Ecology* (1985) having just appeared—and the radical activism of Earth First!, a group founded just a few years earlier in response to the retrograde environmental policies of the Reagan administration and what many saw as the ossifying institutionalization of mainstream wilderness advocacy. My relationship with radical wilderness philosophy and activism was more flirtatious than committed; I slogged my way through Arne Naess, but I never came close to spiking a tree. Nonetheless, I lived through an American moment when deep ecological arguments for wilderness were ascendant. As Guha landed at Yale, then, he almost certainly had conversations with idealistic young wilderness devotees like me and my Santa Cruz cohort.

Over the years I have come to appreciate how Guha's short wilderness polemic functioned as an important companion piece to his pioneering study, *The Unquiet Woods,* which appeared in print the same year.[2] More than that, Guha's wilderness critique

[2] Guha, *The Unquiet Woods: Ecological Change and Peasant Resistance in the*

was a harbinger of the ways in which *The Unquiet Woods* would itself challenge U.S. environmental historians to examine critically their guiding concepts and values. The book was perhaps not meant to have such an influence; although his study ranged widely in building a comparative context for Himalayan peasant resistance, Guha said almost nothing about the United States. But as had his own arrival in the United States, the book raised a provocative set of questions about the contrasts between U.S. environmentalism, built as it largely was upon affluence and post-material concerns, and what he and Joan Martinez-Alier later called 'the environmentalism of the poor'.[3] Just as his sojourn to the United States launched Guha on an inquiry into the comparative history of environmentalism—one that has continued with the publication of several recent books—it also marked a pivot point in American environmental historiography.[4] Guha's wilderness essay was what happened when South Asian and U.S. environmental traditions collided. For U.S. environmental historians, the aftershocks are still being felt.

In one sense, *The Unquiet Woods* is to South Asian environmental history what Nash's *Wilderness and the American Mind* is to U.S. environmental history.[5] Each provided the formative history behind what was, at their point of publication, their nation's dominant strand of environmentalism, and each translated a national environmental sensibility into the moral core of a new academic field. But that is about where the comparison ends, for these two books otherwise could not be more different. Nash's study of the historical rise of wilderness appreciation in the United States focused its admiring attention on a few canonical advocates and their incremental contributions to a national—and nationalistic—environmental tradition. And, as Guha himself

---

Himalaya (Delhi: Oxford University Press, 1989, and Berkeley: University of California Press, 1990).

[3] Ramachandra Guha and Joan Martinez-Alier, *Varieties of Environmentalism: Essays North and South* (London: Earthscan Publications, 1997).

[4] Ramachandra Guha, *How Much Should a Person Consume? Environmentalism in India and the United States* (Ranikhet: Permanent Black, and Berkeley: University of California Press, 2006); Ramachandra Guha, *Environmentalism: A Global History* (New York: Longman, 2000).

[5] Roderick Nash, *Wilderness and the American Mind* (New Haven, Conn: Yale University Press, 1967).

recently pointed out, the logic of modernization—the notion that developing nations would follow the American lead in national park and wilderness preservation once they reached a mature stage of development—pervades Nash's study.[6] The book at once reflected and contributed to the central place of wilderness advocacy within American environmental politics. It motivated a generation of U.S. environmental activists who saw their culture's progressive reconsideration of the ecological and ethical value of wilderness to be one of its formative intellectual achievements. It was this work that introduced me to environmental history and influenced me to take up the study of the U.S. wilderness movement.[7] It also embodied an environmentalist sensibility that launched many U.S. environmental scientists and conservationists out into the world.[8]

The Unquiet Woods, on the other hand, took as its moral centre not the wilderness ideal that Nash and others saw as the pinnacle

[6] Guha, *How Much*, p. 27.

[7] Paul S. Sutter, *Driven Wild: How the Fight Against Automobiles Launched the Modern Wilderness Movement* (Seattle: University of Washington Press, 2002). I now recognize that Nash's book was in fact less the beginning of a new environmental historiography than a transitional book between an older American Studies tradition that made nature central to American culture and the newer discipline of U.S. environmental history. Books in that older tradition include Henry Nash Smith, *Virgin Land: The American West as Symbol and Myth* (New York: Vintage Books, 1950); and idem, *The Machine in the Garden: Technology and the Pastoral Ideal in America* (New York: Oxford University Press, 1964). The formative books in U.S. environmental history include Alfred Crosby, *The Columbian Exchange: Biological and Cultural Consequences of 1492* (Westport, Conn.: Greenwood Press, 1972); Donald Worster, *Nature's Economy: The Roots of Ecology* (San Francisco: Sierra Club Books, 1977); idem, *Dust Bowl: The Southern Plains in the 1930s* (New York: Oxford University Press, 1979); Richard White, *Land Use, Environment, and Social Change: The Shaping of Island County, Washington* (Seattle: University of Washington Press, 1980); Stephen Pyne, *Fire in America: A Cultural History of Wildland and Rural Fire* (Princeton, N.J.: Princeton University Press, 1982); and William Cronon, *Changes in the Land: Indians, Colonists, and the Ecology of New England* (New York: Hill and Wang, 1983). Carolyn Merchant's *The Death of Nature: Women, Ecology, and the Scientific Revolution* (San Francisco: Harper & Row, 1980), while not about the United States, was also an early and influential environmental history for those of us practising in the U.S.

[8] For a history of this process in South Asia, one that itself owes a debt to Guha's provocative work, see Michael L. Lewis, *Inventing Global Ecology: Tracking the Biodiversity Ideal in India, 1947–1997* (Athens, Ohio: Ohio University Press, 2004).

of enlightened environmentalism, but the moral economy and human ecology of the Himalayan peasant. Where Nash's book was primarily an intellectual history, Guha's was a social history, or, rather, a work of historical sociology. Where Nash was interested in universal ideas, Guha emphasized local mobilization and protest. Where the catalyst for Nash's book was the successful passage of the Wilderness Act of 1964, which created a protected system of wilderness areas on U.S. public lands, Guha's book took shape in the wake of India's unsuccessful Forest Bill of 1982, which would have further restricted peasant access to commons' forest resources. And where Nash's study treated the rise of conservation ideas and policies in the U.S. as heroic reformism in the face of the juggernaut of industrial capitalism, Guha depicted Chipko activists and their historical predecessors as opponents of a colonial and postcolonial conservation state, albeit one that generally served the interests of capital. Unlike Nash, who assumed that wilderness advocates spoke for nature's needs, Guha suggested that conservation policy served some groups at the expense of others. Guha's was a decidedly darker history of state conservation than we in the United States were then used to, one that insisted we see conservation as a colonial project.

As Guha was putting his historical understanding of the origins of modern Indian environmental protest in tension with a very different U.S. environmental tradition, he was also bucking his Marxist colleagues by insisting that Chipko was a peasant movement of vital political importance. In this sense his study was more in line with the approach of the emerging Subaltern School, which had a profound influence on Guha—though he brought an environmental approach to the study of peasant resistance that was itself new to Subaltern Studies. As Guha concluded in the final sentences of *The Unquiet Woods*, 'Far from being the dying wail of a class about to drop down the trapdoor of history, the call of Chipko represents one of the most innovative responses to the ecological and cultural crisis of modern society. It is a message we may neglect only at our peril.'[9] Implicit in Guha's conclusion was an effort to decentre American and first world environmentalism. But in battling teleological Marxism he also provided a brilliant historicization of peasant protest for an age of

[9] *Unquiet Woods*, p. 196.

globalization. Far from the '"full-stomach" phenomenon' that many have assumed it to be, environmental protest, *The Unquiet Woods* suggested, could be a pure product of the social dislocations attendant on developmental modernization.[10]

It is difficult to chart the direct influence of *The Unquiet Woods* in U.S. environmental historiography, but it is easy to see that the field has drifted in directions that Guha would applaud. U.S. environmental historians have learned–in part from Guha and the South Asian environmental history tradition he helped to launch–to see the 'hidden history' of the rise of conservation.[11] In a diverse array of studies that have appeared during the past decade or so, my colleagues have located groups on the margins who have been mistreated by the U.S. conservation state: American Indians, Hispano farmers, African American freedpeople, immigrant hunters and fishers, small-scale pastoralists, rural workers, and others who found that state conservation policies often worked to enclose various commons' lands and resources to which they previously had enjoyed access.[12] In the process U.S. environmen-

[10] The quotation is from Nash, *Wilderness*, p. 343.

[11] This phrase is borrowed from the subtitle of Karl Jacoby's book, *Crimes Against Nature: Squatters, Poachers, Thieves, and the Hidden History of American Conservation* (Berkeley: University of California Press, 2001). Like Guha, U.S. environmental historians came to some of these interpretations under the influence of scholars such as E. P. Thompson (and Marx himself) who looked at European class conflict over forest lands, and as a result of reading the work of anthropologists and sociologists such as James Scott, who theorized peasant protest in studies such as *Weapons of the Weak: Everyday Forms of Peasant Resistance* (New Haven, Conn.: Yale University Press, 1985).

[12] See Jacoby, *Crimes Against Nature*; Mark Spence, *Dispossessing the Wilderness: Indian Removal and the Making of the National Parks* (New York: Oxford University Press, 1999); Louis Warren, *The Hunter's Game: Poachers and Conservationists in Twentieth Century America* (New Haven, Conn.: Yale University Press, 1997); Joseph Taylor, *Making Salmon: An Environmental History of the Northwest Fisheries Crisis* (Seattle: University of Washington Press, 1999); Maria Montoya, *Translating Property: The Maxwell Land Grant and the Conflict over Land in the American West, 1840–1900* (Berkeley: University of California Press, 2002); and Stephen Hahn, 'Hunting, Fishing, and Foraging: Common Rights and Class Relations in the Postbellum South', *Radical History Review* 26 (1982): 37–64. For studies that look at relations between resource users and the conservation state that do not quite fit the above scholarship, see Karen Merrill, *Public Lands and Political Meaning: Ranchers, the Government, and the Property between Them* (Berkeley: University of California Press, 2002); Richard Judd, *Common Lands, Common People: The Origins of Conservation in Northern New England* (Cambridge, Mass.: Harvard University Press, 1997).

tal historians have largely absorbed Guha's critique of wilderness as a flawed ecological and moral baseline, and they have looked in greater detail at the history of commons' land use traditions that predated conservation. Indeed, the most important manifesto of this new approach to U.S. environmental history—William Cronon's controversial 1995 essay, 'The Trouble with Wilderness; or, Getting Back to the Wrong Nature'—paralleled many of the points Guha made in his wilderness critique.[13] While wilderness history remains an important part of U.S. environmental historiography, recent studies have been more subtle and contextual in their treatment, and have largely taken these wilderness critiques into account.[14]

U.S. environmental historians have also absorbed another lesson that Guha's book so clearly provided: social conflicts often have ecological dimensions. Indeed, part of the appeal of *The Unquiet Woods* as a still-vibrant model for doing environmental history is how well Guha incorporates the ecological dimensions of his story into the action. Guha's is not only a history of social groups fighting over what nature means and how it should be used. It is also a history in which what nature *does* matters. This was not a point to which U.S. environmental historians were blind when *The Unquiet Woods* first appeared. Nonetheless, some of my colleagues have convincingly argued that U.S. environmental history could become more relevant to the broader field of U.S. history—focused as it is on categories such as race, class, and gender—if we paid more attention to the ecological dimensions of social conflict.[15]

Despite its influence, there are several more lessons in *The Unquiet Woods* that we in the U.S. have yet to absorb, and that

[13] William Cronon, 'The Trouble with Wilderness; or, Getting Back to the Wrong Nature', in idem, ed., *Uncommon Ground: Rethinking the Human Place in Nature* (New York: W.W. Norton, 1996), pp. 69–90.

[14] On recent wilderness scholarship, see Paul S. Sutter, *Driven Wild*; Kevin Marsh, *Drawing Lines in the Forest: Creating Wilderness Areas in the Pacific Northwest* (Seattle: University of Washington Press, 2007); Theodore Catton, *Inhabited Wilderness: Indians, Eskimos, and the National Parks in Alaska* (Albuquerque: University of New Mexico Press, 1997); Michael Lewis, ed., *American Wilderness: A New History* (New York: Oxford University Press, 2007); and Donald Worster, *John Muir: A Passion for Nature* (New York: Oxford University Press, 2008).

[15] Ted Steinberg makes just such a call in 'Down to Earth: Nature, Agency, and Power in History', *American Historical Review* 107, 3 (June 2002): 798–820.

will perhaps mark its importance over the next two decades. First, there is a basic contrast between South Asian forest history and the new conservation historiography in the U.S. that deserves attention: where Guha saw peasant protest as environmental, we in the U.S. have generally *not* seen those marginal subjects who have protested and resisted the policies of the conservation state as environmentalists. If anything, we have made them avatars of a social and cultural critique of environmental ideals and values. And they usually were. Nonetheless, I want to suggest that we might profitably look at resistance to state conservation in the U.S. to find alternative *environmental* traditions. While it is not usually concerned with the power dynamics of state conservation, the burgeoning environmental justice historiography in the U.S. has opened the door to more expansive definitions of what constitutes environmental concern.[16]

This leads us to a second and related point: U.S. environmental historians have been slow to study environmentalism as a social movement in the ways that Guha did for Chipko. Instead, we usually have treated environmentalism as the intellectual product of a discrete set of great actors, as a broad cultural impulse of the affluent middle class, or as the manifest activism of an increasingly professionalized environmental lobby.[17] It is telling, I think, that when Guha looked to explain the importance of Chipko activist Gaura Devi to a U.S. audience in his recent study,

[16] There are exceptions. Karl Jacoby argues, for instance, that local subsistence users in the Adirondack State Park in New York State had a conservation ethic of their own. See Jacoby, *Crimes.* Chad Montrie has examined the environmentalism of working people in opposing surface coal mining in Appalachia. See Chad Montrie, *To Save the Land and People: A History of Opposition to Surface Coal Mining in Appalachia* (Chapel Hill: University of North Carolina Press, 2003). And Kathy Newfont has suggested that residents in and around the national forests of western North Carolina developed a 'commons environmentalism' that allowed them to oppose wilderness designations, which they thought would cut off their local access to natural resources, while also protesting clear-cutting and oil and gas development. See Kathy Newfont, 'Moving Mountains: Forest Politics and Commons Culture in Western North Carolina, 1964–1994' (Ph.D. dissertation, The University of North Carolina, 2001).

[17] This critique may not be entirely fair to those political scientists and sociologists who have studied the U.S. environmental movement, but I have not seen a whole lot of evidence that their work has made much of an impression on U.S. environmental history.

How Much Should a Person Consume?, he chose the analogy of Rosa Parks, a catalytic figure in the U.S. Civil Rights Movement, rather than someone like Lois Gibbs or Dana Alston, both prominent environmental activists but not nearly as well known to the American public.[18] One unmet challenge that *The Unquiet Woods* presents to U.S. environmental historiography, then, is not merely to take account of the victims of state conservation, but also to better understand environmentalism as a complex social movement, or, more accurately, a series of movements, some with deep historical roots. Scholars of other post-World War II social movements in the U.S.–not only Civil Rights, but also the feminist, gay liberation, student, and antiwar movements–have done that to much better effect than have scholars of U.S. environmentalism.[19]

Ironically, one subject area in need of more social movement analysis is postwar wilderness advocacy, for however one chooses to assess its goals and guiding ideals (and I think Guha's rhetorical arrow hit a big soft spot), the recent wilderness movement has been profoundly democratic and has taken as its prime target state conservation agencies such as the U.S. Forest Service, the Bureau of Reclamation, and the Bureau of Land Management. Rather than reifying the wilderness idea as prelude to a cultural critique, we can do more to interpret our own tree huggers in a social movement context.[20] Guha's attention to the gendered dimensions of Himalayan peasant resistance also was particularly

[18] Guha, *How Much*, p. 62. For an effort to integrate these figures into U.S. environmental history, see Robert Gottlieb, *Forcing the Spring: The Transformation of the American Environmental Movement* (Washington, D.C.: Island Press, 1993).

[19] Adam Rome has made a similar call in his article, '"Give Earth a Chance": The Environmental Movement and the Sixties', *Journal of American History* 90, 2 (September 2003): 525–54. Again, the exception to this rule has been scholarship on environmental justice, which has emerged as the American version of the 'environmentalism of the poor'. See, for example, Andrew Hurley, *Environmental Inequalities: Class, Race, and Industrial Pollution in Gary, Indiana, 1945–1980* (Chapel Hill: University of North Carolina Press, 1995); and Eileen Maura McGurty, *Transforming Environmentalism: Warren County, PCBs, and the Origins of Environmental Justice* (New Brunswick, N.J.: Rutgers University Press, 2007).

[20] There have been some good histories of Earth First! and radical environmentalism. See, for instance, Susan Zakin, *Coyotes and Town Dogs: Earth First! and the Environmental Movement* (Tucson: University of Arizona Press, 1993). But we need a better sense of the modern politics of wilderness advocacy.

admirable and might be more often emulated in U.S. environmental historiography. While he was critical of efforts to appropriate Chipko as a universal model for global ecofeminist protest, he nonetheless carefully charted the ways in which women, for reasons at once ecological, structural, and cultural, felt the imposition of state and commercial control over commons' forest resources with particular poignancy. While U.S. environmental historians have made strides in incorporating gender as a category of analysis in recent years, there is still much work to be done.[21]

Guha also warns against the categorical fashions that have prompted so many outside of the region to embrace Chipko as a political *cause célèbre*. In Chipko, Western environmentalists and social theorists found power turned on its head; there was something tremendously attractive about an environmentalism of female indigenous postcolonials, and it is thus not surprising that many have embraced Chipko as an exemplar of an environmentalism from below. What concerns Guha is that outsider affection for Chipko has been selective rather than historically detailed or grounded. Indeed, one of the great and lasting strengths of Guha's portrayal of peasant resistance is precisely its historical specificity. His is an analysis that warns us not only about the dangers of exporting wilderness, but also of importing and embracing a model of environmental activism ripped from its historical context.

Finally, I think U.S. environmental historians ought to pay more heed to Guha's comparative sense of the historical forces that have made the United States and India different. The United States, Guha has noted, is 'at once deeply democratic and instinctively imperialistic.'[22] It is the tension between these two commitments, Guha convincingly suggests, that makes us who we are. But in our recent critical focus on the victims of state conservation, U.S. environmental historians have focused more on the imperial than the democratic. (Although it may not look like it to outside observers of contemporary American society, there are plenty of us who recognize the instinctive imperialism of the United

[21] Virginia J. Scharff, ed., *Seeing Nature Through Gender* (Lawrence: University Press of Kansas, 2003).

[22] Guha, *How Much*, p. 226. He makes the same point in 'What We Think of America', *Granta* 77 (March 2002).

States and have made it a central focus of our historical scholarship.) To put it another way, as we have imported Guha's critical perspective on the conservation state, we have not done enough to assess the comparative specifics of state power and the ways in which our democratic culture has given particular form to even the most colonial aspects of our conservation tradition. For however imperialistic the U.S. conservation state has been, it also has been a state hobbled by a democratic political culture suspicious of overextending state capacities. Conservation in the United States has not been a high modernist state imperative imposed on powerless subject peoples; rather, it usually has been a 'low modernist' impulse at once promoted, opposed, compromised, and tempered by the welter of democratic politics.[23] That does not mean that U.S. state conservation has been perfectly democratic, for it decidedly has not. Indeed, those with the greatest claims to having been exploited by the U.S. conservation state have been those historically denied full access to the democratic process. Nonetheless, conservation in the U.S. has been the province of a relatively weak state. Indeed, Guha's description of the United States as simultaneously democratic and imperialistic hints at important differences between conservation in a domestic context and efforts by U.S. conservation actors in the developing world, where they have been less constrained by democratic oversight. The 'authoritarian biologists' that Guha has recently castigated, in an extension of his 1989 wilderness critique, have rarely enjoyed the authority over conservation decisions within the United States that they have in U.S. territories and other parts of the developing world.[24]

[23] The U.S. agricultural sociologist Jess Gilbert has used the term 'low modernism' to suggest an alternative to the high modernist state projects that James Scott has been so critical of. See Jess Gilbert, 'Low Modernism and the Agrarian New Deal: A Different Kind of State', in Jane Adams, ed., *Fighting for the Farm: Rural America Transformed* (Philadelphia: The University of Pennsylvania Press, 2003), pp. 129–46; James Scott, *Seeing Like a State: How Certain Schemes to Improve the Human Condition Have Failed* (New Haven, Conn.: Yale University Press, 1998); Morton Keller, 'Looking at the State: An American Perspective', *American Historical Review* 106, 1 (February 2001): 114–18.

[24] Guha, 'Authoritarian Biologists and the Arrogance of Anti-Humanism: Wildlife Conservation in the Third World', in Vasant Saberwal and Mahesh Rangarajan, eds, *Battles over Nature: Science and the Politics of Conservation* (Delhi: Permanent Black, 2003). See also Lewis, *Inventing Global Ecology*.

And yet, as different as the United States and India are, *The Unquiet Woods* intimated that they were also connected. Here lies a final lesson that U.S. environmental historians might glean from Guha's groundbreaking study of South Asian environmental resistance. Just as Chipko protest in the Himalaya came in response to peasants having their local commons dragged into a national and international economy, so the very differences between our two environmental traditions are the result of our respective places in an interconnected world of extraction, production, and consumption. And to the extent that the preservation of wilderness has saved large natural areas in the United States from being radically transformed in the maw of industrial commerce—a good thing I would argue—it generally has happened *not* with a corresponding drop in home country consumption, but with at least some displacement of that consumption's ecological and social footprint on the developing world. Wilderness preservation in the U.S. and peasant environmental protest in South Asia are not merely divergent national traditions, then. Rather they are products of different settings within the global economy. And as both Guha and I have pointed out before, U.S. environmental historians have been too slow to move beyond U.S. borders to trace the historical dimensions of these uneven transnational relationships.[25] *The Unquiet Woods* gives us not only a model for rethinking U.S. conservation history, but also a stimulus for thinking about how our entire environmental history has been shaped by such transnational connections.[26] As we celebrate *The Unquiet Woods* and the growing traffic in ideas that it and its author have been so pivotal in putting into motion, we also need to appreciate the production, consumption, and traffic in goods that have historically knitted, and will continue to knit, us together.[27]

[25] Guha, *How Much*, p. 227; Paul S. Sutter, 'What Can U.S. Environmental Historians Learn from Non-U.S. Environmental Historiography?' *Environmental History* 8, 1 (January 2003): 109–29.

[26] There are only a few models: Richard Tucker, *Insatiable Appetite: The United States and the Ecological Degradation of the Tropical World* (Berkeley: University of California Press, 2000); John Soluri, *Banana Cultures: Agriculture, Consumption, and Environmental Change in Honduras and the United States* (Austin: University of Texas Press, 2005); and Matthew Klingle, 'Spaces of Consumption in Environmental History', *History and Theory* 42 (December 2003): 94–110.

Index